GOOD GIRLS AND
WICKED WITCHES

GOOD GIRLS AND WICKED WITCHES

Women in Disney's Feature Animation

Amy M. Davis

British Library Cataloguing in Publication Data

Good Girls and Wicked Witches: Women in Disney's Feature Animation

A catalogue entry for this book is available from the British Library

ISBN: 0 86196 673 2 (Paperback)

Reprinted 2009 and 2012

Cover design: Jonny Wood.

Published by
John Libbey Publishing Ltd, 3 Leicester Road, New Barnet, Herts EN5 5EW,
United Kingdom   e-mail: john.libbey@orange.fr; web site: www.johnlibbey.com

Direct orders: **Marston Book Services Ltd:** direct.orders@marston.co.uk

Distributed in Asia and North America by **Indiana University Press**, 601 North Morton St,
Bloomington, IN 47404, USA. www.iupress.indiana.edu

Printed and bound in China by 1010 Printing International Ltd.

Contents

Acknowledgements

Any project of this size is impossible to complete without the help of a great many people. There is no way to thank individually each and everyone of them, so I give them my most sincere thanks for their moral support, encouragement, advice, and general cheering on, and trust that they know who they are. Amongst them are David Eldridge, whose willingness to talk shop (even on holiday!), and his friendship and example, always inspire me to work harder; Alicia King, who has always been an email away in times of joy and crisis, and who even went above and beyond in helping me proofread; Cara Gunther Waterhouse, who's been a true friend for nearly half our lives, always shared my passion for anything Disney (even if she does prefer the live-action films!), and inspired my desire to try out life in the UK. More recently, thanks are due to Máire Messenger-Davies, John Davies, Ciara Chambers, Niamh O'Sullivan, Andrew Boyce, and Helen Thornham, whose friendship and emotional support in the final stages of this project, not to mention the dog-sitting during research trips, have been of enormous help! Also, extra thanks to Helen for her hard work on the index!

Special thanks, however, must be given to those who gave exceptional help to me in some way. My brother, Brian Davis, has always been most able and willing to talk Disney with me, and given me much inspiration and food for thought in the process. My grandmother, Betty Erwin, has used every birthday, Christmas, Easter, and every holiday in between as an excuse to give me the videos and dvds I've needed along the way. She also is the one who took me on my first trip to Walt Disney World back in 1977 (when I was just five years old), and has always overflowed with love and generosity to help me along the way. My mother, Kitty Davis, deserves the most thanks – not only has she tirelessly supported me in every way possible, she's even provided spelling and proof-reading help at various stages. Most importantly, she took me to see my first viewings of many of the films in this study (and made me stay to the end, even when queens turned into hags and Bambi's mother got shot!), and has given me – and shared with me – her love of movies of every kind. She has been the kind of mother the heroines in this book could only ever have wished for.

Finally, my sincere thanks must be given to Dr. Melvyn Stokes, who supervised my MA dissertation and Ph.D. thesis in the history department at UCL, and helped to launch me in my "Mickey Mouse" career: when casting about for a suitable subject for my MA dissertation, a conversation with my brother still lingering in my mind, I suggested, somewhat flippantly, "Why don't I do my dissertation on Disney?" His brief reply changed my life: "Why not?"

Introduction

The subject of women and how they were regarded over the course of the modern era is not by any means new. Writers, feminists, anti-feminists, politicians, political commentators, psychologists, journalists, celebrities, housewives, students, historians, and many others have written on this subject in varying degrees of depth and seriousness. But in the twentieth century, as a mainly print-based culture gave way to one which, at the start of the twenty-first century, is primarily image- and media-based, it was the way these physical/cultural/social expectations were tied together with and within the medium of film, and disseminated in the person of the "actress" (be she a live woman or a drawing), which became important. It is with the images of women in popular culture that all of the aspects of American society's changing attitudes towards women were mapped.

This book analyses the construction of (mainly human) female characters in the animated films of the Walt Disney Studio between 1937 and 2004. It is based on the assumption that, in their representations of femininity, Disney films reflected the attitudes of the wider society from which they emerged, and that their enduring popularity is evidence that the depictions they contain would continue to resonate as the films were re-released in later decades. It attempts to establish the extent to which these characterisations were shaped by wider popular stereotypes by putting the films into the context of Hollywood films from the era in which these Disney films were made. Moreover, because of the nature of the animated film – because it is a unique combination of printed popular culture (as in drawings done for

1

newspapers, books, and magazines) and the twentieth century's later emphasis on more life-like visual media (such as
film, television, and various forms of photography), it is
argued here that it is within the most constructed of all
moving images of the female form – the heroine of the
animated film – that the most telling aspects of *Woman* as
the subject of Hollywood iconography and (in the case of
the output of US animation studios) ideas of American
womanhood are to be found. Furthermore, because within
the subject of US animation it is the work of the Disney
Studio which has reigned – and continues to reign – supreme within its field, and because most of the major animated films created in Hollywood have been produced by
Walt Disney's studio, it is upon these films that this study
concentrates.

The problems of researching Disney

Ironically, as scholarly interest in the history and creations
of the studio increased thanks to the emergence of film
studies and animation studies as academic disciplines, one
of the major roadblocks which eventually arose in undertaking a study of characterisations of femininity by the Disney
studio has been the Disney organisation itself. The first
logical place to go as a source of information on Disney films
and on Walt Disney himself would be the archives at Walt
Disney Productions in Burbank, California. Though earlier
researchers were able to do this (amazingly, Richard Shale,
author of the 1982 book *Donald Duck Joins Up: The Walt
Disney Studio During World War II*, wrote almost apologeti-
cally in his book's introduction for having to rely so heavily
on the Disney archives and primary sources as a source for
his research materials![1]), recent years have witnessed a
change in the Disney company's attitude toward anyone –
including academics – wishing to undertake research in the
studio's archives. For a time, even using the name "Disney"
or images from Disney was prohibitively problematic. As
the editors of *From Mouse to Mermaid: The Politics of Film,
Gender, and Culture* were told in correspondence with the
Disney Company before the publication of their book
(which they had originally entitled *Doing Disney: Critical
Dialogues in Film, Gender, and Culture*): "... Disney does not
allow third-party books to use the name 'Disney' in their
titles – this implies endorsement or sponsorship by the

1   Richard Shale.
*Donald Duck Joins
Up: The Walt
Disney Studio
During World War
II* (Ann Arbor:
UMI Research,
1982), pp. xiii-xiv.

Disney organization".[2] The letter continued: "As you know, all of our valuable properties, characters, and marks are protected under copyright and trademark law and any unauthorized use of our protected material would constitute infringements of our rights under said law".[3] The hint of threat this statement contains is not there by accident. Over the course of its history, the Walt Disney Company has grown suspicious of outside interest and, as a consequence, has become unusually protective of itself. It could be hypothesised that this protectiveness has its roots in the 1928 theft of Oswald the Lucky Rabbit by Disney's distributor, Charles Mintz, but this seems unlikely, given that this protectiveness reached its height during Michael Eisner's leadership of the corporation. Whether academic research in the archives will be allowed in the future, now that Eisner has left, remains to be seen. It can only be hoped, however, that the value of permitting scholarly access to the archives will be realised, and that the treasure trove of information they contain will be offered up once more for professional intellectual analysis.

By the late 1990s, however, it had become impossible simply to make an appointment to see the Disney archives. Scholars first had to write a detailed letter to the Disney Archives' Permissions Department stating the nature, purpose, and ultimate intentions (i.e. whether publication was intended) of the research that was being undertaken, and then had to wait and hope that access would be granted. Only after first being granted permission to enter the archives were scholars allowed to make an appointment to conduct research. Furthermore, they were still not allowed complete access to the archives. When I enquired as to the existence of audience polls on the reception of Disney's films, I was told that, while these polls had, in fact, been conducted, "Unfortunately, after checking with our Legal departments, it seems that the audience poll information is still considered proprietary and confidential, so it is not available to people outside of The Walt Disney Company".[4]

I myself was denied the use of the archives when, in 1997, I wrote for permission to see such materials as existed showing the evolution of the various character portrayals. The reply I received stated that "While we recognize the purpose you have in mind, unfortunately, I am placed in the unenviable position of having to advise you that we cannot grant

2 Elizabeth Bell, Lynda Haas, and Laura Sells (eds). *From Mouse to Mermaid: The Politics of Film, Gender, and Culture* (Indianapolis: Indiana University Press, 1995), p. 1.

3 Bell et al, *From Mouse to Mermaid*, p. 1.

4 Personal Correspondence, via e-mail, dated 27 February 1997, from Dave Smith, Chief Archivist, Walt Disney Productions.

you the permission you have requested".[5] Moreover, when I e-mailed Dave Smith, the chief archivist at Disney, on 7 June 1999, he informed me, as part of an answer to a enquiry about the content of the archives, that the Disney archives were no longer open to outside researchers, and were, to his knowledge, to remain closed indefinitely.[6] Therefore, for most of my Disney sources, I have been forced to utilise such data that has made it out of the Disney archives and into a variety of other archives, libraries, and the public domain. While this was not an ideal situation for undertaking original research, it has nonetheless forced me to extract as much information as possible from the available sources.

Despite this handicap, however, my sources themselves have been extensive, varied in nature, and sometimes rather untraditional. First of all, I relied upon the Disney films themselves as the basis for detailed textual analysis. My copies of the Disney films on which I focused in my study were all purchased VHS or DVD copies of the films, obtained in both the United States and the United Kingdom. All were officially produced and licensed Disney videos/DVDs released by Walt Disney Pictures. The other films referred to in this study were obtained both from purchased tapes and DVDs and from US and UK television broadcasts which I personally recorded. Another important source was the collection of books published by the Disney-owned press, Hyperion. Because of Disney's careful control over the copyrights of its trademarked images and artwork, books published by Hyperion are amongst the few available sources for them outside of the Disney Studio's archives. An incredibly rich source of previously unpublished materials such as studio memos and personal correspondence was found on the CDrom-based "biography" of Walt Disney, *Walt Disney: An Intimate History of the Man and his Magic*, published by the Walt Disney Family Educational Foundation, Inc.[7] Also, the writings of other scholars on the subjects of Walt Disney, the Disney studio and its films, the theme parks, and animation history generally were useful, both for their information and as examples of the range of attitudes and approaches to the subject of Disney. As for the primary sources I used in this study (apart from the films), the collection of "Personality Ephemera" on Walt Disney in the possession of the British Film Institute proved to be very useful. Also, copies on the internet of such of important

5 Personal Correspondence, dated 29 May 1997, from Margaret Adamic, Contracts Coordinator, Disney Publishing Group.

6 Personal Correspondence, via e-mail, dated 6 June 1999, from Dave Smith, Chief Archivist, Walt Disney Productions.

7 *Walt Disney: An Intimate History of the Man and his Magic*. CD-ROM. (Santa Monica, CA: Pantheon Productions Inc, 1998).

documents as Walt Disney's testimony before the House Committee on Un-American Activities and the United States Supreme Court decisions on various cases connected with the Hollywood film industry were very useful for me in researching this book. Amongst my other primary sources, I relied upon period magazines, books, articles, and film reviews. Secondary sources were the increasing numbers of books and articles about Disney. Of all of these sources, arguably my most important has proved to be the films themselves, which I relied upon to carry out my original textual analysis of the films which my study has covered.

This book, in its emphasis on textual analysis within a historical context, falls within a tradition in film history and film studies of opening up new areas of scholarly enquiry through in-depth analysis both of individual films and of the genre to which they belong. Jeanine Basinger's 1993 study of the women's film genre, *A Woman's View: How Hollywood Spoke to Women, 1930–1960*,[8] is an example of this line of scholarly enquiry, although it is not the first study of women's films during the period 1930 to 1960. It combines detailed textual analysis with an analysis of various aspects of the genre as a whole in a way which sees film texts as being more akin to historical documents, which require an examination of the elements they contain and the factors surrounding their production and reception as forms of popular entertainment. As Martin Barker writes in *From Antz to Titanic: Reinventing Film Analysis*,

> "We can't deduce 'harm' (or 'good' for that matter) from analysis of films. We can't place films along some supposed dimension of political or ideological acceptability, from conservative/reactionary to radical/subversive. Most importantly, we cannot read off possible influences upon an unnamed, 'vulnerable' audience. And part of the reason for that is that films don't contain 'messages' plus message-launching devices in the way that much analysis has supposed."[9]

The spirit of Basinger's study is, in a number of ways, the model for the approach taken here. Like *A Woman's View*, this book strives to examine both the films as individual texts and the patterns formed by these texts when looked at as examples of a genre.

Depictions of women in American culture

On the face of it, cultural images of American women have

8 Jeanine Basinger, *A Woman's View: How Hollywood Spoke to Women, 1930–1960* (London: University of New England Press, 1993).

9 Martin Barker with Thomas Austin, *From Antz to Titanic: Reinventing Film Analysis* (London: Pluto Press, 2000), p. 174.

changed considerably in the last two centuries. For many years, the reigning paradigm in women's history was that of the 'separate spheres' of work and home. Barbara Welter, based on an examination of early nineteenth-century didactic literature – the cultural conditioning of its day – argued that, at least in middle-class families, the roles of each marriage partner were clearly defined along gendered lines.[10] The male supported the family financially by working in the marketplace. The female took care of the home, raised the children, saw to the day-to-day needs of her family, and was subordinate to her husband in terms of overall authority within the family.

By the late twentieth century, the ways in which gender was constructed in the media were, ostensibly, very different. The division of labour in family relationships (where a traditional family could be found) was no longer so clear-cut. Both partners might work and share child-rearing responsibilities equally. The female might work outside the home and the male see to the household, or vice versa. In theory, the choices available to women (or, at least, the outward appearance of the availability of these choices) had vastly increased. Yet, accompanying the apparent growth in women's freedom and their legal and social equality with men, there was also strong evidence of more conservative, less liberated views of women disseminated throughout popular culture.

Tabloid newspapers and magazines have consistently depicted women as objects for the male gaze (as have men's magazines, often to an exaggerated extent). Some women themselves, moreover, seem to have colluded in the production and dissemination of fundamentally conservative gender stereotypes. Even beyond the obvious examples of the women who pose nude (or nearly so) in various male-targeted weekly and monthly publications (and, surprisingly, in many of the daily tabloid newspapers published in Britain), women's magazines, mainly written by women for a female audience, have continually reminded women (through articles, fashion advice, beauty tips, and pictorial advertisements) that they should pay particular importance to their looks and general physical attractiveness. Many such magazines, by the last decades of the twentieth century, were also propagating the positive message that women should be proud of their femininity and comfortable with expressing

10 Barbara Welter, "The Cult of True Womanhood", *American Quarterly*, 18 (1966), pp. 151–174.

their sexuality. Yet their general tenor was still to reinforce the patriarchal view that women are meant to be valued more for their beauty than their brains, and that this new sexual "freedom" meant making themselves more available to men, rather than giving women the freedom to be more choosey in their choice of (or refusal to choose) a sexual partner.

Women's magazines can generally be divided into two principal groups: those concerned with childcare and the various aspects of home-making, and those predominantly aimed at helping women find a partner/husband. The notion that women must find a marriage partner is deeply engrained in American (and Western) history and a variety of cultural formations. It is fore-grounded by women's magazines, advice books, films, advertisements, and television programmes. One of the latter offered an even more specific reason for the phenomenon. In a 1998 episode of *Ally McBeal,* the following dialogue took place between the lead character and her roommate on their return home from being bridesmaids at a wedding:

> ALLY McBEAL: Seriously, Renee, this thing about being married. Why do you think women ...?
>
> RENEE RADICK: We're brainwashed. The first stories we hear as babies – *Snow White, Cinderella* – [are] all about getting a guy, being saved by the guy. Today it's *Little Mermaid, Aladdin, Pocahontas.* All about getting a guy.
>
> ALLY: So basically we're screwed up because of ...
>
> RENEE: (throws her bridesmaid's dress on the open fire) (scornfully): Disney![11]

This dialogue takes place in the opening sequence of an episode from a show which is all about a sad, lonely, slightly strange Generation X-er who cannot find satisfaction in her life – despite her good friends and successful career – because she has been wounded in love once and has yet to find true love since. While trivial in itself, the dialogue quoted above does raise certain issues of relevance to this book.

There are a number of reasons why Disney as a subject has become an increasingly prominent topic of public discourse in recent years. Firstly, Disney itself – during the late 1980s and the 1990s – became much more visible both as a movie studio and as a corporation. In 1987, a retail chain (the Disney Store) was established, Walt Disney World was ex-

11 *Ally McBeal,* Episode "Body Language", first broadcast on 2 February 1998, directed by Mel Damski, written by David E. Kelley, Nicole Yorkin, and Dawn Prestwich.

7

panded with the addition of the Disney/MGM Studio theme park in 1989, a new Disney theme park was opened near Paris, France, in 1992, and Disney's Animal Kingdom was opened in 1998. During these years, Disney animated films became available for purchase on video, and, although they were only hesitantly released by the studio at first, they quickly began to dominate the children's video market. Secondly, Walt Disney's and the Disney studio's places in both American society and other cultures began to receive both popular and scholarly attention. This ranged from highly critical "popular" biographies of Disney, such as that by Marc Eliot,[12] through attacks on anything and everything Disney in works such as Eleanor Byrne and Martin McQuillan's *Deconstructing Disney*[13] and anthropological polemics such as *Inside the Mouse: Work and Play at Disney World* by a group calling themselves "The Project on Disney",[14] to romanticised accounts of Disney's life in Bob Thomas' biography *Walt Disney: An American Original*,[15] more serious academic studies such as Elizabeth Bell, Lynda Haas, and Laura Sells' *From Mouse to Mermaid: The Politics of Film, Gender, and Culture*[16] and, finally, truly scholarly, self-confident works such as Steven Watts' *The Magic Kingdom: Walt Disney and the American Way of Life*[17] and Nicholas Sammond's *Babes in Tomorrowland: Walt Disney and the Making of the American Child, 1930–1960*.[18] However, despite the claims made by writers and commentators for thoroughness and fair-mindedness, many of them have reflected many misconceptions and misunderstandings of Walt Disney, the studio which bears his name and, more often than not, have contributed more to the myths surrounding Disney than they did to an accurate understanding.

In her criticism of Disney in the above dialogue, for example, Ally's roommate, Renee, alleges that Disney films from "*Snow White* [to] *Cinderella* – [are] all about getting a guy, being saved by the guy. Today it's *Little Mermaid*, *Aladdin*, *Pocahontas*. All about getting a guy." This itself emphasises two common misconceptions: that all of Disney's human female characters are princesses (certainly, all of the films she cites have princesses in them, though there are a much larger number which do not) and that all of Disney's female characters – past and present – are weak, passive figures who sit around waiting to be "saved by the guy". Even in just the last three films she cites – *The Little Mermaid*, *Aladdin, and*

12 Marc Eliot, *Walt Disney: Hollywood's Dark Prince* (London: Andre Deutsch Limited, 1995).

13 Eleanor Burn and Martin McQuillan, *Deconstructing Disney* (London: Pluto Press, 1999).

14 The Project on Disney, *Inside the Mouse: Work and Play at Disney World* (London: Duke University Press, 1995).

15 Bob Thomas, *Walt Disney: An American Original* (New York: Hyperion, 1994).

16 Elizabeth Bell, Lynda Haas, and Laura Sells (eds). *From Mouse to Mermaid: The Politics of Film, Gender, and Culture* (Indianapolis: Indiana University Press, 1995).

17 Steven Watts, *The Magic Kingdom: Walt Disney and the American Way of Life* (New York: Houghton Mifflin Company, 1997).

18 Nicholas Sammond, *Babes in Tomorrowland: Walt Disney and the Making of the American Child, 1930–1960* (Durham, NC: Duke University Press, 2005).

Pocahontas – if there is one thing the three main female characters are *not* doing, it is sitting around waiting to be "saved by the guy". In all three of these films, in fact, the heroine actively saves the hero's life in some way or another at least once. And their motivation to do what they do is never solely romantic love. Ariel (*The Little Mermaid*) is motivated by love more than either of the other two, but she is also heavily influenced by her deep-seated curiosity about humans, the human world and her fascination with anything and everything human. This aspect of her personality is highlighted well before she ever lays eyes on Prince Eric. In *Aladdin,* Jasmine, although she is a princess and is beloved by her father, feels stifled by her life and is desperate for adventure in the larger world. It is only because she finally decides to break free of her life as a princess and disguises herself as a peasant that she and Aladdin are ever able to meet. Also, her refusal to marry for any reason other than love and her insistence that the man she marries be someone who, above all, treats her with honour and respect – indeed, it is these qualities in Aladdin which make her fall in love with him – are paramount in Jasmine's portrayal. Likewise, in *Pocahontas,* Pocahontas' love for John Smith is only a small part of her motivation for her actions in the film, as its narrative development makes clear. In fact, she is motivated predominately by her desire to prevent war; in the end, she says good-bye to Smith in order to take up her place as a leader amongst her people.

These are all strong female characters with strong, positive aspects to their depictions. They are also typical of the kinds of female characters to be found in the Disney films of the 1990s. Furthermore, such strong, active women were to be seen in Disney animated films of the late 1970s and 1980s, and instances of such independence and energy are to be found even amongst some of the characters of the first era of the Disney studio's feature animation production (characters such as Slue-Foot Sue and, to a lesser extent, Katrina van Tassel are examples of strong, less-than-passive characters from Disney's earlier years). Yet, because two of the most famous classic Disney characters from two of its most popularly successful films – *Snow White* and *Cinderella* – are both (to a lesser and greater extent, respectively) depicted as passive fairy tale princesses, the reputation that Disney films are full of weak, passive women has gained a wide-spread, largely unquestioned acceptance.

Disney's films are important in cultural terms because Disney himself was probably the closest thing the twentieth-century produced to a teller of national (and international) folk stories. In the past, from the most ancient times until relatively recently, it was through the telling of tales (or rather, listening to tales being told) that human beings learned about their society's ways, traditions, history, and beliefs. In other words, it was through stories that people learned about the culture in which they lived in a more studied, self-conscious way than they might have simply by living in it. Clarissa Pinkola Estés, in her study of folk- and fairy-tales *Women Who Run With the Wolves,* in which she discussed the role of story in society, described such stories as a kind of "medicine".[19] Estés noted that "Stories enable us to understand the need for and the ways to raise a submerged archetype".[20] Estés is referring to archetypes which still exist, but which have been repressed – or ignored – within the cultural concepts and folklore of a society. For her, these "submerged archetypes" are still present, technically, in the sense that they have not been lost or forgotten; their stories are not told, however, because – for whatever reasons – these archetypes do not resonate within society during a particular era. Her book focused, in particular, upon the ways in which various stories can teach and heal the souls/psyches of women. In earlier times, the younger generations turned habitually to the older members of their society for knowledge concerning the problems both of daily life and of life's more complicated issues. In pre-industrial societies in particular, the various generations were more likely to spend time in contact with one another, and, especially in less literate societies, storytelling was perhaps the most common means of answering complex questions to do with such themes as love, morality, religion, justice, and truth.

As Western society became more literate, printed media began to replace the older form of storytelling. While printing stories does give them the advantages of being more widely disseminated and, therefore, ensures that they have a greater likelihood of being preserved, there are two great disadvantages inherent in the teaching capacity of the printed tale: (1) it is less likely to be "told" (or read, which-

19 Clarissa Pinkola Estés, *Women Who Run with the Wolves: Myths and Stories of the Wild Woman Archetype* (London: Rider, 1993), p. 14.

20 Estés, *Women Who Run With the Wolves,* p. 14.

ever is the case) in response to a particular question or situation which may have arisen (and about which it might be able to shed some light) and is more likely simply to be read at random; (2) the story loses its cultural fluidity. This second aspect will be referred to later in relation to Disney's modifications of traditional tales. If one individual is telling a "teaching tale", he or she can alter certain aspects of the tale so that the listeners at that moment will hear something which is especially relevant to them at that time in their lives and, thereby, gain more from the tale than they might have otherwise. A printed story, however, as a consequence of being written down, is forced to be the same tale every time it is read. Although the ways individuals interpret what they read can vary widely, the words themselves – as physical structures printed on a page – of course do not alter themselves on the page in order to suit the needs of each individual reader. And it was in this way, as printed media became "traditional" for later generations, that certain versions of stories became "standard" or, in some cases (such as with the Grimm Brothers' or Hans Christian Anderson's versions) came to be seen as the "original" version of a tale. As with surviving oral versions of various folk tales and fairy tales, the historian can learn much about a society not only from the way a tale is told and preserved; much can also be learned from knowing which tales a society deems worthy of preservation and which tales it allows to disappear.

And then comes the medium of film. The ability of film to tell a story was recognised almost from the start, and effective uses of film as story-teller were quickly found. Stories could be told and retold in many different ways on film, and both film historians and cultural historians have noted the multitude of ways in which attitudes to love, war, religion, the family, and other "larger" topics and issues could be conveyed in films set in both historical and contemporary times.[21] For example, it is possible to compare, amongst many alternative themes, the changes in the culturally-expected "effects" of marriage on a young woman's life by looking at both the 1950 and 1991 Hollywood versions of the Edward Streeter novel, *Father of the Bride*. It is then possible to explore this theme further, as well as such themes as motherhood, ageing (Stanley/George Banks becoming a "grandpa") and how to "let go" of one's adult offspring in both *Father of the Bride* sequels, *Father's Little Dividend* (1951)

21 One example of a text which examines films in this way is Graeme Turner's *Films as Social Practice* (London: Routledge, 1988).

and the less-creatively titled *Father of the Bride Part II* (1995). It is because of this aspect of film's use as a vehicle to explore larger themes, as well as Hollywood's habit both of remaking older films and of producing different filmic versions of the same story (usually a literary text),[22] that what is shown on-screen – and how this can change in different versions (as is the case with adaptations of classic literary tales or remakes of the same type as the *Father of the Bride* movies) – can very effectively illustrate changes in a society's attitudes and beliefs over time.

And again, as with folk/fairy tales, the historian can learn a great deal from examining not only what types of stories have been made into films, but also how the stories were presented, what was left in the story, what was altered, what was left out altogether, and what new elements were added to it. For folklorist Vladimir Propp, these successive "variants" (as he called them) were crucial to understanding a society, since examining the differences between variants revealed much about both the internal and external changes society had undergone.[23] As Propp expressed this idea: "Folklore formations arise not as a direct reflection of life (this is a comparatively rare case), but out of the clash of two ages or of two systems and ideologies".[24]

If there is one single aspect of Disney's films which is consistently criticised more than anything else, it is the changes made in the stories which caused them to differ from the "original" versions. Norman Klein mentions Bruno Bettelheim's criticism of *Snow White and the Seven Dwarfs* (1937): that Disney had differentiated each of the dwarfs into characters with their own names and personalities.[25] It seems clear, however, that Disney, in altering and/or "modernising" these tales, was essentially performing the traditional function of the storyteller by altering the tale he was telling to fit his audience, as well as to make the story work cinematically (giving each of the seven dwarfs his own name and personality was cinematically more interesting than simply having seven unnamed, undifferentiated major characters on screen). Furthermore, we now know that Bettelheim was wrong to accuse Disney of initiating the change whereby the dwarfs are individualised; in the 1916 silent, live-action version of the story, *Snow White* (directed by J. Searle Dawley), the dwarfs are each named and made

22 For example, at least nine variations of Charles Dickens' *The Christmas Carol* have been released, including such versions as *A Christmas Carol* released in 1935, and extending to modernised versions such as *Scrooged* (1988), animated versions such as the short subject *Mickey's Christmas Carol* (1983; starring Mickey Mouse as Bob Cratchett), and the rather off-beat *The Muppet Christmas Carol* (1992).

23 Vladimir Propp, *Theory and History of Folklore*, translated by Ariadna Y. Martin and Richard P. Martin (Manchester: University of Manchester Press, 1984), pp. 8–9.

24 Propp, *Theory and History of Folklore*, p. 11.

25 Norman M. Klein, *Seven Minutes: The Life and Death of the American Animated Cartoon* (London: Verso, 1993), p. 39.

distinct from one another (albeit not to the same extent as in the Disney version).

More important than the cinematic changes made by Disney to these stories, however, are the ways in which Disney films present larger ideas and themes such as love and morality. Indeed, particularly significant are *how* these themes are presented, the ways in which these presentations change over time, and how consciously or unconsciously they are included within the Disney studio's filmic texts. To quote Propp:

> The old is changed in accordance with the new life, new ideas, new forms of consciousness. Transformation into an opposite is only one type of reinterpretation. Changes can be carried so far as to make things unrecognizable, and discovery of the original forms is possible only given a great deal of comparative data on various peoples and at varying stages of their development.[26]

Walt Disney was certainly seen by some of his contemporaries as being a "modern-day" storyteller. In a *Today's Cinema* article from 1938, an anonymous writer, known as "Onlooker", wrote of Disney that "Disney is one of the great creative artists that are destined to immortality. He is the Hans Anderson of the modern medium."[27] And, just as Propp emphasised that the written variants of folk tales were historical documents to be examined by scholars, so too are Disney's film variants – they are simply filmed, rather than written, and their dialogue and images are, as historical documents, open to analysis and interpretation. In other words, Disney films carry on the tradition of telling these stories in ways which are relevant to their audiences: the stories went from being constructed for oral presentation, to being altered to make them suitable for print, then transformed to make them suitable for filming. Concurrently to changing them so as to fit the constraints of each new medium, each new teller has also re-formed and re-shaped elements of the stories to fit both the medium they were using and the audience they were targeting.

It is the intention of this book to begin to delve into the ways in which the Disney studio re-told traditional tales, and by doing so, sought to find ways that would make these stories work cinematically, as well as making them relevant and attractive to contemporary movie audiences. The study itself is concerned primarily with an examination of the charac-

26 Propp, *Theory and History of Folklore*, p. 12.

27 "Onlooker", "Up and Down the Street", in *Today's Cinema* (22 February 1938), p. 11.

terisations of women in a selection of Disney's animated feature films. The question will be posed as to whether or not these characterisations reflect not only contemporary stereotypes, but also modern stereotypes of women within Western society. In particular, my focus will centre on those films in which the main character is not only female, but human. There are a few films in the selection which have a male character as a leading role, but these films also have an important female character who is pivotal to the plot-line, such as the role of Wendy in *Peter Pan* (1953). While other films will be mentioned as necessary, the films which will serve as my primary focus are *Snow White and the Seven Dwarfs* (1937), *Melody Time* (1948), The *Adventures of Ichabod and Mr. Toad* (1949), *Cinderella* (1950), *Alice in Wonderland* (1951), *Peter Pan* (1953), *Sleeping Beauty* (1959), *101 Dalmatians* (1961), *The Rescuers* (1977), *The Fox and the Hound* (1981), *The Black Cauldron* (1985), *The Little Mermaid* (1989), *Beauty and the Beast* (1991), *Aladdin* (1992), *Pocahontas* (1995), *The Hunchback of Notre Dame* (1996), *Hercules* (1997), *Mulan* (1998), *Tarzan* (1999), *The Emperor's New Groove* (2000), *Atlantis* (2001), *Lilo and Stitch* (2002), and *Treasure Planet* (2004). It is the hope of this book to add to the understanding of twentieth-century American social and cultural perceptions of women, as well as to contribute to a better understanding of the content of traditional "2D" Disney animated features and their place in American society. It should be noted here that, as is becoming standard practice amongst Disney scholars, "Disney" or "the studio" will refer to the Disney studio, and "Walt" will refer to Walt Disney the man (except, of course, within quotes; in such cases, naturally, quotes will be recorded accurately, with clarifications inserted where necessary). The Disney corporation will be referred to as either the Disney corporation or the Disney company.

The book begins with two chapters outlining the basic background to the problems to be analysed. Having looked briefly at constructions of femininity within American popular culture in this introduction and in the following chapter, it is intended that this initial discussion will serve as a basis for the in-depth examinations of constructions of femininity which will be undertaken on a film-by-film basis in the fourth, fifth, and sixth chapters. Chapters one and two will serve also as background for the later chapters, with

Chapter two providing the reader with an explanation of the history and mechanics of animation. This chapter is included because, in order to examine and analyse accurately a body of films such as these, certain aspects of how animation as a medium has evolved is essential for understanding why certain choices were made in terms of story, design, and the scale of each project. Chapter three will begin to narrow the study's focus by introducing the history of the rise of the Disney studio, and will also give some biographical details of Walt Disney's childhood, youth, and early adulthood as a way of looking at some of the possible roots of his attitudes and beliefs about women in order to better understand how much the attitudes in these films come from Walt himself, and how much they were normal ideas, attitudes, and values of twentieth century America. Chapter four will emphasise the Disney studio's history between 1937 and 1967, focusing predominately upon the analysis of the films made during that period which fit the criteria of this study. Following this same format, Chapter five will concentrate on films made between 1967 and 1989 and the state of the Disney studio during those years, and Chapter six will offer analysis of films made from 1989 to 2004. This chronological division of the studio's history is one which has been used by others when looking at the history of the studio. In my opinion, it is a useful format for me to follow: firstly, it links this study to earlier histories of the Disney studio; secondly, it reflects the very real differences in management styles at different periods within the company's history, in order to allow some consideration of the effects these have had on the animation studio's thinking and output; thirdly, they reflect (perhaps not coincidentally) the rise, decline, and rebirth of the studio's fortunes as a producer of entertainment within Hollywood and for the US and world markets.

That the Disney studio has been a Hollywood success story is unquestionable: beginning as a tiny independent studio with a staff of four (including Walt, his brother Roy as the business manager, and two animators, Ub Iwerks and Ham Hamilton) in October 1923,[28] it has since grown into one of the richest and most powerful multi-media conglomerates and corporations in the world. That this success is owed, for the most part, to the studio's ability to produce entertainment which appeals strongly to audiences is evidence that the ways it has told these stories resonates with viewers.

28 Watts, *The Magic Kingdom*, p. 28.

15

The fact that many of these films have achieved classic status, that they are continuously referenced by other films and animated works, that they are deemed to warrant scholarly attention, and that they continue to be measurably popular with audiences, shows that these films play an important cultural role. How much they tap into their culture's ideas, hopes, fears, and attitudes is what this study seeks to understand.

1

Film as a Cultural Mirror

In Hollywood, both in the past and in the present, what decides whether or not a film will be made, ultimately, is whether or not it is believed that the film will make money. If a film is to make money, it must appeal to a mass audience. If it is to do this, it must contain ideas, themes, characters, stories, and perceptions to which it can relate. It must, in other words, be relevant to the audience's world view if it is to be successful. Why does a film like *Thelma and Louise* (1991), ostensibly a road movie about two redneck women trying to escape to Mexico, strike such a chord – and stir up such controversy – amongst audiences around the world? The simple answer to this is that *Thelma and Louise* touches upon certain issues – mainly women's roles, rights and positions in what is still very much a male-dominated society – which are relevant not only to the lives of women of the same basic background as the title characters, but also to women as a whole, nearly all of whom have experienced some form of gender-related harassment and/or discrimination. More recently, the phenomenon of the success of the film *Bridget Jones's Diary* (2001), as well as the attendant criticism of the way it depicts thirty-somethings at the turn of the twenty-first century, has enjoyed great success. This far-reaching popularity comes from the fact that, like it or not, *Bridget Jones's Diary* mirrors back to a great many women the conflicting roles they are expected to fill, and their confusion as to how to navigate the difficulties and contradictions to be found within the era's complex and evolving understanding of the ways in which marriage, career, and family are/should be prioritised amongst middle-class Western women.

Likewise, there are within Disney's films certain ideas, perceptions, themes and stereotypes which are relevant to the daily lives of those who made these films successful, namely the audiences, who paid to see these films in the cinema, bought the related merchandise, went to the theme parks and rented or purchased the videos and DVDs. Had these films not "spoken" in some way to contemporary audiences, or at least if the studio had not believed that these films had this potential, then the films themselves would never have been made. Or, if they had been made regardless (which, owing to the expense of their production, is doubtful), then they would – like the many films which have failed to gain a favourable reception with audiences – have disappeared not long after their release. Likewise, had the films been successful in their day, but the ideas and themes they contain ceased to resonate with the public (or, in extreme cases, jarred hatefully with modern values), they would have become rare, controversial cinematic relics along the lines of films such as D.W. Griffith's *The Birth of a Nation* (1915): watched out of scholarly curiosity, at best saluted for their technical innovations, but used – ultimately – as a measure of how far social attitudes and values had progressed since such films' releases.[29] Granted, there is within the continuing popularity of the Disney canon a certain element of parents wanting to share with their children those films they enjoyed during their own childhoods. However, if elements within these films had become so outdated that parents re-evaluated their fondness for these films and changed their minds about sharing them with offspring, or, if the children had found nothing within them to which they could relate, then the films would have faded from popularity, lingering in popular memory only because of their nostalgic value, not because of their importance as cultural icons. But the significance of Disney's animated films is that, by and large, they did not disappear. While some were more popular than others, and while some have either increased or declined in mainstream popularity since their initial releases, most of Disney's films are still highly popular, highly successful, and even decades (in some cases) after their initial releases, still highly profitable for their studio. As they continue to find

29 While it is possible to claim that some films are not watched because they are silent and/or black and white, this is not always the case. Certain elements of British society claim not to want to watch black and white movies because "I pay for a colour tv license", and because black and white is seen as not only old-fashioned, but also as inferior to colour films. Similar prejudices exist toward silent films, since they tend to be thought of as "corny" and "boring". In my own teaching, however, when I have forced my students to watch silent animation and silent films, more often than not, all but the most closed-minded are amazed to discover that these are actually entirely watch-able, enjoyable films. The same cannot be said of a film such as *The Birth of a Nation*, which even film scholars and connoisseurs deplore for its racist, sexist, and violent elements, even while they applaud Griffith's cinematic innovation.

new audiences in each up-coming generation, it seems reasonable to assume that these films have more than simply a nostalgic appeal: they must, in some way, still hold relevance for modern audiences.

Molly Haskell, in the introduction to the classic text *From Reverence to Rape,* noted that "Most of the popular novels, plays, short stories of the twenties, thirties, forties, and fifties have all but disappeared, but the films based on them have survived to tell us more vividly than any new or old journalism what it was like, or what our dream life was like, and how we saw ourselves in the women of those times".[30] This is especially true of the films of Walt Disney. If people are asked to describe *Snow White and the Seven Dwarfs,* they are very likely to start talking about Sleepy, Dopey, and the rest of the dwarfs. If informed that, in the Grimms' version of the tale, the dwarfs did not have individual names, many are generally (and genuinely) surprised. Those who consider themselves to be "well-read" may not like to admit it, but, so far as many such traditional stories are concerned, we are usually content to let "Uncle Walt" tell us "his" versions of the stories and trust that they have been told fairly and faithfully.

A factor which is just as important, however, in any evaluation of Disney's role as cultural mirror is an examination of the individual characterisations within the stories themselves, as well as the types of stories which were selected to be made into films. The early films – the stories for which were chosen (and all of which were given final approval) predominately by Walt himself – are simple in their plot-lines, with easily-defined concepts of good and evil. This preference for more straightforward narratives seems to have been influenced, in large part, by the fact that such narratives seemed easier (both to Walt and to his staff) to adapt into animated feature films.[31] This was particularly true in the earlier history of animation, when technological and artistic innovations were just beginning to find ways to allow for more complex animation such as would support more complex storylines and plots. It is certainly the case that, mostly, they are tales in which highly archetypal, even stereotypical portrayals of women are likely to be found. Snow White, Cinderella, Aurora/Briar Rose – all are good, simple, kind; they are what Virginia Woolf once dubbed "the angel in the house".[32] Many of the female characters from

30 Molly Haskell, *From Reverence to Rape: The Treatment of Women in the Movies* (Chicago: University of Chicago Press, Second Edition, 1987), p. xviii.

31 For more discussion on types of narratives chosen, see Frank Thomas and Ollie Johnston, *The Illusion of Life: Disney Animation* (New York: Hyperion, 1981), Chapter 14 (pp. 367–391, especially p. 368.

32 Michele Barrett (ed.), *Virginia Woolf, Women and Writing* (New York: Harcourt, Brace, and Jovanovich, 1979), p. 59.

this period are counterbalanced within each one's story by some evil, obsessive, and (most likely) sexually-unfulfilled older woman: the evil queen, the wicked step-mother, Maleficent the evil fairy, and Cruella deVil.[33] It should be noted, however, that there are a couple of exceptions in this period. In the later periods of Disney's films, only Penny (in *The Rescuers,* 1977) and Ariel (in *The Little Mermaid,* 1989) are directly threatened by an older, vindictive woman. By the time *Atlantis* was released in 2001 (twelve years later), the female villain, Helga, was depicted as a young, attractive, alluring woman at her peak, and is a far cry (both in looks and in complexity of motivation) from her villainous prede- cessors.

As feminist critics have noted, Hollywood has traditionally reinforced the patriarchal, largely Victorian value system which has dominated Western culture throughout the his- tory of cinema. "As the propaganda arm of the American Dream machine", declared Molly Haskell,

> Hollywood promoted a romantic fantasy of marital roles and conjugal euphoria and chronically ignored the facts and fears arising from an awareness of The End – the winding down of love, change, divorce, depression, mutation, death itself. ... The very unwillingness of the narrative to pursue love into marriage (except in the 'woman's film', where the degree of rationalization needed to justify the disappointments of mar- riage made its own subversive comment) betrayed a certain scepticism. Not only did the unconscious elements obtrude in the films, but they were part of the very nature of the industry itself.[34]

In 1978, Brandon French noted that, particularly within women's roles (both in film and television) of the 1950s, there was a substantial degree of subversion of the notion that women were happiest in these traditional roles.[35] This subversion, however, in combination with the more tradi- tional representations of women finding fulfilment in mar- riage, still reflects the mood of their era: it is just that they reflect an era of change, albeit change which was still in its earlier stages of development.

In Disney's films – in particular, those made during what is referred to in this book as "The Classic Period" (films made during Disney's lifetime, between 1937 and 1966) – this traditional interpretation of the roles of love and marriage is without question the most prevalent. Heroes and heroines meet, fall in love, go through a separation and hardship

33 This idea of the "dangers" of older, sexually-potent women will be discussed in detail in Chapter 4 and, to a lesser extent, Chapter 5 in this book.

34 Haskell, *From Reverence to Rape,* pp. 2–3.

35 For more on this, see Brandon French, *On the Verge of Revolt: Women in American Films of the Fifties* (New York: Unger, 1978).

(which no doubt serves in some sense as a test of their devotion and pureness of heart), are reunited, marry, and live happily ever after. What exactly that "happily ever after" entails is a mystery, and we as spectators are led to believe that it will be simply a continuation of their love and happiness – of their exact emotions – at the time of their marriage. For many individuals within both child and adult audiences, such a future seems not only bright and lovely but possible. There is nothing in most films (Disney or otherwise) to indicate that love, even when it lasts, can change, or lose its intensity without losing its strength. Some recent writers and pundits have criticised this tendency to focus on the "happily ever after" as one of the roots of marital instability in the late twentieth century. As one such writer, working in the increasingly popular so-called "self-help" genre, would complain, "Because romantic tales usually end at the wedding (whole years eclipsed by the lying words: 'and they lived happily ever after') and because there has been scant attention paid to the question of *how* to live together in the increasingly complex state of marriage or long term cohabitation, most people are naive about what it entails".[36] However, given that, in the case of Disney films, most of these stories were decades or centuries old by the time they were put on film, and that the narrative structures they rely upon have been the framework for countless stories both past and present, when accounting for the increase in failed marriages and difficult or failed long-term relationships in the late twentieth/early twenty-first century, it seems peculiar to think that so much of the blame can be laid at the feet of fairy tales and the movies.

For some spectators, these depictions of love and marriage – stereotypical and essentially Victorian in sensibility though many of them are – served as a valued and valuable form of escapism.[37] This notion becomes particularly heightened when one remembers that the films with which this study is concerned, animated Disney feature films based mostly upon traditional fairy tales, are films which can be seen as doubly escapist due to their source material (fairy stories, with which many within the audience would have been familiar since childhood) and their medium (animation being a format which allows for amazing and otherwise impossible characters and depictions of fantasy and mythology). As Norman Klein notes:

36 Janet Reibstein, *Love Life: How to Make your Relationship Work* (London: Fourth Estate Limited, 1997), p. xvii.

37 Jackie Stacey offers a very interesting and useful discussion of this for British female fans of Hollywood cinema in Chapter 4 of her book *Star Gazing: Hollywood Cinema and Female Spectatorship* (London: Routledge, 1994), pp. 80–125.

> Much has been made of the psychological advantages of *function* in fairy tales; it presumably enables the listener to externalize deeply felt anxiety. It reifies forgotten moments in a person's intimate development (stages in childhood; family crises; sexual fears), or the social meanings of taboos in a community (like kin or incest). *Function* penetrates forgotten fears.[38]

What is it in these tales the Disney studio tells which carries out this "*function*" in fairy tales? When strong, sexually-mature women are portrayed as frustrated, maniacal, bloodthirsty demons and witches, what are these portrayals saying about perceptions on the part of the film-makers of women's sexuality? Most of all, perhaps, how large a role do these portrayals play in perpetuating or, in some cases, challenging certain sub-consciously held attitudes within society? Such questions as these are best answered not only through looking at Disney films as a genre in and of themselves, but also through looking at Disney in relation to the horror genre.

Disney and horror

The horror genre possesses many attributes in common with Disney's animated films, thanks no doubt to the fact that Disney's major source of stories has been fairy tales (which share major story elements and themes with classic horror films). Disney films featuring human leading characters, in particular, have many of the major elements of the horror film: the heroine/victim, the monstrous Other, the victorious hero who defeats the monster and re-establishes order.[39] It is important to clarify that not all of the films within this study can be classed as horror. Indeed, some of the films have either few or none of the elements of the horror genre. Nonetheless, most of these films do have, to varying degrees, examinations of the notion of "good versus evil", and often, as is traditional when following the Classic Paradigm narrative structure (as most Hollywood films do), the plot is structured so as to depict an on-going contest of protagonist against antagonist. This is most easily seen in the following table (facing page).

Of all the films in this study, "The Legend of Sleepy Hollow" segment of *Ichabod and Mr. Toad*, in fact, is one of the straightest treatments of horror to be found amongst Disney's animated features. The plot of the film demon-

38 Norman M. Klein, *7 Minutes: The Life and Death of the American Animated Cartoon* (London: Verso, 1993), p. 39.

39 This breakdown of the elements of horror films is a common one amongst scholars of the genre. For two examples of this, see Barry Keith Grant, *The Dread of Difference: Gender and the Horror Film* (Austin: University of Texas Press, 1996) and Barbara Creed, *The Monstrous-Feminine: Film, Feminism, Psychoanalysis* (London: Routledge, 1994).

Film	Antagonist	v.	Protagonists
Snow White & the Seven Dwarfs	The Wicked Queen	v.	Snow White and the dwarfs
Melody Time (Pecos Bill segment)	Widowmaker	v.	Pecos Bill and Slue-foot Sue
The Adventures of Ichabod & Mr. Toad	Brom Bones, The Headless Horseman	v.	Ichabod Crane, Katrina von Tassel
Cinderella	Wicked step-mother	v.	Cinderella and the mice
Alice in Wonderland	The Queen of Hearts	v.	Alice
Peter Pan	Captain Hook	v.	Peter and Wendy
Sleeping Beauty	Maleficent	v.	Prince Philip, the Good fairies
101 Dalmatians	Cruella deVil	v.	Roger, Anita, Pongo, Perdita
The Rescuers	Madame Medusa	v.	Bianca, Bernard and Penny
The Fox and the Hound	The Hunter	v.	Tod, Widow Tweed, Copper
The Black Cauldron	The Horned King	v.	Taran and Eilonwy
The Little Mermaid	Ursula	v.	Ariel, Eric, King Neptune
Beauty and the Beast	Gaston	v.	Belle and the Beast
Aladdin	Jafar	v.	Aladdin, Jasmine, and Genie
Pocahontas	Governor Ratcliffe	v.	Pocahontas and John Smith
Hunchback of Notre Dame	Frollo	v.	Febus and Esmeralda
Hercules	Hades	v.	Hercules and Meg
Mulan	The Hun	v.	Mulan, Shang, et al.
Tarzan	Clayton	v.	Tarzan and Jane
Emperor's New Groove	Yzma	v.	Kuzko
Atlantis	Rourke and Helga	v.	Milo, Kida, Audrey et al.
Lilo & Stitch	Gantu, Jumba, Pleakely	v.	Lilo, Stitch, Nani (and later, Jumba and Pleakely)
Treasure Planet	John Silver and his pirate band	v.	Jim, Dr. Doppler, Capt. Amelia, Morph, and B.E.N.

strates the classic horror film pattern. In essence, this pattern is comprised of the following elements: showing the normal order of the society in which the story is set; beginning the build-up of tension by the telling the background of the society's "threat" from within (in this case, the ghost of the headless horseman); the actual direct threat to Ichabod Crane as the Horseman tries to murder him; the allusion at the end of the film that the story has been only temporarily resolved, but that the threat in fact remains, awaiting another time and another victim. Though not all Disney films can be discussed in terms of horror (even if only partially), many do contain elements of horror and fantasy, albeit to a lesser extent than films like not only *Ichabod*, but also such films as *Snow White and the Seven Dwarfs*. *Alice in Wonderland* has an evil Other in the form of the Queen of Hearts, but this

23

is only for a section of the film. Mostly, *Alice in Wonderland* is just a bizarre dream full of nonsense, and is more akin to fantasy than true horror. In *Mulan*, even though there *is* in a sense the presence of what could technically be seen as a monstrous Other which threatens the order of Mulan's society, the outside threat is the Golden Horde, with whom China is at war, and though they are a threat to Mulan while she is a soldier, they are not targeting her personally and so, in this sense, are not a threat in the same way that the wicked witches, evil step-mothers, vindictive pirates, and other malevolent characters are in the other stories. The "Pecos Bill" segment of *Melody Time,* together with *The Fox and the Hound,* although they do present antagonism, do not really deal with "good versus evil" in their stories. *Mulan,* however, represents a rather different case. Indeed, in the pantheon of Disney animated films, *Mulan* presents the historian and film analyst with a special case in terms of its story and subject matter, and, therefore, will be given special attention in a later chapter.

Horror and Disney deal with notions about what are (and what are not) appropriate gender roles, and it is true that Disney films and horror films tend to deal again and again, at least on an underlying level, with such themes as what is proper/improper behaviour for women, what is/is not the "natural order", issues of coming of age and sexuality, and other gender-based concepts. Who rescues and who is rescued (not to mention who is rescue-able), what behavioural traits make a character "good" or "bad", and whether a "bad" character can or cannot be reformed or redeemed are themes which Disney and horror films share, and the parallels between the ways in which these themes are played out within these two types of films are numerous.

As a specific example of a parallel between a Disney film and a horror film, we may compare the stories of *Beauty and the Beast* (1991) and *Phantom of the Opera* (1925). Both look at the love/obsession of a "monstrous other" for a beautiful, gifted young woman (Belle is highly intelligent and possesses strong academic leanings, Christine is a talented opera singer and performer). The Beast gives Belle a library so that she may read to her heart's content for the first time in her life; the Phantom gives Christine the opportunity to take to the stage at the Paris Opera in a leading role, and finds ways to ensure that she has a successful career. Both young women, however, are prevented by their "benefactors" from having lives outside the small worlds of their gifts, and the only sources either Belle or Christine have for anything resembling romantic love are the monsters who are their protectors. Both films are based upon classic stories: *Beauty and the Beast* being based upon a French folk tale, *Phantom of the Opera* on Gaston Leroux's novel by the same name, which is, in turn, based upon the legend of a haunting at the Paris Opera House. Both are tales of beautiful, innocent young women who are – ultimately – held captive by a deformed creature who is characterised by such traits as loneliness, vengefulness, possessiveness, self-loathing, possible madness, frustrated sexual desire, jealousy, and fear.

Such parallels between Disney films and horror films are easily drawn. As Brigid Cherry points out in her study of female horror film fans:

> For many of these habitual [horror film] viewers, the taste for horror often began well before adolescence – several reported that their first experience of horror involved being enjoyably frightened by Disney-animated films and other dark children's films based on fairy tales – and had persisted long after. Horror films share the frequent representation of distortions of natural forms – supernatural monsters with a human face, for instance   with children's fiction, and these representations were often mentioned by participants [in Cherry's study of female horror film fans] as a continuing source of fascination, suggesting that these viewers continue to be simultaneously drawn to, and repelled by, similar representations to those that had engaged them in childhood.[40]

Clearly, at least in the minds of some fans of horror, there is a definite link between Disney and horror as genres. Yet an interesting area in which Disney and horror films depart company is the issue of what groups are considered the target audience. Although this conception of the horror film is currently changing, for many years it has been assumed that the primary audience for the majority of horror films has been male.[41] Certainly, Cherry has gathered evidence which demonstrates that, far from being unwilling audiences of horror, there are women who actively enjoy horror, even when they dislike certain aspects of the genre (such as the violent treatment of women in many horror films). The target audience for Disney films is traditionally seen as the child/family audience, despite the high degree of violence and terror which is typical in Disney films. It is interesting

40 Brigid Cherry, "Refusing to Refuse to Look: Female viewers of the horror film", in Melvyn Stokes and Richard Maltby (eds), *Identifying Hollywood's Audiences: Cultural Identity and the Movies* (London, BFI, 1999), p. 196.

41 Barry Keith Grant, "Introduction", *The Dread of Difference*, p. 7.

that the same parent who would not think twice about forbidding their child from seeing *Silence of the Lambs* (1991), in which a man kidnaps and murders various women with the intention of making a suit of clothes from their skins, would probably also think nothing about allowing their child to see *One-Hundred-and-One Dalmatians,* in which a psychotic woman is systematically kidnapping the "children" of various families of Dalmatians with the intention of slaughtering them and making a coat from their skins. The parallels between these two stories, when summarised in this way, are obvious. For the majority of spectators, however, such parallels would not seem as salient. After all, one is about a deranged serial killer and the FBI trainee who is investigating the case aided by the killer's psychopathic psychiatrist, the other about an erratic, eccentric woman and a bunch of talking puppies. *Silence of the Lambs* is live-action; *One-Hundred-and-One Dalmatians* is both an animated film and a Disney movie.

Despite the fact that Disney films are seen by many retailers, reviewers, and film cataloguers as being essentially a separate sub-genre of "family films", if not a genre in and of themselves, the fact is that Disney films' subject matter has at times been considered – at least by some film review boards – as possibly too intense and/or frightening for the child audience. For example, when it was released in the UK in 1938, *Snow White and the Seven Dwarfs* was deemed unsuitable for young children as it might cause them nightmares.[42] This precaution on the part of the British Board of Film Classification, however, was not universally viewed as appropriate, even within Britain. Numerous British reviews at the time of *Snow White*'s release attest to a wide range of opinions on the subject, though most seem inclined to think that an "A" certificate for the film was a little overly-cautious. One article which refers to the controversy surrounding the "A" certificate being given to *Snow White and the Seven Dwarfs* reads, in part, as follows:

> Of course, one of the questions I wanted to investigate was this business of the "A" certificate. I have since discussed that with several people, and there are two opinions. Some think the "A" certificate ridiculous; others think it is quite reasonable.
>
> My own impression is, that it was a bit over-cautious, and that I have seen many more things, both in cartoons and otherwise, that I should be more doubtful about for children. On

42 Alan Page, "Snow White and Fiery Red", *Sight and Sound,* vol. 7 no. 25 (Spring 1938), p. 22; see also "E. P.", "Snow White and the Seven Dwarfs", *Monthly Film Bulletin,* vol. 5 no. 50 (28 February 1938), p. 44.

the other hand, I should prefer a child to see the picture with his parents, rather than alone, and can assure both parent and child that they would be in for a very enjoyable time.[43]

Even as recently as 1995, the British Board of Film Classification decided that the Disney/Pixar film *Toy Story* (1995) deserved a PG [Parental Guidance] rating because, as Veronica Horwell would later describe it in an article on censorship, the film was deemed to be "... a mite scary".[44] In the United States, in contrast, the film received a G [General] rating and was apparently not seen by the Motion Picture Association of America [MPAA] as particularly frightening, even for very young children. Yet despite these occasional opinions and the various ties between Disney films and traditional horror films – Disney films are considered, by and large, to be acceptable viewing for audiences of all ages.

There is a substantial amount of scholarship supporting the notion that spectators can and do view films in an active way which allows them to take from a film those incidents and portrayals which "ring true" to them and ignore those aspects of films which are inaccurate or demeaning.[45] While these studies deal principally with black female spectators of mainstream Hollywood films and women audiences as spectators of horror films, it nonetheless seems plausible that this theory of active spectatorship can be applied, at least to an extent, to the genre of Disney animated films. I say to an extent because, while much of the audience for any Disney film consists of a fair percentage of adult women and older girls, a substantial proportion of a Disney film's audience is made up of very young girls. The above studies are of adults; they are of women who have learned over the course of their lives to take the portrayals of race/sex which they see on the movie screen with a grain of salt, and may consequently have become sophisticated at reading films. Young children, however, at the beginning of their movie-watching lives, are only beginning to learn that what they are watching is only "make-believe". Furthermore, and unlike adults, children are very likely to incorporate the things they see in movies into their play, thereby repeating, analysing, and incorporating into their subconscious the ideas and themes they take away from films. The degree to which they do this is a matter of some debate amongst experts on children, the media, and child psychology.

43 "Onlooker", "Up & Down the Street", *Today's Cinema,* Tuesday, 22 February 1938, p. 11.

44 Veronica Horwell, "Cut and Thrust", *The Guardian,* 1 February 2000, p. 7 (of the *G2* section).

45 Examples of discussions on the subject include Karen Hollinger, *In the Company of Women: Contemporary Female Friendship Films* (Minneapolis: University of Minnesota Press, 1998), and Jacqueline Bobo, *Black Women as Cultural Readers* (New York: Columbia University Press, 1995).

Studies of children and media

In looking at psychological theories about children's play, the idea that children use play – pretend play in particular – as a way of practising their present, future, and even potential roles within society is undisputed. H.G. Furth and S. R. Kane, for example, use detailed analysis of a single but extended episode of pretend play on the part of three girls (one four-year-old and two five-year-olds) to demonstrate that such play not only develops social skills (the children's abilities to share and communicate is discussed at length), but also shows how the girls are able to incorporate various cultural stereotypes, roles, and traditions into their play.[46]

The example given concerns three girls pretending to be getting ready for a royal ball. It should be noted that, as the authors of the study point out, the only constraint imposed on the children was that they had to play in a particular corner of their school room (albeit one which was typically used for certain kinds of play amongst the children).[47] The play initially began between the two five-year-old girls: the older one, who was five years and eleven months, proposed to the younger girl (aged five years and one month) that they pretend that they are getting ready for a royal ball which is to occur "the next day" (according to the frame of their play). While the two girls were playing, various social conventions were invoked: a hierarchy was established, with the slightly older girl being recognised by both children as being the one in charge (though whether this superiority was thanks to her age or the fact that the "royal ball" theme was her idea is never really discussed or made clear). Sharing and equal division of the various toys available to the girls was done through taking turns selecting items and relying upon rules of previous possession in order to establish "ownership" of the items being involved in play. The ability of children to use items symbolically was demonstrated by looking at how the girls used a large bedspread, with corners on it that could be used to simulate hoods, as their coats, since each of them could use one corner of the bedspread as her personal coat and share it. Furthermore, the use of this bedspread as a coat by the girls was also employed to show that the children were able to incorporate tradition into their play since it would seem that this bedspread has been used as a coat by a succession of children who have been in this classroom.[48]

46 H.G. Furth and S.R. Kane, "Children Constructing Society: A New Perspective of Children at Play", from Harry McGurk (ed.), *Childhood Social Development: Contemporary Perspectives* (Hove, UK: Lawrence Erlbaum Associates, Publishers, 1993).

47 Furth and Kane, "Children Constructing Society", p. 153.

48 Furth and Kane, "Children Constructing Society", p. 156.

Nineteen minutes into the play session, a third child – the four-year-old girl mentioned earlier – entered the room and became involved in the play session. Her arrival demonstrated the other two girls' knowledge of how to play this particular game of "getting ready for a royal ball", how to establish and maintain rules of ownership, and how to establish and maintain hierarchy – based on age – within the group. Because there were certain elements of their play which the two older girls had to explain to the younger girl, the fact that the girls were able to combine both reality and the rules of their pretend game demonstrated their ability to construct their make-believe world.[49] Through their play, the two five-year-olds and the four-year-old showed quite clearly the fact that they were able not only to recognise roles and the rules that apply to those living those roles, such as when they are discussing how they will behave and how other (pretend) individuals will behave toward them when they are queens during their evening at the ball, but are also able to internalise them (even if only for the purposes of their play) and regulate their behaviour according to them.[50] It is interesting that they chose, as the format for this complicated play session, the framework of a fairy tale (in this case creating a story which in many ways parallels the tale of "Cinderella"). As Furth and Kane point out, however, this choice of framework as a way of practising social interaction is understandable, since social and cultural norms are usually contained within such stories. As Furth and Kane put it, "It was Western tradition, handed down in fairy tales and conveyed in the present culture, not personal affect or attachment that determined these roles. There was no need for the players to define roles before they started".[51]

Using a traditional fairy story as the starting point for the discussion in his book on children's play, David Cohan demonstrates the fact that even very young children are able to understand ideas as complex as gender roles at a surprisingly early age. He points out how his son (who served as one of the subjects) was, at the age of two years and six months, completely aware of the differences between masculine and feminine, and he and others around him were able to fulfil very definite social roles. This passage, which is Cohan's account of this particular discussion with his son, is best quoted in full:

At 2:6,[52] Reuben has also started to play games in which his

49 Furth and Kane, "Children Constructing Society", pp. 158–162.

50 Furth and Kane, "Children Constructing Society", pp. 154, 157, 158, 160.

51 Furth and Kane, "Children Constructing Society", p. 164.

52 In his book, *The Development of Play* (London: Routledge, 2nd. ed.1996), Cohan relies upon the method used by Piaget of noting his subjects' ages at given moments. The notation 2:6, for example, means two years and six months.

gender identity is brought into question. From 2:0, he has been very fond of *Snow White and the Seven Dwarfs*. At 2:5, we have just been listening to the record. Reuben looks happy. I ask him if he is Cheerful (one of the dwarfs)?[53] "No", he smiles. Is he Dopey? "No", he smiles. Is he Sneezy? "No", he smiles. Is he Snow White? "No". Reuben now bursts out laughing. He goes on laughing as he says that Mummy – Alieen [Cohan's wife] is indeed in a white dress – is Snow White.

At 2:6, Reuben also plays a game with Nicholas [Reuben's older brother] in which each of them is supposed to have a vagina. They cross their legs – Nicholas especially – and, from time to time, laugh a little. This is another instance where they create a game in which sexual roles are involved.[54]

Children have been shown to be well aware of gender roles at significantly early ages, and can even be shown to be aware of what is inappropriate – as well as appropriate – behaviour within these roles. Examples such as those mentioned above point out that psychological observation of normal[55] children at play offers substantial backing to the notion that children develop a definite sense of gender-appropriate roles at comparatively young ages.

Furthermore, it is known that children are affected from very early on by the media images with which they are constantly bombarded. The example given above (of Reuben and his being questioned on *Snow White*) already emphasises the fact that very young children are already exposed to the media.[56] Of course, there is some disagreement as to how much or how little children actually take in of what they see in movies and on television. What does seem to be agreed upon by psychiatrists and psychologists studying the impact of media upon children, however, is that visual media have an influence on children (and on adults, for that matter) because film appeals to the sense of fantasy, even when the images being portrayed are "realistic" (such as with documentaries).[57] Thus far, however, the amount of recent academic work focusing upon the child audience is comparatively small, the data for examining how children respond to films is limited or flawed, and most research into the effects of media images on children is in any case primarily concerned with television rather than cinema audiences. While there have been a number of studies in the past which have attempted to explore the effects of various media (mainly cinema) on children (one

53 Cohan never states whether it is the Disney version or another version of the story which is being used. Disney did not use "Cheerful" as a name (there is, however, a dwarf called "Happy"). The other two names mentioned are names used by Disney for the dwarfs, so it is possible that Cohan has simply made a mistake in naming the dwarfs to his son.

54 Cohan, *The Development of Play*, p. 134.

55 "Normal" here is meant to mean children who are not suffering any social or psychological difficulties.

56 For examples of studies on the subject of media's impact on children, see Dolf Zillman, Jennings Bryant, and Althea C. Huston, *Media, Children, and the Family: Social Scientific, Psychodynamic, and Clinical Perspectives* (Hove, UK: Lawrence Erlbaum Associates, Publishers, 1994).

57 An essay which touches upon this subject is Charles Ashbach, "Media Influences and Personality *(contd)* Development: The Inner Image and the Outer World", in Zillman et al,

famous example being the Payne Fund studies of the 1930s), these studies are of no use to modern-day researchers into media's effects on children as they were often distorted by their eras' attitudes to and prejudices towards race, ethnicity, and class which would today be seen as both irrelevant and elitist, particularly when it comes to their (to modern eyes) patronising and exaggerated concerns about the effects of the movies on immigrants, the poor, and – ultimately – upon all of those who are not white, male, middle-class (or higher), native-born Americans. As the fields of film history and film/media studies grow, this gap will no doubt be addressed. At present, however, the evidence from which I have been compelled to draw my conclusions has been focused more on specific adult audiences (such as women and various ethnic groups), and references to these groups' viewing interests as children are only briefly addressed, and usually as memory rather than as subjects of long-term viewing habits (which might include, for instance, observing an individual's movie-going habits over the course of twenty or thirty years and compiling data as to how an individual views films at various points in their lives).

*Media, Children,
and the Family,*
pp. 117–128.

2

A Brief History of Animation

This chapter begins with an overview of animation's beginnings and a discussion of how animation, as both an art and as an industry, took shape in the United States in the first half of the twentieth century. This is followed by a brief examination of two of the main animation studios in America in the 1930s and 1940s (and Disney's main competitors), the Fleischer Brothers studio and the animation unit at Warner Brothers. These will help to underline and illustrate a comparison between how animation's role and worth as a medium were perceived at the Disney studio and other studios. It is also important to outline, in general terms, animation techniques and practices of this period and at various studios in order to achieve a more complete understanding of how and why animated characters were created and presented as they were.

This chapter, despite its presence in a book on the films of the Disney studio, has very little discussion of topics which are directly related to Disney. While this may initially seem odd, there are in fact very good reasons: in order to appreciate the many ways in which the Disney studio differed (and continues to differ) from its competitors, it is important to become acquainted with the nature of Disney's competition. From 1928 – the year in which the Disney studio achieved its first major success with the release of "Steamboat Willie" – up to the present day, animation at other studios has been defined, understood, and appreciated in relation to Disney (even if only to reject the Disney style and ethos), measuring achievements and failures by how much – or how little – the influence of the Disney studio can be detected. In other words, *why* the Disney studio did what it did, *how* it did what it did, what it did, how its ways changed (and how they stayed the same) over time, and even a sense of what Walt Disney and his successors hoped to achieve both within and for animation as a medium, are best understood within the context of how animation was approached at other studios. Because there were two studios in particular between 1925 and the 1950s which could be viewed as being equal to the competition offered by the Disney studio, it is only those two studios – the Fleischers' studio at Paramount, then the animation unit at Warner Brothers studio – which will be discussed in any detail.[58] Once the reader has a working knowledge of animation history and an idea of how animation outside the Disney studio was approached, it becomes much easier to understand the very real and important ways in which the Disney studio differed from other studios, and to appreciate the ways in which these differences contributed not only to the choices made by the Disney studio regarding its production, but also to the Disney studio's ultimate success.

Pre-cinematic animation

It is generally accepted that the earliest precursor to animation – as well as to all film-making – was a device called the magic lantern. It was a very basic machine, consisting of a box in which one placed a lantern or a candle next to a curved mirror so as to project still images. Discussed by the man given credit as its inventor, Jesuit priest Athanasius Kircher, in the last chapter of his *Ars Magna Lucis et Umbrae* [The Great Art of Light and Shadow], published in Rome around 1645, the magic lantern quickly caught the imaginations of many, despite the warnings of some churchmen that it was somehow linked to witchcraft.[59] While the interests of some, such as Kircher, led them to see the magic lantern as a tool for education, many others viewed the device as a means of entertainment. By 1735, Dutchman Pieter van Musschenbroek had shown that the magic lantern could be used to create images which had the illusion of movement.[60] This was done with the aid of a revolving disc which, unlike Kircher's use of a series of related pictures to highlight/illustrate a story (rather like a modern slide show or PowerPoint

58 While it is recognised that the animation unit at MGM was a vibrant, successful, and award-winning studio, and while it certainly could not be characterised as second-tier, nonetheless it was not one of the studios which could be perceived as the *main* competition for Disney in the era being discussed. In the 1920s in particular, Fleischer was the dominate studio in US animation, and when Fleischer declined, it was to secede its position to Warner Brothers, in large part thanks to the popularity of Bugs Bunny.

59 Charles Solomon, *The History of Animation: Enchanted Drawings* (Avenel, New Jersey: Wings Books, 1994), p. 3.

60 Solomon, *The History of Animation*, p. 3.

presentation), van Musschenbroek's discs had on them various sequential images which, when used correctly, simulated simple movements. Indeed, according to Charles Solomon, it was van Musschenbroek who would present the first animated show using several magic lanterns. These shows included "synchronised slide changes and long slides (which he slowly passed before the projecting beam) to present more elaborate illusions, such as a storm at sea …".[61] This form of magic lantern show quickly caught on, and by the eighteenth century it was a fairly common gimmick amongst travelling entertainers. Indeed, magic lantern shows took various forms, including the use of magic lanterns for adding special effects to stage plays. Magic lanterns were used, for example, to project ghostly images onto a stage for a more "realistic" effect, as well as producing phantom images for the popular "Phantasmagoria" shows of the eighteenth and nineteenth centuries. It was in these ways that magic lantern shows became widely known in Europe and North America in the nineteenth and early twentieth centuries, though, smaller, less expensive versions of the magic lantern eventually were mass-produced and sold as parlour toys for the middle and upper classes.

Another device which is accepted as a precursor of animation as we know it today is a toy called the *thaumatrope*, invented around 1826.[62] Playing upon the then newly-discovered physiological phenomenon called *persistence of vision* (which, briefly, is when the human eye fuses a series of consecutive pictures into a single, moving image, provided that the pictures are shown with sufficient speed and light), the *thaumatrope* was simply a disc with corresponding images on each side of it (such as a bird on one side and a cage on the other) and was manipulated either with pieces of string tied through opposite ends or with the disc mounted on top of a stick. When the disc was spun quickly, the two images on either side of the disc appeared to be combined into a single image; in other words, the bird appeared to be inside the cage.

One step up from the *thaumatrope*, technologically speaking, was the *phenakistoscope*, invented by the Belgian scientist Joseph Plateau sometime between 1828 and 1832. The *phenakistoscope* consisted of two discs, one with a short series of simple sequential images on it and the other with a series of evenly-spaced slits. When the discs were spun, the viewer

61 Solomon, *The History of Animation*, p. 3.

62 According to Solomon, the *thaumatrope* was invented in 1826, probably by John Ayrton Paris, but its invention has also been attributed to various others. See *The History of Animation*, p. 7.

looked through the slits to see what appeared to be a moving image. Following this was the appearance of the *daedalum* (Devil's wheel). Although it was invented in 1834 (by William Horner of Bristol, England), it apparently did not catch on until the 1860s, when its name was changed to the *zoetrope* (wheel of life). The *zoetrope*, which also relied upon the phenomenon of persistence of vision, was a drum with evenly-spaced slits in its side and in which was placed a slip of paper with sequential images printed on it. When the drum was spun, the spectator looked through the slits at the images, which appeared to be moving. While a very simple, repetitive image (such as a man hammering or a seal balancing a ball) was all that the *zoetrope* could produce, nonetheless the device proved to be very popular, and examples of both *zoetropes* themselves and the paper slips with images for use in *zoetropes* can still be found in a number of museums and private collections today. Also still surviving in large numbers are *kineographs*, or flipbooks, which were invented in 1868. In 1895, Thomas Edison created a mechanical version of the flipbook, called the *mutoscope*, which could be described as being like a rolodex/rotodex with a crank, with a sequential photograph or drawing upon each card in the rolodex. This device, however, which seems to have mainly appeared as an amusement park novelty, most likely arose as an experimental device to accompany Edison's sound recordings, rather than as a purposeful advance in the history of animation.

What was – arguably – a real leap forward in the history of the animated film as we know it today came when Emile Reynaud invented a device called the *praxinoscope* in 1877. According to Charles Solomon, the *praxinoscope* was like the *zoetrope* in that both devices involved the rotating of a drum with a paper slip of sequential images attached to its inside. Unlike the *zoetrope*, however, which required the viewer to look through slits in the drum, the images were reflected upon a series of mirrors. By 1882, Reynaud had begun using the *praxinoscope* with a projector and began to draw animated stories, initially upon long strips of paper, then upon strips of celluloid. He opened his Théâtre Optique at the Musée Grevin, which was a wax museum in Paris, in 1892, and began exhibiting what he called his *Pantomimes Lumineuses*, which were the short films he was drawing on celluloid. The films were accompanied by music and electrically-triggered sound effects, and proved to be highly successful. Solomon states that between 1892 and 1900, Reynaud gave approximately 13,000 performances of his various *Pantomimes Lumineuses*, to a total audience estimated at 500,000, which was an exceptionally large number at that time.[63] Eventually, however, Reynaud was unable to keep up with the rates of production to be seen elsewhere in the growing film industry, as men like Emile Cohl and Georges Méliès proved to be better suited to producing work for the new medium. Although a few of his films have begun to be rediscovered in recent years, many of them were lost when, in a fit of despair one evening in 1910, Reynaud himself apparently threw his equipment and the majority of his films into the Seine. His place in animation's history seems to be somewhat debatable, in fact, since, although it is known that (despite his slight ability at animation and drafting) he created colour animated films with synchronised soundtracks long before anyone else, it is not known whether other pioneering animators or other film-makers attended any of his shows or even knew of his work. His influence upon other animated film-makers, therefore, is open to question. By 1900, certainly, the film industry, though still in its infancy, was nonetheless becoming well established and was certainly more sophisticated than anything Reynaud had produced, which could explain why his *Pantomimes Lumineuses*, which were so popular initially, fell from public favour so rapidly.

Early cinematic animation

Many of the early artists in the American animation industry had fallen into the animation business because of their unsuccessful earlier attempts at careers as illustrators or cartoonists. Emile Cohl, Georges Méliès, and many of their contemporaries had begun their careers as comic illustrators, and the influences of their earlier training can be seen in the style and nature of the animation they produced. Paul Terry, Tex Avery, and Winsor McKay all began as cartoonists. Max Fleischer was the art director of a magazine, and his brother Dave trained briefly at an engraving company. Walter Lantz's first job, according to Norman Klein, was cleaning Winsor McKay's brushes at the *New York Herald*.[64] Walt Disney took a job as an animator with the Kansas City Film Ad Company because his application to work as a

63 Solomon, *The History of Animation*, p. 8.

64 Norman M. Klein. *Seven Minutes: The Life and Death of the American Animated Cartoon* (London: Verso, 1993), p. 13.

cartoonist at the *Kansas City Journal* had initially been rejected, and the business he had begun with Ub Iwerks (called Iwerks-Disney Commercial Artists) had been allowed to dwindle and had gone into limbo.

Of these, the first to achieve wide-spread renown as an animator was Winsor McKay. A successful cartoonist and illustrator, McKay, who claimed to have been inspired by his son's flipbooks and, supposedly, was spurred on in his attempt by a bet, is said to have created the first American animation (as we think of it today) in late 1910.[65] Called "Little Nemo" and based upon his comic strip of the same name, "Little Nemo" premiered at the Colonial Theatre in New York on 12 April 1911 as part of McKay's own vaudeville act. According to Solomon, McKay was irritated by the fact that his skill as an animator and draftsman caused his audience to mistake his drawings for trick photography involving live actors, a mistake which audiences apparently made again in 1912 with McKay's film "How a Mosquito Operates", reportedly believing (according to Solomon) that McKay had rigged up a mosquito dummy on wires and then filmed it.[66] Because of this mistaken perception of his animation as live-action films, and in particular given the fact that McKay's rich, detailed, lavish animation was incredibly time-consuming and laborious to complete, McKay chose as his next subject a dinosaur, a creature which would have been much harder to fake in live-action cinema than it would have been to draw one. Thus, "Gertie the Dinosaur" premiered in 1914, again as part of McKay's vaudeville act. Gertie proved successful at being the first screen character to be accepted by US audiences as an animated character, which perhaps accounts for her popular but inaccurate reputation as the first animated character of the cinema, in place of Little Nemo.

It was not long after "Gertie the Dinosaur" was released that the animated film industry began to expand rapidly. Although McKay neither formed his own studio nor worked for any of the already-established film studios, other artists and animators quickly began to establish animation studios as a more stream-lined way of producing animated films (McKay would occasionally hire one or two assistants, but on the whole is said to have done the majority of the drawings for his cartoons himself). Animated film production elsewhere was largely tied to the characters of the

65 Though McKay is acknowledged as the first *American* producer of animation, and though he often claimed to have invented the medium, it is now believed that the real credit for the invention of animation as we know it today goes to French artist Emile Cohl. For more on him, see Donald Crafton, *Before Mickey: The Animated Film 1898–1928* (Chicago: University of Chicago Press, 1993).

66 Solomon, *The History of Animation*, p. 16.

syndicated comics (the "Funnies") which were circulated in US newspapers, some early examples being *Mutt and Jeff* and the *Katzenjammer Kids*. These films were the products of convoluted deals between the studios and newspaper publishers, and more than one studio could be producing simultaneously cartoons of the same characters, providing that each studio had a deal with the newspaper which owned the character.

While the deals which allowed these cartoons to be created were often complex, the cartoons themselves were simple in terms of storyline (when there actually was a storyline), character development (even in the cases of re-occurring characters, very little was put into a character's motivations or personality), or draughtsmanship. The character of Felix the Cat provides an example. Felix can solve problems by manipulating the things around him, turning them into whatever objects he requires at any particular moment (after all, his world is made of ink, and can be re-formed by him at will so as to serve his purpose). He can use his ability to manipulate the world around him as a tool to outwit his adversaries. He can run, jump, climb, walk, and hop. His face can express fear, triumph, satisfaction, and anger. He can laugh and cry. He can do absolutely anything. He can go absolutely anywhere. He has no limitations. Nothing is much of a challenge for him to overcome. But we never have any strong sense of personality from Felix. Although we may find his antics funny, we cannot identify with Felix, and, even when we can cheer him on, it does not disappoint us if he is momentarily unsuccessful (in fact, we can laugh without any sympathy at his plight). Even his failures serve as a source of enjoyment for his audience. This description holds true for the majority of early cartoon characters. But these early cartoons were not considered by many people – including the artists and studios who made them – to be important, as they were merely short subjects to provide entertainment for audiences between featured attractions, both in the cinema and in vaudeville.

In the early days of cartoons in America, the majority of the cartoon studios were located in New York City, and, consequently, the major distributors were there as well. Walt Disney's studio (founded in 1924 as the Disney Brothers studio) was the first animation studio to be set up in Los Angeles, and, when Disney wanted to distribute his cartoons, he had to deal with people in New York. It was not until the 1930s, once sound production had become industry-wide, that the animators based in New York and Kansas City (where animators such as Disney, Iwerks, Hugh Harman, and Rudolph Ising began their careers) began to follow Disney to California, as studios such as Disney, Warner Brothers, and MGM began to lure artists westward to create cartoons for them. It was during the 1930s that, initially, the main strategy of many animation studios for competing with Disney was to attempt to copy Disney as much as possible. Indeed, Warner Brothers, MGM, and various other animation studios, in their efforts to compete with the increasingly successful Disney studio, did all they could to persuade Disney artists to come and work for them.[67]

Although, in April 1929, Universal became the first of the major studios in Hollywood to invest in the formation of an animation department for the sole purpose of making their own cartoons, it was during this period, mainly 1928 through to the late 1930s, that the Disney studio became the leader in its industry, mainly owing to the exceptionally high standards it set itself (at least in comparison with other American animation studios at that time), as well as to the Disney studio's constant striving for improvements both in the organisational methods employed in producing cartoons and in the technological aspects of animated film production. It was the Disney studio, for example, which has been credited with the invention of the storyboard as a way of organising a cartoon's story and communicating it to the animators. In the technical aspects of filming the cartoon with the greatest degree of realism[68] possible, Disney led the way for other animation studios with its various technological innovations, an example of this being the invention by a Disney studio employee of the multi-plane camera, which was a way of photographing the various cels so that the overall shot had greater depth and dimension. The innovations of the Disney studio, however, will be discussed at a later stage.

How to make an animated film

The importance of a discussion of animation techniques here is this: because of the artistic and technical limits of animation as an art form, many of the stylistic and visual

67 Michael Barrier, *Hollywood Cartoons: American Animation in its Golden Age* (New York: Oxford University Press, 1999), p. 325.

68 For the purposes of this study, the terms *realism* or *realistic*, are used to mean having a kind of accuracy about the look of the drawing. It may still be more artistically than photographically rendered, but it is drawn to scale with the characters and environment surrounding it. Mickey Mouse, for example, is not realistic; he is about three feet tall (rather large for a mouse), and no matter which way he moves his head, both of his ears are still facing the audience. Snow White, however, is realistic as she is drawn to scale with everything around her, her limbs and other characteristics are all properly proportioned, and she moves in the same way any other human would.

aspects of the characters, stories, and films are sometimes influenced less by the original vision of the animators and more by the technical constraints of the medium. The trade-off for these technical constraints, however, is the greater "control" which the makers of animated films have over their "actors". In a live-action film, an actress may disagree with the overall perceptions and/or vision of the director of a film in which she is appearing. Although she may speak her lines and hit her marks as she is directed, she still has the power to influence her audience's perception of her character through her eyes, her face, and her body language, as well as through the tone of her voice, so that what spectators see in the character is different from what the director had intended for them to see. It is in this way that Annabella Sciorra claims to have not only differed with director Spike Lee, but even to have subverted his intentions for her character, in the making of *Jungle Fever* (1991). As one writer commented,

> Spike and Sciorra would look at the same words in the script every morning, yet take away two entirely different ideas of what they were supposed to mean. As both writer and director, Spike had the final say in the matter: he had the power to make her say his words. But he could not control the *way* Sciorra delivered these lines, or how ... she held her head or set her facial muscles. Through this subtle subversion, Sciorra got her way.[69]

This sort of subversion, however, is largely impossible in an animated film. After all, there is nothing in the portrayal of an animated character – not a blink of an eye, not a tilt of the head, not even the movement of the folds of a skirt – which is not decided upon in advance, carefully mapped out, and then drawn to suit the expectations of the director of a film. All that the actor or actress contributes to the performance is a voice. And, since the dialogue is usually the first step in the process of producing an animated film, the visuals can be made either to complement or counteract the performer's tone of voice.

It is not known how often an actor or actress who is lending his/her voice to an animated character has tried to change the main perception of a character from that of the director to his or her own. Admissions such as Annabella Sciorra's are hard to come by in Hollywood cinema. To find such a comment on an animated film – especially a Disney film

69 Alex Patterson, *Spike Lee* (New York: Avon Books, 1992), p. 167.

(coming as it would from the feedback surrounding the output of one of the most notoriously litigious of Hollywood studios) – is, in my experience, impossible. However, it is important to bear in mind when watching and analysing an animated film that no look or gesture is there by accident. All of the visual aspects of a character which come together to influence our perception as spectators are there on purpose, and their inclusion was decided upon not by the actors, but by the director. This point cannot be stressed enough. Indeed, it is upon this concept that the key arguments of this study rest.

During the last five to ten years, animation techniques, thanks to the increased use of the computer, have undergone some of the most dramatic changes in their history. Yet, throughout the period from 1911 to roughly 1985,[70] the basic aspects of the mechanics of animation remained the same. Characters and backgrounds were drawn by artists, their drawings were photographed onto cels, and the cels were photographed onto film reels. Various people checked to see that the drawings were in the proper sequential order, that continuity was maintained (i.e. that the colours used, the look of each character, and the story elements were consistent throughout the film), and that the story – as it was presented – made sense. This is not to say, however, that there were no innovations in animation during its first eighty years. It is important, however, that an overview of the subject be included in order to give the reader a better understanding of why various aspects of the look of each film evolved as they did.

Animated films, like live-action films, are made up of a series of sequentially arranged individual photographs, called frames. Like the *thaumatrope*, *zoetrope*, and other such devices, film relies upon the phenomenon of persistence of vision for the viewer to be able to link the series of frames into what appears to be a moving image. In order for this to be achieved, the film is run at a speed of twenty-four frames per second. In a ninety-minute film, therefore, there are 129,600 individual frames. This means that, for a ninety-minute animated film, a team of artists must produce a number of individual drawings which is many times the number of frames (since there are at least two drawings which are put together to create the layers of a single frame) – an enormous amount of work. It is a gigantic effort which

70 Although the Disney film *The Black Cauldron* (1985) was the first to incorporate any computer animation, computer animation was used only sparingly until the Pixar film *Toy Story* (1995) became the first animated film produced entirely on computer.

requires that the project possess meticulous organisation and co-operation, but still be run in such a way that individual creativity can easily be admitted into the overall process. It was also during the 1920s that the process of animation became increasingly more factory-like in its "assembly-line" production methods, methods which arose in the various studios as a way to make their work go more quickly from start to finish, thereby making themselves more competitive in terms of both out-put and expenses.

The creation of an animated film of any length involves various stages. In the pre-production stage, the story is chosen and planned, the backgrounds are designed, aspects of how the film's characters look and act are decided upon, and the music, sound effects, and dialogue are recorded and timed to correspond with the correct frames of the film. It is at this stage of production that the storyboard for the film is put together, an invention which today seems logical and simple but which, when it was first created in order to help the artists at the Disney studio organise their work on "Steamboat Willie" (1928), was a revolutionary idea both for animation and the film industry as a whole. Alfred Hitchcock, for example, later adopted the storyboard method in planning certain sections of his films, with some of his scripts having as many as 600 set-up sketches for the more complicated shots.[71] The storyboard is mainly used as a tool for organising the story as a whole, as well as a way of deciding which lines will be spoken during particular shots in the film. Besides providing a visual aid to the directors and artists of a film, the other advantage of a storyboard is that, especially in the planning stages of a film, it is easy for those working on the film to add, remove, or re-arrange certain sections of the story in order to determine the best possible way the story in front of them can be told.

In the production stage of the making of an animated film, there are basically eight phases: (1) the main drawings of a sequence are created; (2) the extra drawings needed to complete an action in a sequence are worked on by artists known in the industry as in-betweeners; (3) the clean-up artists remove any extra lines from the drawings and, in general, "clean up" the image; (4) the cels are inked (which means that the black outlines of the figures are drawn) and painted; the cels are then (5) checked for any mistakes, (6) assembled, (7) put into sequence, and (8) photographed.[72]

71 Louis Giannetti, *Understanding Movies* (Englewood Cliffs, New Jersey: Prentice Hall, Inc. (5th edn, 1990), p. 154.

72 For more detailed explanations of the processes of making an animated film, see Ralph Stevenson, *The Animated Film* (London: The Tantivy Press, 1973), pp. 17–19, and Frank Thomas and Ollie Johnston, *The Illusion of Life: Disney Animation* (New York: Hyperion Press, 1981).

This list of steps does not include the stages when sound is added because, in many ways, it is an entirely separate process from the creation of the drawings of the film itself. Many of the eight steps, moreover, did not evolve in animation until the 1930s.

The use of a storyboard, for example, could make a studio more competitive. The process of creating an animated film, however long or short, is a highly labour-intensive endeavour. If cutting the number of finished drawings down from twenty-four to twenty-two per second is worth-while enough to a studio as a means of cutting down its budget, then obviously cutting down on the number of wasted drawings created for sequences which were later thrown out for not working within the film as a whole, obviously, is a great saviour of time and money. The storyboard (which is made up of single sketches of various shots for the film), by allowing the artists and directors to have a visualisation of what the final outcome of the film will be, often allows them to discard a sequence which does not work within the context of the film as a whole before ever having to animate even a rough version of the sequence. The merits of being able to throw out the three or four rough sketches which stood for a minute of film, as opposed to throwing out the 1,440 drawings which are necessary to create one minute of film, are obvious. It was the creation of the storyboard by the Disney studio's story department, and its expanded use by the studio's artists, which not only helped to give Disney a competitive edge at a very crucial time in the history of studio animation, but which also made the creation of a full-length animated feature, an effort which was (and indeed still is) such a monumental undertaking for a studio, not only more easily done in the artistic/conceptual sense, but also (and predominately, in the minds of most animation studio heads other than Walt Disney) in the financial sense.

The rise of American animation and the Fleischer studio

Cartoons in the early years of animation were, by and large, very simple in terms of story and character development. This simplicity was, in large part, due to the limits of the medium as it existed at that time. Stories had to be simple, with easily understood pantomime and gags, as films were, of course, silent. Each cel had to be made from drawings that were completely done by hand, as no other duplication methods existed at that time. Assuming, therefore, that a cartoon ran seven minutes (the average length of a cinematic animated short), and that the animators had included twenty-four frames for each second of film (which, at some of the more profit-driven studios such as Fleischer, was not always the case), a seven minute cartoon could be made up of 10,080 frames and anywhere from two to ten times that number of drawings to make up the entire frame). It should be noted that, typically, each frame is comprised of multiple drawings: two at the most basic level (the background and the characters), three and upwards for more complex, higher-quality animation. These numbers, of course, do not include the numerous drawings which, for whatever reasons, did not work and were therefore not included in the finished cartoon, nor does it include drawings for things like the storyboard. For film with a running time of seven minutes, 10,080 is the number of finished frames on the strip of film, *not* the number of drawings needed to create that finished film.

Obviously, having to do that number of *finished* drawings by hand – as well as having to ensure that all of the drawings, by different artists, conform completely in style – can be very expensive in terms of both time and money. Given the low status (in relation to both art and to cinema) which has been endured by animation for much of its history, the idea that a great deal of time, money, and artistic endeavour should be "wasted" on a "mere" cartoon seems not to have arisen at the majority of animation studios, including in particular those studios which, unlike the Disney studio, were owned and run by the major Hollywood film studios. Indeed, many animation studios found that it was possible to get away with twenty-two frames per second of film. Doing so, although it reduced the overall quality of the image, also reduced the overall cost of the film and cut down on the number of man hours involved in the film's production. By limiting the number of frames in a film from 10,080 frames (which a seven minute cartoon would have when animated using twenty-four frames per second), to only 9,240 frames (as would be the case in a film using only twenty-two drawings per second), a difference of 840 frames and at least twice that

45

number of drawings was eliminated. That being able to reduce the amount of finished frames by 840 for nearly the same results on the screen would be seen as a major saving by a financially strapped studio is obvious, and it was this mindset – which considered financial aspects of film-making over the artistic and aesthetic ones – which was most often found in the less successful animation studios of the 1920s and 1930s.

One of the best ways to understand Disney's success is to look at why its only real competitors, ultimately, were not as successful. By examining two other studios, Fleischer Brothers and the Warner Brothers animation studio, and looking at some of the myths surrounding Disney's position in the animation industry at that time, a better understanding will be reached as to those factors which helped the Disney studio to succeed. On the whole, by the early 1930s, there were two major animation studios vying with each other for dominance within the medium: the Disney studio, which was one of Hollywood's few independent studios to be successful over the long-term, and the Fleischer studio, which, eventually, came to be owned by Paramount. The Fleischer studio, run by brothers Max and Dave Fleischer, was the studio which brought to the screen such characters as Koko the Clown, Betty Boop, and Popeye and which, for much of its existence, was considered by many to be the only serious rival of the Disney studio.

It has been argued in an article in the June 1999 issue of *Sight and Sound* that the Fleischer studio, and Max Fleischer in particular, were in fact the front-runners in animation – both in terms of story development and technical innovation – throughout the 1920s and 1930s. Harvey Deneroff, the author of this article, in his brief discussion of the Betty Boop cartoon "Poor Cinderella" (1934), implies that this, the first of Fleischers' cartoons to be made in colour,[73] was leading the Fleischer studio along the path (which was already being taken at Disney beginning in 1934) towards full-length animated film production. According to Deneroff, had Fleischer committed his studio's "resources and talent [which] he [had] employed on "Poor Cinderella", the history of US animation might have taken a different turn. But instead the studio lavished its attention on its newest star, Popeye, whose cartoons following "Popeye the Sailor" (1933) became the most popular short films in the United

73 "Poor Cinderella" was also, according to Deneroff, "an elaborate production which introduced the 3-D process (invented by Fleischer and John Burks the year before) ..." Harvey Deneroff, "The Innovators 1930–1940: The Thin Black Line" *Sight and Sound*, vol. 9 No. 6 (June 1999), p. 24.

States, eclipsing even Mickey Mouse".[74] What Deneroff fails to realise is that the Disney studio was perhaps the earliest to recognise the importance of "narrative" and plot for a cartoon, which can be defined as the existence within a cartoon of both an overall identifiable story and the presence of motivation for characters' actions, as well as a series of events which rise to a climax and end in a resolution in a form which at least resembles, if not directly using, the classic paradigm narrative structure. In his book *Hollywood Cartoons*, Michael Barrier points out that all of the effort which went into the making of "Poor Cinderella" went into such details as the bridles on Cinderella's coach, not into the story or character development. As Barrier puts it, "There's no sign in most Fleischer cartoons from the middle thirties, and in the Color Classics [of which series "Poor Cinderella" was the first] in particular, of any real interest in the characters; they're usually dull or unsympathetic".[75]

Barrier recognises the enormous amount of technical work which went into the making of "Poor Cinderella", noting that it was far more detailed than was typical of Fleischer cartoons and does mention the "3-D" effect which Deneroff describes. Barrier notes, however, that rather than being 3-D, "Poor Cinderella" employs a "3-D" process called a "set-back"[76] (the device to which Deneroff was no doubt referring when he stated that "Poor Cinderella" was "an elaborate production which introduced the 3-D process (invented by Fleischer and John Burks the year before)".[77] A "set-back", which was patented by Max Fleischer in 1933, was when a cell which had the characters and foreground objects painted on it was placed between two sheets of glass and photographed in front of a miniature set, made to be in the same scale as the cel painting, and photographed together as a frame, so that the animated characters would appear to be moving about in a three-dimensional world. In many ways, the idea is similar to the concept, popular since the early 1920s, of imposing animated characters onto a scene from the real world, except that, rather than using live-action film for the background, an actual set is constructed. Because of this small but critical difference, the look of each of these concepts is quite different. Indeed, the effect of the set-back, far from being even remotely convincing, is actually quite eerie and far more unrealistic than it seems intended to have been, the obvious animatedness of

74 Deneroff, "The Innovators 1930–1940", p. 24.

75 Barrier, *Hollywood Cartoons*, p. 185.

76 The "set-back" was in many ways a version of the multi-plane camera patented by the Disney studio (and no doubt what Deneroff had in mind when he says that the Fleischers' came up with an early version of this sort of photography before Disney). The difference between this technique and a multi-plane camera is that the multi-plane camera relies entirely upon painted cels which are stacked between sheets of glass with the background cel at the bottom working up to the main foreground image's cel, thus giving a greater illusion of depth to the frame as a whole, as opposed to miniature background "sets", which is what a "set-back" relies upon.

77 Deneroff, "The Innovators", p. 24.

the characters contrasting jarringly with the objects and room surrounding them. The notion that a film such as "Poor Cinderella", with its unappealing characters and its strange aesthetics could have been a stepping stone for the creation of a feature film department at Fleischer is also something of a stretch. It is unsupported by the kinds of cartoons being created by Fleischer at that time, to include "Poor Cinderella", the main appeal of which was apparently meant to have been the use of the "set-back", and it is also not supported by the animated feature which Fleischer eventually did produce, *Gulliver's Travels* (1939), which did not utilise the "set-back" method at all.[78] Most importantly, however, the idea that "Poor Cinderella" was an attempt by Fleischer to prepare for feature animation is weakened by the fact that the film concentrates more on its look than on such key elements – often ignored in Fleischer cartoons – as character development and story.

In the early days of animation, although story was stressed to a point, the emphasis of many cartoons was on slap-stick and violence as a means of entertainment, and the Fleischers' cartoons moved along in this vein, albeit with a twist of New York's Lower East Side-style humour and speech patterns. The Fleischers, after all, like many of America's animation pioneers (including Walt Disney), were not only influenced by, but were in many ways taught their craft by *the* handbook on animation techniques and principles at that time: E.G. Lutz's *Animated Cartoons*, published in 1920.[79] In his handbook, Lutz pointed out in the chapter entitled "On Humorous Effects and on Plots", that

> "To be sure, an animated cartoon needs a good many more incidents than one calamitous occurrence. It is indispensable, for the sake of an uninterrupted animation, that it should have a succession of distressing mishaps, growing in violence. This idea of a cumulative chain of actions, increasing in force and resultant misfortune, is peculiarly adapted to animated drawings."[80]

The Fleischers' cartoons before Popeye certainly follow this pattern, and, even during the *Popeye* series, violence, rather than plot movement or character development, was still used as the main catalyst for both the story and the characters' actions. Deneroff seems not to have appreciated the fact that there is almost no story whatsoever in the Fleischers' cartoons. Characters are simply driven from one gag to the

78 It is true that Fleischer did use the set-back in other shorts, such as "House Cleaning Blues" (1937). However, its use was limited within the individual shorts (for just a shot here and there), and it was not used for even a majority of the Fleischer studio's shorts output. Moreover, it was never employed in any of their feature films, and seems not to have been intended to be (nor was it ever treated as) an important aesthetic development within animation practice at the Fleischer studio.

79 Animation histories, without fail, mention Lutz's book as being in almost universal usage amongst animators of the 1920s, to include such animators as Walt Disney, Friz Freleng, and Ub Iwerks. One history of animation which specifically mentions Lutz's book as an important guide amongst animators of this era is Klein's *Seven Minutes*.

80 E.G. Lutz, *Animated Cartoons: How They Are Made, Their Origin and Development* (New York: *(contd)*

next, often for no particular reason, and then the cartoon simply ends, with little closure involved, as there is little or no story which needs to be resolved.

Deneroff states that the Popeye series was an important departure from the Fleischer studio's earlier work because, prior to Popeye, the Fleischers "... had previously paid little attention to narrative",[81] as if he thought it was entirely possible to make a successful animated film, running an hour or more in length, which was solely comprised of sight gags, slap-stick violence, and the occasional Yiddish aside, with little or no plot, character development or motivation, or anything with which an audience could identify. When describing why the Fleischers' studio failed, he says only that the studio suffered serious labour problems and that, in order to get away from having to work with unions, the Fleischers moved to Florida and established a studio there which eventually went bankrupt thanks to their having to pay high wages to attract artists to Florida. That these serious labour problems were in fact a five-month long strike, in 1937, held by lower-level artists (mainly in-betweeners and ink-and-painters), and that the strike was over pay, working conditions, and business practices at the studio, and which had an enormous impact on the studio's eventual decline, does not come into Deneroff's discussion at all. Furthermore, he makes no mention in his article of the bitter feud which had arisen between Max and Dave Fleischer,[82] nor does he mention the enormity of the Fleischers' debts to Paramount (again, many of which were either created by or exacerbated by the strike). The fact that their departure from Paramount left the Fleischers without any of the merchandising rights to the characters they had created is also not discussed, nor is Max Fleischer's very real lack of interest in animation as a medium (indeed, his only interest in it seems to have come from his interest in mechanical invention). These, plus Fleischer's poor understanding of business practices and people management, seems not to have occurred to Deneroff, yet they are vital to understanding how and why the Fleischer studio eventually failed.

The weakness of Deneroff's argument can be further underlined by pointing out the examples at the Disney studio which were occurring at roughly the same time as the troubles at the Fleischers' studio. Walt Disney, when he

Charles Scribner's Sons, 1920), pp. 225–226.

81 Deneroff, "The Innovators", p. 24.

82 Klein, *Seven Minutes*, p. 85.

49

moved his studio out to California (he was the first to establish an animation studio in Los Angeles), had to pay premium wages in order to lure artists west from such places as New York City, and, in 1941, only four years after the labour disputes at Fleischers' studio, Disney was forced to contend with a strike at his own studio which lasted several months and affected not only morale, but also production and finances. As far as a comparison between Disney and Fleischer animation goes, it is crucial to point out that Disney cartoons, by focusing on story, plot and character development, as well as by concentrating on improving the artists' abilities in technical animation, were taking much more realistic – and conscious – steps towards feature production from 1933 onward. Fleischer cartoons, which depended mostly on gags, were not being used by the studio to prepare for features, but were simply business as usual. As will be discussed below, the only reason the Fleischer studio seems to have been prompted to attempt feature animation was in order to compete with Disney, rather than out of any real desire to expand the studio in that direction.

A common misconception about Disney's relationship to other animation studios – in particular in the 1920s, 1930s, 1940s, and 1950s – is that Disney was a rich, powerful, and influential Hollywood film studio which simply squashed all its competition by throwing more money at its projects than would have been possible by these other studios. Furthermore, there seems to be an acceptance of the idea that the Disney studio was able to eliminate its competition by saturating the market for animation with its own films. Deneroff, for example, makes the mistake of thinking of the Disney studio as being one of the industry-controlling Hollywood studios of the day, instead of the struggling independent studio which it in fact was, a misconception he demonstrates when he comments that "… undoubtedly the *most important and profitable independent* [my italics] cartoon studio – and Disney's most feared rival – was that owned and run by the Fleischer Brothers".[83] Since, in reality, Paramount owned the Fleischer Brothers studio from 1929 until 1938 (a fact to which Deneroff alludes on the second page of his article), the only time in the history of Fleischer Brothers in which the Disney studio could have been viewed as a major contender in the field of animation, it is worth pointing out that Deneroff's article even confuses

[83] Deneroff, "The Innovators", p. 22.

which studio during this period was independent (Disney) and which was not (Fleischers).

This may sound like a small point but, in fact, there was a great deal of difference in the advantages and disadvantages of independent versus non-independent studios. Most importantly, it should be noted that the independent studios in Hollywood (to include Disney) did not have a means of independently distributing their films at this time. Instead, they had to make deals with professional distributors and/or those larger studios which owned the movie theatres and controlled the distribution and advertisement of most films circulated in the United States until the monopoly on theatre ownership and film distribution by the so-called "majors" was broken up by a series of cases brought by the federal government between 1946 and 1955. As a result of these cases, and in particular the Supreme Court's decision in the case of the *United States* v. *Paramount Pictures* (decided 3 May 1948), the major studios, in order to comply with the Court's decisions regarding their violations of various sections of the Sherman and Clayton acts, sold off their theatre chains.[84] Indeed, in the early days at the Disney studio, one of the greatest controlling factors as to which of the studio's films were released and promoted was the whim of whomever held their distribution contract, and the percentage of money made by the studio from a film's profits was also determined by how much the distributor felt inclined to pay. Honest distributors paid the agreed-upon percentage, as was stipulated by their contract, and also offered a fair, equitable deal to the studio. Dishonest distributors found ways to shuffle their accounts so as to keep the Disney studio's share of the profits to themselves for as long as possible.[85]

The licensing and financial perils of such a system for an independent studio – such as the Disney studio – are readily obvious. The Fleischers were sheltered from the difficulties of distribution by Paramount, which handled the distribution of the Fleischers' cartoons for them and naturally gave these cartoons preferential treatment in Paramount-owned theatres over the cartoons of other animation studios. Although the Fleischers had to contend with the executives at Paramount when it came to making some of their decisions, the very real, major problems of having to deal with an outside distributor were headaches from which they were

84 As a result of the major studios selling their theatre chains – in effect, relinquishing their control over film exhibition – many independent distributors were able to form and compete on a level playing field with the major studios' distribution and exhibition units. The effect of the Supreme Court ruling upon the Disney studio was that they were able to form their own successful distribution unit, Buena Vista, which now had fair ground for competition. Disney were thereafter able to keep a greater percentage of their films' profits, thanks to their not having to pay a percentage of the profits to their outside distributors, as they had been forced to do previously. For the crucial cases on the road to "divestment", see *Bigelow v. R.K.O. Radio Pictures*, 327 US 251; *Schine Theatres v. the United States*, 344 US 110; *United States v. Paramount Pictures*, 334 US 392; *Theatre Enterprises, Inc. v. Paramount Film Distributing Corp.* 346 US 537; *Partmar Corporation v. Paramount Pictures Theatres* protected. An independent studio, such as Disney, was forced to sign contracts with distributors in order to get their cartoons and films shown in enough cinemas for the film to earn any revenue at all, let alone turn a profit for the studio. Furthermore, a part of these contracts could be – and often was – that distributors would be given the right to keep for themselves an agreed-upon percentage of the profits from a cartoon or a film for an extended period of time, thus decreasing the profit margin of the studio which had created the film or cartoon in question. Not only was the potential for fraud great (Disney, for example, probably lost thousands of dollars in the late 1920s and early 1930s thanks to his association with Pat Powers, a distributor in New York City), but there was also the problem, when an independent was dealing with a major studio as its distributor, that the major studio naturally tended to give preferential treatment to their own films over those being produced by an independent studio who had turned to them for distribution.[86]

The fact that the Fleischers were protected by their association with Paramount from such financial constraints was invaluable to them when it came to attempting to compete with Disney with an animated feature film of their own. The Fleischer Brothers/Paramount animated film *Gulliver's Travels*, according to Norman Klein, was a hit at the time of its release during Christmas 1939. Although it has not often been re-released since then, Deneroff asserts that the film was a major influence upon such film-makers as Hayao Miyazaki.[87] According to Klein, Paramount wanted the film to be made as "a Fleischer answer to *Snow White*",[88] thus implying that *Gulliver's Travels* was made more as a reaction to *Snow White* than as a natural progression in animation at Fleischer. Also, although the animation, despite the mix of graphic styles, was good enough, the story as it was presented in the film was not terribly brilliant, and does little to hold the audience's interest, let alone its attention. Klein sums it up well when he describes *Gulliver's Travels* in this way: "The principles of volume and cuteness were observed [in the film]; overall it was more than a competent, if uninspired, effort".[89] *Gulliver's Travels* was made at a chaotic time for the Fleischer studio. Brothers Max and Dave Fleischer were no longer on speaking terms, and in the midst of this was the studio's move to Miami (which Paramount helped finance, even though – or perhaps because – the

(contd) *Corp.* 347 US 89; *Lawlor, Trading as Independent Poster Exchange v. National Screen Service Corp.* 349 US 322; *United States v. Loew's Incorporated* 371 US 38. The full texts of these decisions are available at http://www.findlaw.com/casecode/supreme.html

85   Barrier, *Hollywood Cartoons*, pp. 48–49, 63–67.

86   Klein, *Seven Minutes*, p. 53; Barrier, *Hollywood Cartoons*, pp. 58, 61–63.

87   Deneroff, "The Innovators", p. 22.

88   Klein, *Seven Minutes*, p. 85.

89   Klein, *Seven Minutes*, p. 85.

move represented the troublesome Fleischers' breakaway from Paramount). Indeed, when *Gulliver's Travels* is compared to some of the early planning stages of *Snow White and the Seven Dwarfs*, a similar mix of styles and similar mistakes were being made by Disney artists. The key differences, however, between the Disney studio's creation of *Snow White* and the Fleischer studio's creation of *Gulliver's Travels*, were these: (1) Disney had more time to plan, revise, and discard elements which did not really work within the overall film, and had the luxury of time to work on the visual, story, and sound elements (music, voice, and sound effects) of the film until they were exactly right, whereas Fleischer was working under a fairly tight deadline imposed by Paramount, and had to hurry to meet that deadline; (2) the Disney studio had already divided up into various departments which concentrated on perfecting their own parts within the process: a story department, an effects department (which specialised in all the special effects such as fire, rain, and so forth), and a character animation department, just to name a few; furthermore, it had seen to it that all of its staff were well trained, and that this training was an on-going process; the Fleischer operation was far less organised and compartmentalised, which meant a lack of opportunity for individual artists to improve or perfect their craft; likewise, not only had Fleischer not ensured artistic training amongst its staff, it had traditionally *discouraged* its artists from seeking fine art training or any other training. As one former Fleischer employee described this situation,

> Those people who were quite content with the raw, peasant humor, the bad drawing, the kind of not-too-thought-out timing and the simpleminded stories ... that bunch stayed [at Fleischer]. The more adventurous, who really wanted to learn to do a better movie, left [Fleischer]. Every one of them. Nobody stayed who had that urge, because there was no way to make such a picture in New York. So, that marked a schism which exists to this day. And it's a very strange thing. The people in New York who later went down to Miami to work on *Gulliver* and *Mr Bug Goes To Town*, to a man they believed that any time that Max would give a little more time to work, they could have done all that stuff in *Snow White and the Seven Dwarfs* easily, no problem. They had been self-hypnotized so they couldn't see the exquisite drawing which had nothing to do with their work.[90]

90 Leonard Maltin, *Of Mice and Magic: A History of American Animated Cartoons* (New York: McGraw-Hill, 1987), pp. 83–84.

It's most damning "review" came from Walt Disney himself, who is said to have commented on the film, "we can do better than that with our second-string animators".[91] Furthermore, Fleischer directors were not likely to encourage any kind of experimentation or innovation on the part of their staff. Michael Barrier, for example, quotes a 1977 interview with Ed Rehberg, who described one of the leading directors at Fleischer (and one of the directors for *Gulliver's Travels*), Seymour Kneitel, in this way: Kneitel

> "had a stock formula for walks and runs, and you either did it his way or it was wrong. There was never any experimenting. He'd say, "You're stupid if you do it that way. Don't you have any more sense than that?" He was that crude.[92]

Clearly, the work/artistic culture at Fleischer was radically different from the one at Disney. Like many studios, it operated under the belief that animation as a medium was not to be valued, and therefore that large amounts of time, money, and effort were not worth the bother. Unlike some of the other animation studios belonging to the majors, however, it was tightly controlled and used by those in charge, and its artists lacked the freedom or resources to build and improve. Though still working under tight budgets, other studios, which granted their animators more freedom to experiment, achieved better results. One studio which proved that beyond all doubt was the animation unit at Warner Brothers.

Animation's golden age and the Warner Brothers' studio

Whilst the Fleischer studio may have failed eventually, another animation studio which operated successfully in competition with Disney during the 1930s, 1940s, and 1950s was that at Warner Brothers. The Warner Brothers-affiliated cartoons got their start on 28 January 1930, when Hugh Harman and Rudolph Ising signed a contract with Leon Schlesinger (who had earlier signed a contract with Warner Brothers to provide them with cartoons), binding them to pass on to him the negative of one sound cartoon each month for three years.[93] Dubbed *Looney Tunes*, an obvious take on the Disney studio's *Silly Symphonies* series, these cartoons were to be made within a budget of $4,500 per cartoon for the first year, with the budget to be increased to at least $6,000 per cartoon over the next two years.[94] According to Michael Barrier, when the first *Looney Tunes* cartoon, "Sinkin' in the Bathtub", was shown to Jack Warner in April

91 Maltin, *Of Mice and Magic*, p. 118.

92 Barrier, *Hollywood Cartoons*, p. 295.

93 It could be argued, however, that it was Schlesinger's contract to provide cartoons for Warner Brothers, signed on 24 January 1930 (four days earlier), which was the actual beginning of cartoon production at the Warner Brothers' studio.

94 Barrier, *Hollywood Cartoons*, p. 157.

1930, Warner, after seeing only half of the cartoon, ordered twelve more *Looney Tunes* from Schlesinger and, on 17 April 1930, Warner decided to exercise Warner Brothers' option and ordered a further eleven.[95]

Looney Tunes, as their name implies, were intended, like the *Silly Symphonies,* primarily to highlight music, something in which Warner Brothers was interested as the studio owned several music publishing companies and saw these cartoons as potential vehicles for the songs they were publishing.[96] *Looney Tunes* were, however, still very much typical cartoons of their day, full of the same gags and sense of humour in general. The original *Looney Tunes* featured Bosko, a character created by Harman and Ising, who was originally portrayed as a stereotypical black character who spoke in the "minstrel show"-type dialect. He quickly evolved, however, into a rather close imitation of Mickey Mouse. Bosko was even given a girlfriend, Honey, who fulfilled the same function in Bosko's stories as Minnie Mouse did in Mickey's cartoons. This evolution in Bosko's characterisation probably occurred because of the rise in popularity which Mickey Mouse enjoyed during the first year of the production of *Looney Tunes.* Although Bosko, as Harman and Ising first conceived of him, was to be featured in cartoons with a much greater emphasis on dialogue, because of the terms of their contract with Warner Brothers (obliging them to use the music available to them from the Warner Brothers' music catalogues), the cartoons' subsequent emphasis on music left little room for dialogue. Even the titles of the early *Looney Tunes* cartoons were either humorous takes on the titles of actual songs published by Warner Brothers, or else the cartoons had the same title as the main song featured in the cartoon.

Although the Warner Brothers music library was well-tapped by the *Looney Tunes* series, it was the *Merrie Melodies* series, beginning in 1931, which most heavily utilised the Warners' musical resources. As Barrier points out, the *Merrie Melodies* took their titles directly from their featured songs, rather than spoofing song titles as the *Looney Tunes* tended to do. Also, as the cast of characters in the *Merrie Melodies* tended to change from one cartoon to the next, they came to resemble the Disney studio's *Silly Symphonies* in their form and structure much more closely than did the *Looney Tunes.* The *Looney Tunes*, with their emphasis in the first

95 Barrier, *Hollywood Cartoons*, p. 158.

96 Warner Brothers, thanks to the success of their film *The Jazz Singer* (1927), were at that time pioneering talking films. Furthermore, their ownership of music publication businesses gave them an added impetus for wishing to promote this aspect of their corporation. For more on this, see Douglas Gomery, "The Coming of Talkies: Invention, Innovation, and Diffusion", in Tino Balio (ed.), *The American Film Industry* (Madison, WI: University of Wisconsin Press, 1976), pp. 192–211.

three series on the re-occurring characters of Bosko and Honey, more strongly resembled the Disney studio's Mickey Mouse cartoons.

By 1933, difficulties began arising between Leon Schlesinger and the partnership of Harman and Ising. In part, the tension seems to have resulted from money troubles. Schlesinger was paying Harman and Ising less money per cartoon by the 1932–33 season, only $7,300 per cartoon instead of the originally promised $10,000 they were to have received at that time. By 1 March 1933, when Schlesinger signed a new contract with Warner Brothers, his own payment for bringing in cartoons for Warner Brothers was further reduced to $6,000 per cartoon, meaning that he could afford to pay Harman and Ising even less than that.[97] Additionally, the trouble between Harman, Ising, and Schlesinger may have been exacerbated when they were nearly sued by Disney for breach of copyright, on the basis of Bosko and Honey's increasingly striking resemblance to Mickey and Minnie Mouse.[98] Also, there seems to have been a degree of personality conflict between Harman and Schlesinger, and through Schlesinger with Ray Katz, Harman and Ising's business manager and Schlesinger's brother-in-law. The result of these difficulties for the partnership between Schlesinger and Harman and Ising was that Harman and Ising broke away from Schlesinger. Schlesinger signed a new contract with Warner Brothers, this time forming an animation studio which was directly controlled and owned by Warner Brothers (as opposed to a studio which worked for them under a contract, as Harman and Ising's studio had done). Schlesinger proceeded to staff his studio by stealing as many animators as he could away from the other studios of the day, and then went on to let his animators get on with the business of animation (Schlesinger himself knew almost nothing about the process of creating an animated cartoon, and so concerned himself principally with acquiring funds for the studio, seldom interfering with the day-to-day running of the animation unit, its artistic decisions, et cetera).[99]

Although the new studio's early cartoons were neither well made nor successful, by 1934 the role of director had finally been handed over to Friz Freleng, who started out directing *Looney Tunes* for Schlesinger but who quickly became the sole director for *Merrie Melodies*. Although some of his early

97 Barrier, *Hollywood Cartoons*, p. 164.

98 Klein, *Seven Minutes*, p. 46.

99 Barrier, *Hollywood Cartoons*, pp. 324, 358.

Merrie Melodies can be compared to contemporary cartoons at Disney, the fact that the *Merrie Melodies* budget per cartoon was only around $7,500 (as compared with the $20,000+ which Disney spent per cartoon), meant that such standards were impossible for Freleng to maintain for very long. According to Barrier, the way that Freleng dealt with his limited budget was to think in terms of time, rather than dollars, and he determined that a cartoon needed to be produced by their studio every four to five weeks. Whilst his first *Merrie Melodie* was done in the two-colour process, his next six cartoons were done in black and white, which helped to stretch each cartoon's budget during the initial period of Freleng's leadership. Although the *Looney Tunes* continued to be made in black and white for some time, the *Merrie Melodies* from November 1934 onward were made in colour, which Warner Brothers made allowances for by paying Schlesinger an additional $1,750 per *Merrie Melodie*, bringing each cartoon's budget up to $9,250.[100]

By 1935, another new director began working at Warner Brothers, Fred "Tex" Avery. Avery was an in-betweener at Universal's animation department until he was fired from his job in April 1935. In May, Avery went to Leon Schlesinger, declared himself to be a director, and managed to convince Schlesinger to hire him, despite his having no previous directing experience before joining the Warner Brothers animation department. Just as Freleng was the director who proved to be best at organising the new Warner Brothers animation department, so did Tex Avery prove to be the director it took to help the animation studio move forward successfully in its transition from featuring mainly human characters to featuring animals as its stars. In many ways, Avery did much to forward the career of one character in particular who had made a small appearance in a Freleng *Merrie Melodie* called "I Haven't Got a Hat" (March 1935), namely Porky Pig. Although it was Freleng who took credit for coming up with Porky Pig's most lasting and memorable trait – his stutter – it was Avery who, in effect, became Porky's "career manager" and really made him famous.[101]

It was also some of the members of the unit under Avery's permanent direction – Bob Clampett and Charles M. "Chuck" Jones (along with Virgil Ross, and Sid Southerland) – who eventually became some of the Warner Brother cartoons' most famous animators. Freleng continued to

100 Barrier, *Hollywood Cartoons*, p. 327.

101 Barrier, *Hollywood Cartoons*, pp. 329–332.

direct his own cartoon unit at Warner Brothers, as did Jack King, who worked with Warner Brothers until April 1936, when he left Warner Brothers for Disney to become the director of the new series of Donald Duck cartoons. Avery continued to feature Porky Pig as the exclusive re-occurring character in his cartoons whilst slowly introducing to the *Merrie Melodies* series as a whole a newer, more zany style that harkened back to the Felix the Cat cartoons which Avery admired, but still maintaining the more realistic style which had become the industry standard thanks to Disney's insistence upon more realism in his own cartoons. In fact, it was not until April 1937, in the cartoon "Porky's Duck Hunt", that what was in many ways a revolutionary new character – one who differed from Porky in the sense that he was in the cartoon purely to serve as a source of gags rather than a source of story – was introduced into Avery's work. Although he did not have a name at the time of his introduction, he would soon be called Daffy Duck, and, unlike Porky, he was created decidedly *without* any influence from the Disney studio. Daffy stood out at the time he was created precisely because he was created with the emphasis less on realism and more on gags. In many respects, Daffy, especially in his earliest incarnation, was the perfect hybrid between the earlier unrealism to be found in cartoons of the 1920s and the push for realism which was so important in cartoons from the mid-1930s onwards.

"Porky's Duck Hunt" was a significant cartoon for Warner Brothers not only because of the advent of Daffy Duck, however. Supplying Daffy's voice in "Porky's Duck Hunt", as well as giving Porky a new voice, was the soon-to-be-famous voice-over performer and Warner animation institution, Mel Blanc. Although "Porky's Duck Hunt" was not Blanc's first performance in a Warner Brothers cartoon, it was nonetheless an important moment for both Blanc and Warner Brothers. First of all, Blanc, a former radio actor, actually knew how to act with his voice, as opposed to simply reading the characters' lines. He was also gifted with an amazingly flexible voice, and was able to provide most (if not all) of the voices necessary for each cartoon (indeed, Blanc's vocal gifts would eventually earn him the title of "The Man of a Thousand Voices"). Secondly, Blanc was being given for the first time the task of bestowing voices upon major characters in the Warner Brothers cartoons.

Indeed, it was Blanc's voices, along with Avery's gradual trend of moving away from the earlier *Looney Tunes* and *Merrie Melodies* formula of featuring a Warner Brothers' published song, which proved to be the major forces moving these two groups of cartoons toward the cartoons of the 1940s and 1950s which are now regarded as more typical of the Warner Brothers' style of cartoons.

Where Avery differed from other animators of his day was that he never seemed even remotely interested in copying the Disney studio's illusion of realism in its animation. For Avery, the quality of the gag was far more important than the technical quality of the animation.[102] This attitude differed markedly from that of Chuck Jones, who became a director at Warner Brothers' animation department in 1938 and very quickly began to guide the *Merrie Melodies* through their next major stage of transformation, into a more sophisticated graphic style.

Chuck Jones was one of the few animators working for Leon Schlesinger who had received any formal art education, having studied for a time as a scholarship student at the Chouinard Art Institute (with which the Disney studio was closely affiliated; it would eventually grow to become the California Institute of the Arts, or CalArts). His fine art training, along with his admiration for the Disney style of animation, are readily apparent in his early *Merrie Melodies*, which posses a much more studied, realistic quality to their animation than do Tex Avery's rough, undetailed drawings. In the late 1930s and early 1940s, however, neither Avery's nor Jones' cartoons showed much of the character development – even in their re-occurring characters – which was such a Disney hallmark. As Barrier points out, Jones' characters, such as Conrad the Cat (who often invited comparisons to Disney's character Goofy), had "only mannerisms …, and not personality".[103] Still, it was under Jones' direction (and Freleng's, after he returned to Warner Brothers from MGM in 1939) that more of the memorable characters who are now associated with Warner Brothers cartoons began not only to emerge, but take shape into what eventually became their own personalities. Elmer Fudd, for example, who started out as a nameless character in several Avery cartoons, under Jones's direction evolved into a character with a name, identifiable mannerisms such as, in Elmer's case, his speech impediment of turning the "L" and

102 Barrier, *Hollywood Cartoons*, p. 341.

103 Barrier, *Hollywood Cartoons*, p. 357.

59

"R" sounds into "W's", as in one of his catch phrases, "that waskawy wabbit!" ("that rascally rabbit!"). Another character who first appeared in an earlier cartoon under another director but who took shape under Jones's and Avery's direction was the above-mentioned "waskawy wabbit", Bugs Bunny. Starting as an insane, trouble-making rabbit, becoming a country bumpkin, and finally evolving into a cool, collected city-slicker whose adversaries were no match for him, Bugs Bunny was a major innovation amongst animated characters in that, rather than the zany, over-the-top antics which were characteristic of most cartoon characters, he tended to be more understated, and was one of the few early characters who seemed not just to react to situations, but to think them through. The personality which emerged in Bugs Bunny was strong enough, in fact, that after Avery's departure from Warner Brothers in 1941, Bugs continued largely unchanged in Warner Brothers cartoons, and it was Bugs Bunny's success as a character which helped to insure that the Warner Brothers' animation department would remain in successful competition with the Disney studio. In *Film Daily*'s lists of which Warner Brothers films were being released each year, in fact, the number of "Bugs Bunny Specials" is listed separately from the number of "Technicolor Cartoons". Perhaps, however, their key to competing successfully against Disney was that, rather than try to beat Disney at his own game, the animators under Schlesinger instead sought to find – and fill – their own niche in the cartoon industry, creating cartoons and characters who, whilst strong and memorable, were also as easily identifiable as being from Warner Brothers in terms of style and personality as characters such as Mickey Mouse and Donald Duck were as examples of the Disney style.

Conclusion

This chapter has endeavoured to provide a general overview of animation history and technique, in order to make later discussions, which focus on Walt Disney, his studio, and its creations, more comprehensible. It is no means a definitive account of the Fleischers' studio at Paramount nor Leon Schlesinger's studio at Warner Brothers. Nor is it meant to imply, stopping as it does in the 1940s, that the history of animation outside of things Disney ended at that time. Indeed, the field of animation – as well as its output –

continues to be at least as vibrant as it was in the first half of the twentieth century. While the difference between these two periods is that animation, apart from full-length animated features, has moved away from the cinema and found a home in the arena of television, what continues unabated is the development of new characters, new techniques, new series of cartoons, and new concepts in the field. By the 1960s, Hanna-Barbera had brought about the concept of the cartoon show as television sit-com, a form which continues to this day in such network television series as *The Simpsons*, *King of the Hill*, and *South Park*. For decades, the cartoons of Warner Brothers featuring Bugs, Daffy, Elmer Fudd, Sylverster and Tweety, Roadrunner and Wile E. Coyote, and others continued to appear on the Saturday or Sunday morning US network television line-ups aimed at children. Though Warner Brothers cartoons are no longer featured on many network/terrestrial television stations, cartoons continue to reign supreme in the Saturday morning line-up. Since the 1990s, most cable television systems in the United States carry the channel Cartoon Network (not to mention Boomerang and Toonami), which shows not only the products of new cartoon studios (including such hit series as *The Powerpuff Girls*), but also attests to the continuing popularity of the cartoons of the early days of animation, highlighting in particular the cartoons of Warner Brothers, MGM, Paramount, Universal, King Features, and others. The only cartoons not shown on these animation-centred networks, in fact, are Disney cartoons. They, however, have their own channels, amongst them The Disney Channel and Toon Disney. If there is one thing that has not changed, it has been Disney's habit of setting itself apart from its competition.

3

The Early Life of Walt Disney and the Beginnings of the Disney Studio, 1901–1937

104 For example, see Marc Eliot, *Walt Disney: Hollywood's Dark Prince* (London: Andre Deutsch, 1995).

105 For example, see either version of Bob Thomas' biography, *Walt Disney: A Biography* (New York: Hyperion, 1981) or *Walt Disney: An American Original* (New York: Hyperion, 1994).

The early years in the life of Walt Disney and the start of his studio are the subject of a high degree of myth and misunderstanding, much of it perpetuated by Walt himself. Late twentieth century folk wisdom on the subject maintains that Walt was not only not an artist, but also that he possessed no artistic ability himself and merely took credit for the artistry of his studio employees. One biography of Walt paints the picture of a man who was mentally ill in more ways than one (obsessive compulsive, megalomaniac, and paedophile are just a few of the accusations levelled[104]), while others prefer to paint an image of a kindly, loveable, albeit somewhat complex man, again at the expense of a balanced picture.[105] But who was Walt Disney, how much was he involved in the output of the studio which bears his name, and what influence over Disney films did he have and does he continue to have? What was and is Walt Disney's place in American popular culture, and how was that place achieved? While these questions and others will be addressed in the next few chapters, the roots of the answers will be discussed here in Chapter three. Walt Disney's childhood, youth, and early professional years will be analysed in light of vast amounts of both information and misinformation which abound on the subject, and the founding of the Disney studio will be examined in conjunction with the biographical elements of this chapter since, in many ways, the story of Walt Disney's life during the 1920s and 1930s is very much the story of the early years of the Disney studio.

Childhood and youth

Walter Elias Disney was born on 5 December 1901 in Chicago, Illinois, the fourth son of Elias and Flora Call Disney. This statement sounds straightforward and uncontentious enough on the surface, and yet even Walt's birthplace and the identity of his parents have been the subject of speculation on the part of one biographer. Marc Eliot argues in his book, *Walt Disney: Hollywood's Dark Prince,* that one of the sources of Walt's apparently "anti-parent" stance in his films is the fact that the true identity of his mother remains a mystery. According to Eliot, there is evidence suggesting that a Spanish immigrant woman from Mojácar, whom Eliot claims had an affair with Elias Disney, was Walt Disney's real mother, and that Elias forced his wife to accept his illegitimate son as her own. Eliot further claims that J. Edgar Hoover used the issue of Walt's unknown maternal descent to persuade Walt to work as an FBI contact in Hollywood, promising to send agents to Spain to search for the truth about his heritage in exchange for Walt providing the FBI with information about suspected communists in and around the film industry.[106] Eliot does not present any evidence for this claim, nor does he list any of his sources. His argument seemingly stems from the fact that, when Walt tried to enlist in the army in 1917 and sent for a copy of his birth certificate in order to prove his age, the only birth certificate on record in Chicago for a Walter Elias Disney was for an individual whose date of birth was listed as being ten years earlier than Walt's own.[107] Without any real acknowledgement of the fact that record-keeping of this sort in the United States in the eighteenth, nineteenth, and early twentieth centuries was at best disorganised and that birth certificates often went missing, were destroyed, were filled

[106] Eliot, *Hollywood's Dark Prince,* pp. 152–157.

[107] Eliot, *Hollywood's Dark Prince*, p. 12.

in inaccurately, or were never actually completed in the first place, Eliot uses the episode to suggest that the event so traumatised the young Walt that, from then on, he was apt either to de-emphasise, kill-off, or ignore completely the roles of parents in the stories he chose to tell on film.

What is known about Walt Disney's childhood is that he was born in Chicago in December 1901. His father, Elias Disney, worried about the rising crime rates in the city, bought a farm near Marceline, Missouri, in April 1906.[108] The few years he spent on his parents' farm were recalled by Disney to the end of his life as probably his happiest period, and they never seemed to loose their intense hold on his imagination. In the late spring of 1910, however, Elias Disney lost the farm due to debts and a string of unfortunate events and illness, and moved his family to Kansas City, Missouri.[109] He bought a large newspaper distribution route and had Walt working for him as one of his delivery boys while he himself managed it.[110]

It was during this time that Walt first began to display a love of acting (forming an act with his friend, Walt Pfeiffer, and calling it "The Two Walts"),[111] and also when, as he later recalled, he saw a motion picture for the first time, at a special screening given for all the newsboys who delivered papers for *The Kansas City Star* (interestingly, the film they were shown was a silent version of *Snow White and the Seven Dwarfs*, probably the 1916 version starring Marguerite Clark).[112] In 1917, Elias Disney was offered a business opportunity in Chicago and, after the school year was out, moved his family back to Chicago. The sixteen-year-old Walt, however, stayed behind in Kansas City, where he found work for the summer as a news butcher[113] on the Santa Fe Railroad out of Kansas City.[114] He rejoined his family in Chicago at the end of the summer, and enrolled at McKinley High School that autumn. At McKinley, he gained a reputation as an artist, drawing cartoons for the school newspaper and taking a few art classes at the Chicago Institute of Art.[115] It was during this period that Walt began toying with the idea of becoming a commercial artist and newspaper cartoonist, which was why he was able to persuade his father to pay for his art lessons. He also spent a significant amount of his free time attending the local vaudeville shows. He would later claim that he saw this as part of his education, since he recorded many of the gags

108 Steven Watts, *The Magic Kingdom: Walt Disney and the American Way of Life* (New York: Houghton Mifflin Company, 1997), p. 7.

109 Watts, *The Magic Kingdom*, p. 8.

110 Watts, *The Magic Kingdom*, pp. 8–9.

111 Watts, *The Magic Kingdom*, p. 9.

112 Voice recording, "Library/Snow White/Snow White (On Choosing Snow White)", and "Snow White/Snow White (to Margaret [sic] Clark)", "Library" section of the CD-ROM *Walt Disney: An Intimate History of the Man and his Magic* (Santa Monica, CA: Pantheon Productions Inc., 1998).

113 A news butcher was someone who worked on the trains, selling newspapers, cold drinks, and a variety of snacks to the passengers.

114 Watts, *The Magic Kingdom*, p. 9.

115 Watts, *The Magic Kingdom*, p. 10.

and jokes for use in his cartoons.[116] Walt also held down a number of part-time jobs in order to contribute to his family's income during this period.

By autumn 1918, however, Walt had dropped out of high school and joined the Red Cross Ambulance Corps.[117] He was not shipped out to France until after the signing of the Armistice, but nonetheless spent ten months in France and Germany, driving ambulances and delivery trucks and, once he had become familiar with the area, occasionally chauffeuring visiting dignitaries. He had also acquired a reputation as an artist amongst his fellow ambulance drivers, thanks to his painting some of the ambulances and vans with characters and pictures. Walt also, during this time, attempted, albeit unsuccessfully, to sell some of his artwork to various newspapers and magazines in America. He returned to Chicago in September 1919, and, a few months after coming home, unsatisfied with the opportunities on offer to him, decided to return to Kansas City and to try to become a professional cartoonist.[118]

Becoming an animator – the Kansas City years (1920–1923)

In Kansas City, Walt worked for a time at the Pesmen-Rubin Commercial Art Studio, where he made the acquaintance of fellow artist Ubbe Iwwerks (later, Iwerks shortened this spelling to Ub Iwerks).[119] When the two young men were laid off from Pesmen-Rubin, they decided to open their own studio. Iwerks-Disney Commercial Artists opened in January 1920, but very quickly turned out to be an unsuccessful business venture. By February, Walt had accepted a job at the Kansas City Film Ad Company, convincing his bosses to hire Iwerks a few weeks later.[120]

It was during his time at Kansas City Film Ad that Walt began to learn about the processes of animation (the company made simple, one-minute advertisements for exhibition in local cinemas). He founded his next company, Newman Laugh-O-Grams, during this time, working at night in a garage using a camera borrowed from Kansas City Film Ad, and the success of this venture raised his worth in the eyes of his bosses.[121] Differences with them, however, as well as the success of his Laugh-O-Gram films, finally persuaded Walt to try to branch out on his own. In May

116 Watts, *The Magic Kingdom*, p. 10.

117 Watts, *The Magic Kingdom*, pp. 10–11.

118 In this context (and indeed, on a technical level), the terms "cartoonist" and "animator" are *not* the same thing. A cartoonist is an artist who draws still cartoons for printed media such as newspapers and magazines. An animator is an artist who draws a series of still images to be put together on film and viewed as a moving image. Throughout this book, the term "animator" is used to refer to the Disney studio's artists. When referring to the Disney studio's non-feature-length animated output, the term "shorts" or "animated shorts" is used, since this refers to the proper name for these six- to eight-minute works: "short subjects". Although such works have come to be referred to as "cartoons" and the artists who draw them are often referred to as "cartoonists", this is in fact a misnomer, since technically a cartoon is a *printed* rather than a *moving* image.

119 Watts, *The Magic Kingdom*, pp. 25–26.

120 Watts, *The Magic Kingdom*, p. 26.

121 Watts, *The Magic Kingdom*, p. 26.

122 Watts, *The Magic Kingdom*, pp. 26–28.

123 There is no date associated with the document. However, Disney states in answer 24 that he has been married for seven years; as he was married on 13 July 1925, it can therefore be guessed that this document was created in the second half of 1932 or the first half of 1933. "Walter Elias Disney: Answers to Interview" (Questions and Name of Interviewer Unknown), not dated (probably 1932?), catalogued as "Personality Ephemera: Autobiographical Material dictated by Disney, n.d.", British Film Institute Library.

124 The questions seem to have been lost; in any case, they are no longer attached to the answers nor do they seem to be in the possession of the BFI library. The answers themselves, however, are of such a nature that the questions they are responding to are, in most cases, easily inferred.

1922, he quit Kansas City Film Ad and incorporated Laugh-O-Gram films as an independent business. Several colleagues from Kansas City Film Ad – namely Iwerks, Hugh Harman, and Rudolf Ising – decided to try their luck with Walt. Although the small company had a modest number of successes, within a few months many of Walt's employees had decided to work for other companies where at least they were guaranteed a steady income. Eventually, the company dwindled down to Walt on his own.[122]

The facts as presented above record some of the more important moments in the life of the young Walt Disney. They offer, however, only the most cursory understanding of his early life and give little detail on some of the most formative years of his life. A number of crucial episodes and incidents from these years perhaps give more useful glimpses into the formation of Walt's character. Although there are a number of sources of information about his childhood, perhaps one of the most telling examples of what Walt Disney was like as a person comes from his own references to his boyhood. In the collection of the British Film Institute library, there is a twelve page document made up of answers which Walt dictated, probably in 1932,[123] to a series of interview questions about his early life and his career.[124] Although, in the main, in these answers Walt depicted his childhood in fairly pleasant terms, he does so whilst describing many episodes which actually point to a difficult, unhappy childhood. For example, in answer to question number five, Walt describes working for his father's paper route in Kansas City in this way:

> During my early school days in Kansas City, I carried a newspaper route from the age of nine to fifteen, getting up at 3.30 every morning, working until 6.00 a.m. and making the same route every evening after school. I was proud of my record, because during the six years I missed a total of only one month, which was due to illness. When I started out in the morning, during the winter months, it was always dark and bitter cold, and many times I had to plow through three feet of freshly fallen snow, breaking my own path as I went. Once in a while, when I reached an apartment house, I lay down in the comparatively warm hallway to get a few seconds' more sleep. I would wake up later to find out that it was daylight, and I was late, and then I had to hurry and finish my route, to get my papers delivered before time to get ready for school. Naturally, my paper route interfered with playing

after school hours. However, I always managed to find a little time to pal around with the neighbourhood gang, and we indulged in the usual pranks of any gang of boys, building caves, having snow fights, secret societies, and shows.[125]

This lengthy quotation demonstrates a number of things both about Walt's personality and his preferred professional persona. Firstly, it suggests that he learned at an early age to adhere to a strong work-ethic. Secondly, it contributes to his favourite self-depiction as being the living hero of a Horatio Alger-type story. Thirdly, it depicts him as someone who, despite having achieved great success in his field and being regularly celebrated as one of the greatest entertainers of his era, still very much wished to be regarded as a "regular guy", someone who knew first-hand what it was like to be poor, hungry, tired, and cold, as well as caught up in an endless cycle of mind-numbing work with little time for anything else. Throughout his lifetime, Walt, of course, made frequent references to his childhood, many of which were depictions of happy, funny, light-hearted moments. Although a number of his biographers have tended to stress his recollections of difficulty and hardship, it is important to note that, while Walt did have happy memories, he tended to characterise his early struggles as formative to his character and as valuable lessons on the importance of hard work and determination in achieving success.

Though Walt seems to have seen his childhood as being important in establishing a strong work ethic, it was his youth – in particular the time he spent in France – which he himself appears to have regarded as being the most significant period of his life. As Walt himself put it, "Within the eleven [sic] months I was over there, I had a lifetime wrapped up in experience. It was such a valuable thing to me".[126] It was his first trip abroad (not to mention the first instance of his spending a substantial period of time outside the Midwest), and it was a time in his life when the young Walt was ready to experience a different way of life as well as total independence from his family, in particular his first independence from his father. Elias Disney was an authoritarian man and a very strict disciplinarian who had never understood his son's imaginative, creative, artistic temperament (by all accounts, he himself was a very practical, unusually thrifty, and highly self-disciplined man who believed things such as entertainment to be wasteful and

125 "Walter Elias Disney: Answers to Interview."

126 Voice recording of Walt Disney, in "Library/Early Exploits/Audio Clips/On Walt's Red Cross Experience", "Library" section of the CD-ROM *Walt Disney: An Intimate History of the Man and his Magic*.

useless). More importantly, however, Walt's time in France exposed him to a larger world than he had known in Marceline, Kansas City, or even Chicago, and it was his time in Europe that effectively constituted the "lifetime wrapped up in experience" to which Walt always referred.

The time Walt spent in France was certainly the period of his life which he himself saw as the most formative (thanks no doubt to the fact that this was when he decided to become a commercial artist). It seems more plausible, however, to assert that it was his time in Kansas City from 1919 to 1923 that was really more crucial. It was, in fact, during this period that he learned the ins and outs of life as a professional commercial artist and began to experiment both with animation and – perhaps more significantly – with owning and running his own animation/film studio. Walt himself, while stressing the significance of his stint with the Red Cross, nonetheless acknowledged the importance of his animation career in Kansas City when he referred to the failure of Laugh-O-Grams: "I think it's important to have a good hard failure when you're young".[127] It was during these years in Kansas City that Walt learned about the animation business, established his initial contacts in the field and decided to make a career within the animation industry. Although he ended up in animation primarily because he was unsuccessful in his earlier desire to become a cartoonist, it was his continuing confidence in his own abilities as a film-maker and animator which led to his determination – despite the failure of his initial attempts to establish his own studio – to work toward a career in animation.

Although Walt's decision to return to Kansas City may have been influenced by the fact that he still had family and friends there (not to mention that his parents still owned a house there and had given him permission to live in it), he was doubtless aided in his decision by the fact that Kansas City had many thriving commercial art companies. Indeed, a number of animation's early innovators worked in Kansas City at that time, and for Disney it was an opportunity both to gain experience within the field and to make contacts with other young artists, cartoonists, and animators. It was also during this time that Disney first joined forces with Ub Iwerks, the man who was later credited with shaping the physical appearance of Mickey Mouse and who contributed a great deal to many of the Disney studio's shorts and

127 Voice recording of Walt Disney, in "Early Exploits/ Audio Clips/On Leaving Kansas City", "Library" section of the CD-ROM *Walt Disney: An Intimate History of the Man and his Magic.*

animated features. It was in Kansas City, moreover, that Walt first learned how to make an animated film.

When Walt first went to work for Kansas City Film Ad, the kind of animation produced there was a fairly basic – even primitive – version of what is today known as stop-motion animation. Briefly, the kind of animation Walt was involved in at this time consisted of drawing figures which were cut-out, hinged at their joints, and then moved about between photographing in order to simulate movement. At some point in 1920, however, Walt would later recall that he found a copy of E.G. Lutz's book *Animated Cartoons: How They Are Made, Their Origin and Development* in the Kansas City public library, and began studying the type of animation it outlined (defining, in fact, what we think of as animation today). While there were a number of animation studios already engaged in the kind of animation Lutz described, and though the young Walt was almost certainly familiar with these studios' shorts, it was not until he had read Lutz's book and begun borrowing a camera from Kansas City Film Ad and experimenting on his own that he learned the processes involved in "modern" animation. Working with a few unpaid amateurs in his father's garage every night after work, Walt began to make very simple shorts. Called Newman Laugh-O-Grams, they were mostly one- to two-minute-long animated advertisements paid for (and used by) the Newman Theatre in Kansas City.

When Walt left Kansas City Film Ad and incorporated Laugh-O-Grams, he also began work on more story-based shorts (as opposed to theatrical advertisements) and started upon a path which was less commercially-based and more concentrated on animation within the entertainment industry. Laugh-O-Grams achieved a few modest successes, but it was always in a fragile financial state. Walt was able to hire a few employees for his fledgling company (some of these artists following Walt from Kansas City Film Ad) and began to make both theatrical advertisements and a series of shorts which were based upon fables.[128] These were usually given a twist in that they were brought forward in time, usually into the 1920s (at the end of the Laugh-O-Gram short "Puss in Boots", for example, the hero and heroine, as well as the cats, escape from the king by jumping into their jalopy and riding off into the sunset). Although the surviving shorts from Laugh-O-Grams have nothing about their artistry

128 Michael Barrier, *Hollywood Cartoons: American Animation in its Golden Age* (New York: Oxford University Press, 1999), p. 37; Watts, *The Magic Kingdom*, p. 27.

which sets them apart from the work of other studios at that time, there is one feature that was already becoming apparent which did distinguish Laugh-O-Grams' work from that of its rivals – a reliance on narrative.

As discussed in Chapter one, a feature of early cartoons is their lack of a unifying narrative. In general, what there was of a story was basically a theme used to link a series of gags, as opposed to a story being punctuated by gags. In other words, the usual emphasis on shorts at this time was on the gags, not the story. Walt's Laugh-O-Gram shorts, however, while still heavily reliant on gags, nonetheless also tended to rely upon an established story to link these gags, and this trait alone is what distinguishes Walt's work at this time. Despite this, his cartoons were on the whole still fairly mediocre. Moreover, a series of unsuccessful deals which never paid off caused the tiny studio huge financial problems. Although he enjoyed a brief turnaround in his company's fortunes (during which time he was able to make the first episode, "Alice's Wonderland", of what would later be known as his *Alice* comedies), in the end Walt and Laugh-O-Grams were so broke that no attempts to save the studio were possible. Walt managed to sell off most of his equipment and buy a movie camera which he used to make short films of local children and sell to their parents, but, by the summer of 1923, he was forced to declare bankruptcy.[129] In the end, urged on by the fact that one of his uncles was living in southern California, his interest in live-action movie making, and his brother Roy Disney's residence in a veteran's hospital in southern California, Walt found a buyer for his movie camera, said good-bye to Kansas City, and headed off to Hollywood. As Walt would later tell the story, he left with one suitcase (which contained only a few bits of old clothes and some art supplies), $40 in his pocket,[130] but with a first-class train ticket[131] on the Santa Fe railroad from Kansas City to Hollywood.

The move to Hollywood and the Disney Bros. studio (1923–1928)

When he first arrived in Hollywood, it was Walt's intention to get into live-action cinema. As he would later recount,

> I was discouraged with animation … And I just said, "It's too late. I should have been in the business six years before. … It was too late, so I was out of the cartoon business. I came to

129 Photo of document declaring Laugh-O-Grams to be bankrupt. In "Bankruptcy", "Library" section of the CD-ROM *Walt Disney: An Intimate History of the Man and his Magic*.

130 Russell Merritt, "Walt's Hollywood Beginnings". Accessed via "Library/ Hollywood/ Hollywood (Walt's Hollywood Beginnings)" on the CD-ROM *Walt Disney: An Intimate History of the Man and his Magic*.

131 Barrier, *Hollywood Cartoons*, p. 27.

Hollywood and there was just one thing I wanted to do: I wanted to get into the motion picture business. I wanted to be a director. That was my ambition or goal: to be a director.[132]

Although he made the rounds of the various studios looking for work as a director or an actor, he also apparently decided to hedge his bets by trying to use the only copy of "Alice's Wonderland" he had made to sell the concept to an animation distributor in New York. Having been in contact before leaving Kansas City with Margaret Winkler, a successful animation distributor (who was at that time linked to the *Out of the Inkwell* and *Felix the Cat* series), Walt had already described his plans for a series of *Alice* comedies. Being more than unusually creative with the truth, Walt also convinced Winkler that he had "left" Laugh-O-Grams (with no mention of the bankruptcy) and had moved to California in order, as Walt put it, to "engage trained talent for my cast, and be within reach of the right facilities for producing"[133] the live-action elements of the *Alice* series. (He also persuaded her that he had brought with him a "select number" of Laugh-O-Gram artists in order to set up his studio in Los Angeles.[134]) After he had sent her a copy of "Alice's Wonderland", Winkler, having no idea of just how exaggerated a "truth" Walt's description of his circumstances was, believed him and made a deal to produce more episodes of the *Alice Comedies* at $1500 each for the first six. So, having had no luck in his attempts to break into live-action movies and having been offered a lucrative deal by Winkler, Walt found himself back in animation.

It was after his move to Hollywood that Walt was finally able to add the key ingredient to his studio which would help to guarantee its success: his brother, Roy. Roy Disney had worked in a bank prior to joining the army when the United States entered World War I. In 1923, he was living in a veteran's hospital in Sawtelle, west Los Angeles, suffering from a mild case of tuberculosis. Upon arriving at the convalescence home where Roy was living, Walt explained to him his idea of starting up a studio and showed Roy his offer from Winkler. Asking if he could borrow the $200 which Roy had frugally saved in the bank, Walt also asked whether his brother could come and work with him as the book-keeper and business manager for the studio he hoped to found. Roy agreed. Finally, on 16 October 1923, Walt and Roy Disney signed a contract with Margaret Winkler to

132 Voice recording of Walt Disney, in "Early Exploits/ Audio Clips/On Coming to Hollywood", "Library" section of the CD-ROM *Walt Disney: An Intimate History of the Man and his Magic.*

133 Letter from Walt Disney to Margaret J. Winkler dated 25 August 1923, in "Library/Alice/Letter to Winkler", "Library" section of the CD-ROM *Walt Disney: An Intimate History of the Man and his Magic.*

134 Letter from Walt Disney to Margaret J. Winkler dated 25 August 1923, in "Library/Alice/Letter to Winkler", "Library" section of the CD-ROM *Walt Disney: An Intimate History of the Man and his Magic.*

produce six episodes of the *Alice Comedies* at $1500 each, six further episodes at $1800 each, with an option to produce two more series of *Alice Comedies*.[135] And so, with his contract from Winkler in hand, his brother Roy to help him with the financial management (not to mention the $200 which Roy brought with him), and further aided by a loan of $500 from his uncle Robert Disney, Walt was able to set up a small studio and start work on the first series of the *Alice Comedies*.[136]

What set the *Alice Comedies* apart from the output of other studios at that time was its twist on a popular concept. The *Out of the Inkwell* shorts, made by the Fleischer brothers, were famous for inserting animated characters into live-action worlds. Walt's variant on this had been to take a real little girl, in this case the child actress Virginia Davis, and place her within an animated world, surrounded by (and interacting with) various animated creatures.

By and large, the *Alice Comedies*, a fair number of which survive to this day, were very popular with both the critics and the public. Each new episode of *Alice* showed various improvements both in the technical and in the artistic and creative elements of the shorts. The fledgling Disney Brothers Studio, considerably helped by the good professional relationship between Walt, Roy, and Winkler, was beginning to make a name for itself, as well as being able to expand in a modest way. As time passed, Alice herself (portrayed first by Virginia Davis, then by Margie Gay) began to appear less and less in the series which bore her name, being replaced by an increased focus on the animal characters who had featured all along. According to Barrier, by the time "Alice's Orphan" was made in late 1925, Alice appeared briefly in only two scenes and was definitely being supplanted in importance by the animal characters in the series.[137] Also, by this time, Walt had been able to hire a small staff of animators to do the drawing for him, leaving him free to concentrate on the other aspects of production. He had also made one more significant move: recognising the importance of name recognition in the success of a company, in 1926 Walt changed the name of the studio from the slightly impersonal Disney Brothers Studio to Walt Disney Productions.

Overall, things seemed to be going well with his studio. Yet

135 Barrier, *Hollywood Cartoons*, p. 39.

136 Watts, *The Magic Kingdom*, p. 28.

137 Barrier, *Hollywood Cartoons*, p. 41.

all was not as secure as it seemed. First of all, shortly after signing her contract with the Disneys, Margaret Winkler had married Charles Mintz, and it was he who became the main voice of Winkler Pictures from that point onward. Having lost its contracts with both Pat Sullivan (who made the Felix cartoons) and the Fleischers, Winkler Pictures now found itself reliant upon the Disney Brothers Studio as its main source of income. Mintz's letters to Walt became increasingly harrying as he tried to retain a powerful bargaining position over him, but, by late 1925, Walt's confidence in dealing with distributors was growing and he was beginning to learn negotiation tactics which combated Mintz's bullying. However, added to Walt's troubles with Mintz, both of the original animators who were working for Disney at that time, Hugh Harman and Rudolph Ising (both former Kansas City colleagues), were working on their own cartoon behind Walt's back and were looking for ways to set up on their own in the animation business.[138] (Fortunately for Walt, he did have loyalty from both Ub Iwerks and Rollin Hamilton; Hamilton worked at Disney for the majority of his career, and though Iwerks had a falling-out with Walt and Roy and went to work elsewhere early in 1930,[139] by 1940 he had returned to work at Disney and continued there until his death in 1971.) Despite such handicaps, however, Walt was able, by February 1926, to move his expanding studio to a larger premises, namely the site on Hyperion Boulevard where it would remain until 1940.[140]

In 1927, with Charles Mintz/Winkler Pictures acting as the middleman (indeed, it was Mintz – not Walt – who signed the contract), the Disney studio was commissioned to create a new series of shorts featuring a rabbit. The contract, which was signed on 4 March 1927, was the start of the *Oswald the Lucky Rabbit* series, and in the contract twenty-six Oswald shorts were promised. Although, for a time at least, Disney was producing *Oswalds* and *Alices* simultaneously, the *Oswalds* – or at least the few which survive – show that the Disney studio's work had much improved and had even achieved a certain finesse absent from the earlier *Alices*. The *Oswalds*, in particular, seem to have been admired by a substantial number of both critics and animators on the East Coast[141] (which is where most major animation studios continued to be located in the late 1920s). Indeed, the profits the Disney studio made from the *Oswalds* were such that

138 Barrier, *Hollywood Cartoons,* pp. 42, 45–46.

139 Barrier, *Hollywood Cartoons,* pp. 63–67.

140 Barrier, *Hollywood Cartoons,* p. 43.

141 Barrier, *Hollywood Cartoons,* pp. 46–47; Watts, *The Magic Kingdom,* p. 29.

Walt was able to expand his staff and improve his equipment. By now, Walt was very much working as the director of his studio's films, and it was a position which best suited his talents. Roy was still in charge of the books, and used his position to make sure Walt did not spend more than the studio could handle. By and large, the brothers had by this time established a pattern in their working relationship which would continue for the rest of their shared careers: Walt came up with the ideas, and Roy came up with a way to finance them safely. Certainly, by early 1928, the Disneys had settled into a comfortable existence producing the successful *Oswald* series. A routine had been established, and the indications are that Walt believed his studio to be largely secure. That year, however, he was given a rude awakening as to the real situation at his studio, and would be forced to come to terms with some rather unpleasant facts about several of his hitherto trusted associates.[142]

The creation of Mickey Mouse – 1928

For most of the Disneys' relationship with Winkler Pictures, Margaret Winkler-Mintz's brother, George Winkler, had worked as a film editor at Disney, but as an employee not of Disney, but of the Mintzes. Therefore, Mintz had an ally in place in the Disney studio to observe things for him and to have contact with the animators in the Disney studio. During mid-1927, George Winkler reportedly received a favourable response when he approached Hugh Harman about the possibility of Harman's producing the next series of *Oswald* on his own, without Walt, and thus began the chain of events which would lead to the end of Disney's ties with Winkler pictures. Walt, along with his wife Lillian and his lawyer Gunther Lessing, travelled to New York to meet with Mintz in person to renew their contract so as to negotiate for more money per *Oswald*. It was then that he learned that Mintz was trying to take control of the Disney studio, using as leverage the fact that copyright ownership of the Disney studio's most successful character up to that time, Oswald the Lucky Rabbit, in fact belonged to Universal, not Disney. To have kept Oswald, Walt would have had to relinquish control of his studio to Mintz. It was also at this point that Walt learned of the defections of a number of his animators to Universal. Negotiating with Mintz himself in an attempt to produce a better situation, Walt quietly sent Lessing to look for a new contract with another distributor, although none would be found for another seven months (during which time Disney was without a distributor). Disney then formally ended its association with Winkler Pictures and with Charles Mintz. Sending a wire to his brother on 13 March 1928 that everything was okay,[143] Walt set off on his return trip to Los Angeles, still obliged to complete the remaining *Oswalds* he had been contracted to make, but without any new ideas for a different series after the last few *Oswalds* were finished.

Although there are various versions of the story, a weighing of the details points to the probability that it was during his train journey home to Los Angeles that Walt first created the character of Mickey Mouse. When examining the original sketches of Mickey and comparing him to Oswald, there are a number of similarities: Oswald's long rabbit ears were shortened to the round ears we now associate with Mickey; his bunny-like tale was transformed to a long, thin mouse's tale; his body was made rounder and softer in its already existing features; buttons were added to his trousers. Legend states that it was Lillian Disney who suggested the name Mickey Mouse for this new character, though at present there is no way either to confirm or deny this. Decades later, rumours began to circulate that it was in fact Ub Iwerks who had created Mickey Mouse,[144] but an examination of the various competing versions of the story, as well as some knowledge of the principal individuals involved, suggest a compromise: the more creative Walt was Mickey Mouse's inventor, but it was the superior artist and draftsman Iwerks who polished and shaped Mickey Mouse's look (at least in the form in which he would initially appear when Mickey made his public debut in 1928). While it is not possible at this time, due in part to the closed-door policy in operation at the Disney studio's archives, to elucidate the facts of this episode, it seems fitting that the birth of arguably the most successful character in animation history should be shrouded in a degree of mystery. As things stand, the 'true facts' of the subject of who exactly created Mickey Mouse are not as important as the actual fact of his creation, and so the slight controversy surrounding Mickey's birth has been mentioned only because it is an important part of the Disney studio's history.

By the time Walt had returned to Los Angeles, it was already

143 Original telegram "All okay", in "Library/Oswald/Te legram to Roy 'All okay'", "Library" section of the CD-ROM *Walt Disney: An Intimate History of the Man and his Magic*.

144 Watts, *The Magic Kingdom*, pp. 50–52.

known that certain of his animators would be leaving as soon as the studio had completed the remaining *Oswalds*. Therefore, in order to protect his latest creation, Walt set Iwerks to work on creating a Mickey Mouse short in carefully guarded secrecy. The other animators at Disney knew Iwerks was working on *something*, but they did not know what as his work area was separated from the main areas of the studio.[145] Once the final *Oswalds* had been completed and sent off to Mintz and the departing animators were gone, work on the first Mickey Mouse short to be produced, "Plane Crazy", went into full swing. A second Mickey Mouse, "The Gallopin' Gaucho", quickly followed. Before either of these was released, however, Walt made a decision which would forever change his fortunes and the course of American animation. Convinced by the success of the early talkies that sound films would be a permanent fixture of the movie industry, he decided to make his third Mickey Mouse film, "Steamboat Willie", in such a way that it could be synchronised with sound. Because the Disney studio did not initially have the necessary equipment on site, "Steamboat Willie" was initially completed as a silent, but throughout its production Walt had ensured that the action of the film was timed so that it would be syncopated with the songs "Steamboat Bill" and "Turkey in the Straw", as well as with various sound effects. The process, however, was not as simple as it sounds here. None of the Disney studio's staff at this time were musicians (according to Michael Barrier, animator Wilfred Jackson had "some limited knowledge of music",[146] but it seems to have been rudimentary at best), and none were experienced in the use of sound for movies. With no precedents or guidelines to help them through the process, the artists at the Disney studio had to come up with an entirely new approach to planning and creating an animated film.

In the past, the process of creating an animated short had been a relaxed affair, with animators generally working from a loose story plan and making drawings which got the characters from one scenario to the next. Even though the process had tightened up somewhat by the late 1920s, the usual extent of advanced planning seems to have been limited to detailed advance sketches which determined more precisely the overall look of each scene. Sound synchronisation, however, required still more controlled

145 Barrier, *Hollywood Cartoons*, p. 49.

146 Barrier, *Hollywood Cartoons*, p. 51.

planning and more precise timing than had previously been the case. As a way of tying each scene's planning sketch to the action expected to occur during that scene, Iwerks drew up a series of sketches which had next to them a type-written description of each scene's action. This was the earliest known use by a studio of what is now called a storyboard. A kind of bar sheet for the entire film was made up by Wilfred Jackson, so that "in the places where we had definite pieces of music in mind, the name of the music was there, and the melody was crudely indicated, not with a staff, but just with a little note that would go higher and lower … so that I could follow it, in my mind".[147] The "ex-sheets", or exposure sheets (which were the frame-by-frame instructions for the cameraman to use to put together the various drawings in the correct sequences), which had always been done after the animation for the film was completed, now had to be done prior to any work on the animation for a film so that the animators would know precisely when various actions were to occur within a scene. After Jackson had made a rough bar sheet for each song to be used in the film, Walt would then use these bar sheets to make the ex-sheets so that he could indicate the exact frames upon which each beat of the song should hit. These gave a very definite and exact control over a film's timing, thus making it possible to make an animated film which could be synchronised to sound. Once some of the animation for "Steamboat Willie" had been completed, the animators decided to test their efforts by playing what there was of the film and using the bar sheets as guides for providing the sound themselves. Satisfied that the sound, when properly synchronised with the action, looked as though it was actually coming from the film itself, work continued on finishing "Steamboat Willie" with the intention of having it paired with a soundtrack.[148]

Once the animation for "Steamboat Willie" was completed, Walt returned to New York so that he could have a sound-track added. After shopping around, he finally made an agreement with Pat Powers, who owned a system called Cinephone. A soundtrack was recorded on 15 September 1928, but due to problems with getting the orchestra's conductor to follow the directions for getting the right beats in time with the right frames, Walt had a second soundtrack recorded on 30 September.[149] Although there were a few minor flaws on the second attempt, overall Walt was satisfied

147 From a 1973 interview with Wilfred Jackson by Barrier, quoted in Barrier, *Hollywood Cartoons*, p. 51.

148 Barrier, *Hollywood Cartoons*, pp. 52–53; Watts, *The Magic Kingdom*, pp. 30–31.

149 Barrier, *Hollywood Cartoons*, p. 53.

with the result. So, a finished sound version of "Steamboat Willie" now existed. All it needed was an audience. Although it received a lukewarm reception from the theatre owners/managers and the various cartoon distributors who saw it, Walt finally struck a deal with the Colony Theatre in New York, who agreed to show "Steamboat Willie" for free for one week. Walt's gamble paid off. "Steamboat Willie" turned out to be an immediate critical and popular success,[150] and was held over by the Colony for a second week.[151]

It is important to note that "Steamboat Willie", contrary to popular myth, was not technically the first sound animated film to be produced. As early as 1924, the Fleischer brothers were producing song cartoons, or shorts in which a song was featured; its lyrics went across the screen with a bouncing ball leading the audiences' singing. In fact, many of these song cartoons were, in reality, silent and had to be accompanied by the theatre musicians, but some of the Fleischers' cartoons of this kind did have soundtracks. The difference, however, between the song cartoons and "Steamboat Willie" was that "Steamboat Willie"'s soundtrack featured more than just music. Its comparatively heavy reliance upon synchronised sound effects is what set it apart from earlier attempts at sound cartoons within the animation industry. This factor, no doubt, is why it gained the reputation for being the first sound cartoon.

Once it became obvious that the public liked both Mickey and the idea of a sound cartoon, offers from various cartoon distributors came pouring in. Walt finally signed a two-year letter agreement with Powers on 15 October 1928. The other distributors had made Walt better deals up-front, but they differed from Powers in their insistence on buying outright the cartoons Disney produced. Having learned his lesson when he lost Oswald, Walt was careful to secure the ownership of Mickey Mouse for the Disney studio.[152]

The build-up to feature animation (1928–1934)

150 Watts, *The Magic Kingdom*, p. 30.

151 Barrier, *Hollywood Cartoons*, p. 55.

152 Watts, *The Magic Kingdom*, p. 30.

On his way to New York in 1928 to oversee the recording of "Steamboat Willie"'s soundtrack, Walt had stopped off in Kansas City to see an old acquaintance of his, a theatre organist named Carl Stalling, and had left copies of both "Plane Crazy" and "The Gallopin' Gaucho" with him. Stalling joined Walt in New York about a month after the soundtrack for "Steamboat Willie" had been completed, and together he and Walt worked on adding sound to "Plane Crazy", "The Gallopin' Gaucho", and "The Barn Dance", a fourth Mickey Mouse short which Walt had written in New York and which Iwerks had animated during his absence. During their time in New York, Stalling had suggested to Walt the idea of producing a series of musical novelty shorts, similar in some ways to the song cartoons, but made more interesting and sophisticated through the use of the latest sound technology as well as through careful storytelling. Although he seems to have rejected the idea initially, by the time Disney and Stalling had returned to New York in February 1929 to record the soundtrack for the fifth Mickey Mouse, "The Opry House", they were also ready to record the soundtrack for "The Skeleton Dance", a novelty of the sort Stalling had proposed. "The Skeleton Dance" was to be the first *Silly Symphony*.

The *Silly Symphonies* as a series was an important and useful one for the Disney studio. As a series of music-themed shorts which had no recurrent characters or situations, the *Silly Symphonies* provided Walt and his animators with a useful forum in which to experiment with various new ideas and techniques.[153] For example, it was a *Silly Symphony* from 1932, "Flowers and Trees", that became the studio's (and, indeed, animation's) first colour work using the 3-Strip Technicolor process. Production on "Flowers and Trees" had begun in black and white. About half-way through production, however, Walt struck a deal with Technicolor, whereby his studio, for three years, would have the exclusive right to use their new Three-Color process. At this point, he decided to turn "Flowers and Trees" into a colour film.[154] It was also within the context of the *Silly Symphonies* that Disney artists began to experiment with animating the human form, something they had avoided up to that time due to the complications involved in making human characters move realistically enough to be believable for audiences.[155] This last feature – realistic, believable animation – played an important part in the studio's evolution. Walt was unique in wanting his animators to have artistic training,[156] and went to great lengths to ensure that his animators and other artists had extensive art classes and artistic training. This training was put into practice in the Mickey Mouse shorts and other

153 Barrier, *Hollywood Cartoons*, pp. 57–59.

154 Barrier, *Hollywood Cartoons*, pp. 80–81.

155 Barrier, *Hollywood Cartoons*, pp. 84, 86.

156 For more detailed discussion of this aspect of the Disney studio's formation, see Barrier, *Hollywood Cartoons*, pp. 82–86, and Chapter ten of Thomas, *Walt Disney, An American Original*.

character-based cartoons, of course, but, by and large, the *Silly Symphonies* were used by the studio as a practice ground for various ideas and theories which they wished to try.

The popularity of both Mickey Mouse and the Disney studio was assured by 1929, and the studio continued to turn out one short after the next, adding to their cast of characters as well as improving the technical qualities of both the animation and the sound (as well as the uses of different kinds of sound). Because of his popularity, however, Mickey continued to be emphasised as the studio's "star". Capitalising on this popularity, in autumn 1929, Walt accepted an offer of $300 to allow Mickey's image to be used on the cover of a line of children's school paper pads, and in 1930, Roy Disney was able to strike a deal with the George Borgfeldt Company to produce toys and bisque figurines of Mickey, as well as licensing Charlotte Clark to produce a now famous and highly collectible line of Mickey Mouse plush dolls.[157]

Such deals brought in much-needed revenue for the studio. Despite the success of their shorts, the costs incurred in adding sound facilities to the Hyperion site were a heavy burden. Furthermore, their association with Pat Powers was turning out to be a less than happy one, as Powers continually skimmed off increasingly higher percentages of the studio's profits to cover his own costs, as well as proving reluctant to pay them the money he owed them from their share of their cartoons' revenue.[158] Powers, indeed, turned out to be a thoroughly unscrupulous, dishonest character, and, during his two-year association with the Disney studio, habitually lied to the Disneys about how much they were earning from the distribution of their shorts. In 1930, Walt, his wife, Lillian, and studio lawyer Gunther Lessing returned to New York to confront Powers directly. It was then that Walt learned that Iwerks, his associate of nearly eleven years, had signed an independent contract with Powers to work for Powers' own company producing a series of sound shorts.[159] Iwerks left the Disney studio the day after Walt learned of the contract with Powers, and, upon leaving, Iwerks and Roy Disney signed a contract whereby the Disneys would buy back Iwerks' twenty per cent interest in the studio at a total cost of $2,920 (according to Bob Thomas, that twenty per cent interest in the Disney studio, at the time of his writing in 1976, would have been worth an estimated

157 Robert Heide and John Gilman, *Disneyana: Classic Collectibles 1928–1958* (New York: A Welcome Book/Hyperion, 1995), pp. 38, 49.

158 Watts, *The Magic Kingdom*, p. 31; Barrier, *Hollywood Cartoons*, p. 62.

159 Watts, *The Magic Kingdom*, p. 31.

$750,000,000[160]; by the time Thomas published the 1994 edition of his book, this figure had risen to $4 billion[161]). Meanwhile, Walt spent two weeks carrying on the pretence of negotiating with Powers over their contract while he sent Lessing and another lawyer to negotiate with other, larger studios and distributors. Finally, on 19 February 1930, Walt signed an agreement with Columbia whereby they agreed to distribute his films for him and also agreed to lend the Disneys up to $25,000 to fight off a legal challenge from Powers.[162] Walt immediately returned to California once the contract was signed, and, a few months (and $10,000 in legal fees) later, Roy Disney travelled to New York and settled with Powers.[163] Various aspects of their relationship with Columbia were not very beneficial for the Disney studio (mainly in connection with their troubles with Pat Powers), and so, in July 1932, once they had fulfilled their financial and contractual obligations to Columbia, the Disneys signed a much more favourable distribution contract with United Artists.[164]

By 1932, more merchandising deals had quickly followed the Borgfeldt and Clark deals. Mickey Mouse dolls, watches, dishes, soaps, and a variety of other items quickly became available, and it is the income from such deals which helped keep the Disney studio afloat throughout the 1930s. Without doubt, the fact that the studio had a guaranteed income from these sources, along with Walt Disney's abilities as a salesman for his ideas, is what helped make it possible for Walt and Roy Disney to convince their creditors to finance their next big idea for animation: an animated feature-length film.

160 Thomas, *Walt Disney: A Biography*, p. 95.

161 Thomas, *Walt Disney: An American Original*, p. 101.

162 Watts, *The Magic Kingdom*, p. 31; Barrier, *Hollywood Cartoons*, pp. 64–65.

163 Barrier, *Hollywood Cartoons*, p. 64.

164 Watts, *The Magic Kingdom*, p. 31.

4

Disney Films 1937–1967: The "Classic" Years

In what is currently believed to be the first American animated short, Winsor McKay's "Little Nemo", the only female character, and therefore probably the first female character to appear in an American cartoon, was a princess. Her name was the Princess of Slumberland, and in her role she was awakened by Nemo, who sketches her and thus brings her to life. In the twenty-six years between the release of "Little Nemo" in 1911, and that of Disney's animated feature *Snow White and the Seven Dwarfs* in 1937, a number of other female characters would be shown, but rarely were they central to the cartoons in which they appeared. The *Betty Boop* cartoons were the only instance of a successful cartoon series in which a female character featured, and Betty was certainly one of the few human characters to appear in animation before 1937. Instead, those female characters to be found were, by and large, foils for the male heroes of the cartoons: Minnie was there to support Mickey, Petunia was there for Porky, Clarabelle Cow for Horace Horse, Honey for Bosko. Rarely were they featured in cartoons of their own, and this happened only later on in their "careers", after their association with their male counterpart had been well established. Betty Boop was the only real exception to this, since she was the main character in all of her cartoons. The only other possible exception would be

Alice from Disney's *Alice Comedies*, but since Alice was played by a real little girl (and was eventually all but phased out of the series which bore her name), she does not truly count as an exception in the same way as Betty Boop.

Although there were female characters in Disney's cartoons from the start, it was predominately the male characters who were promoted by the studio as its "stars". However, by the mid-1930s, female characters had begun to take on a more central role at Disney in the context of the *Silly Symphonies*. As there were almost no recurring characters in the *Silly Symphonies*, such figures cannot individually be seen as major characters, either specifically at Disney or within animation as a field. The importance of these pioneering female characters generally to the whole of animation history, however, not to mention their importance to the history of animation at the Disney studio, cannot be underestimated. It was within the context of the *Silly Symphonies* that the Disney animators began to experiment with animating the human form, working toward the ability to create a female character who looked believable and moved realistically enough to be accepted by audiences as a viable character.

The reason for this stress upon realism by the Disney studio is fairly obvious in terms of its place within the wider arena of Hollywood cinema as a whole: the more realistic the animated characters became, the more plausible it was that audiences would accept these characters as not just cartoon figures, to be laughed at and then forgotten once the main feature started, but instead as characters to be loved or hated, but above all accepted as "realistic".[165] In order for the audiences' attention and interest to be sustained throughout a feature-length animated film, the characters and story of the film had to be acceptable to that audience, which, to Walt Disney in the 1930s, meant making the characters as similar as possible to humans in live-action cinema.

The characteristics of animation give it elements of charm and allow for the introduction of fantastical creatures and situations without the need for expensive special effects. In other words, animation, by its very nature, does not require the use of contrivance or special effects as there might be in the special effects of live-action cinema. There are no men in "rubber suits" (such as were used in films like *The Creature From the Black Lagoon*, 1954) or things being suspended from

165 See the definition of this term on Chapter 2, page 40, note 68.

strings (as used to show things like flying saucers in a number of older science fiction movies such as Ed Wood's film *Plan 9 From Outer Space*, 1959) to mar the effect of the image on the screen. Technical brilliance in the field of animation, therefore, is not reliant upon a more theatrical style of trickery, but upon a kind of artistic ability which, particularly in the early days of studio animation, was not often found outside the Disney studio. This ability was reliant upon not just artistic skill, but upon a kind of focused, purposeful training which gave the artists the necessary skills to make characters look and move in such a manner that they imitated as much as possible the look of live action cinema, rather than simply accepting and normalising the unrealistic way that many animated characters moved and looked at that time. Furthermore, it was this increased emphasis on realism which allowed animation as a medium to carry a story of feature length. It was artistic training and technical proficiency at the Disney studio which were important factors in its transition from producing short cartoons to sustaining successful feature-length animation.

Technical and artistic advances at the Disney studio

This reliance at Disney on both artistic training and a working knowledge of art history was a departure from previous traditions in animation. After all, the majority of the characters used in American animation were animals, and unnaturally bi-pedal animals at that. Mice, cats, birds, pigs, dogs, and other animals had lost all realistic scale, grown arms with hands in place of their front legs and feet, and had walked upright on their back feet for most of the history of American animation. Since the animals themselves were totally unrealistic, there were no expectations amongst spectators as to the way these creatures should look and move, and therefore realism had never been a significant issue with animators. In fact, animators at the majority of studios were actively discouraged from making any attempts to draw realistic characters or to study animation in the context of art. Shamus Culhane, for example, would later recall that, while working for Charles Mintz in the 1920s, "I decided to go to the Art Students' League at night, and one of the animators told me very solemnly, 'Don't go to art school. It'll stiffen you up'."[166] In other words, it was the belief of

166 John Canemaker, "Animation History and Shamus Culhane", *Filmmakers Newsletter* (June 1974), p. 28.

many of the early animators that formal art training would make the animator's drawings and drawing technique in general less fluid and "natural" and more formal and classically rendered, a style which would have been the exact opposite of the typical look of American animation at that time.

This attitude, although widely prevalent amongst the animators and heads at other animation studios, was the opposite of the approach taken at Disney. Art Babbit, not long after joining the animation staff at Disney in 1932, had begun organising informal study sessions in which several of the animators would gather at Babbit's home to practice sketching models. These sessions quickly became popular with the other Disney artists, and soon caught the attention of Walt himself. As Babbit would describe it later, Walt informed him that he would happily provide the classes with supplies and hire instructors for these sessions, provided they were held at the studio itself.[167] On 15 November 1932, a few weeks after the classes moved from Babbit's home to the studio, an instructor from the Chouinard Art Institute, Don Graham, began teaching life-drawing classes on the Disney sound stage. These classes became so popular that a second instructor, Phil Dike, was brought in to take on some of the extra teaching load. There were some initial growing pains for both the animators and their instructors, since a new approach to teaching art had to be invented in order to ensure that such lessons had relevance for a group of animators. These classes, however, quickly became a normal part of the Disney studio's routine, and would continue for years to come, helping the animators to meet the challenges which would come with each new film: for example, preparation for *Snow White* meant extra study of rendering human movement, and work on *Bambi* meant more careful study of the way real animals looked and moved and behaved. Prior to the animated features, however, these classes were combined with practical experimentation in the *Silly Symphonies* to help the Disney animators work on achieving a more realistic look for their characters. Furthermore, this increased emphasis on formal art training encouraged the studio to consider hiring art college graduates; likewise, a greater number of formally-trained artists began to consider animation as a possible career path. With the Depression in progress, a significant number of art graduates sought work

167 Michael Barrier, *Hollywood Cartoons: American Animation in its Golden Age* (New York: Oxford University Press, 1999), pp. 83–84.

at the Disney studio thanks to its offer of a steady paycheque, and Disney was more than happy to be able to hire them.

It was, in fact, the higher degree of artistic training amongst Disney studio artists as compared to the artists at other Hollywood animation studios at that time that enabled Disney to produce higher-quality animation, as well as more sophisticated story-lines. After all, if a story consists of more than simple gags, the artists creating the film need to be capable of rendering more complex actions and emotions than those required by the sort of basic gags which were the mainstay of early animation. Once the story-lines of animated shorts (and the characters who appeared in them) became more complex and therefore, in certain aspects, more realistic, it became possible for audiences not just to laugh at them, but to laugh with them, or – eventually – even to cry with them. There is an emotive difference between watching a character such as Felix the Cat and laughing at him removing his tail to use as a hook to hoist himself out of one frame of film onto the next, and laughing with Donald Duck in the cartoon "Donald's Cousin Gus" (1939) because he is being eaten out of house and home by an unwanted cousin who has come to visit, and watching as Donald is forced to use logic and strategy to get his cousin to leave. We enjoy Felix's antics, but we cannot see ourselves using the same methods, i.e. removing a body part and using it to hoist us to a higher space. (In fact, everything about Felix's antics serve to remind us that we are watching an animated short.) We can, however, imagine ourselves being pestered by a boorish relative and doing whatever we can to get them to leave without directly telling them to go. While we may not have some of Donald's tactics at our disposal (such as the hot dogs which he feeds his cousin which then make barking noises from his stomach and pull the cousin away in pursuit of a cat), we nonetheless can empathise with his situation and subsequent emotional reactions, and can imagine serving, if not barking food, at least something awful enough to make them want to leave. That this tactic could be employed as a gag in live-action is evidenced in the "Tennessee Ernie Hangs On" episode of *I Love Lucy*, in which Lucy (Lucille Ball), in an effort to get Cousin Ernie (Tennessee Ernie Ford) to leave, tells him that they are broke and pulls out two hard, stale rolls for their food for the day.[168] Disney gags were still exaggerated, but generally

168 *I Love Lucy*, Season 3, episode 95, "Tennessee Ernie Hangs On"; original air date: 10 May 1954. Episode features Lucille Ball and Tennessee Ernie Ford.

they were not impossible in real life. The same cannot be said of the gags in non-Disney animation of the same period.

The importance of emphasising this difference between the sophistication of the two kinds and levels of cartoons is that the level of artistry at the Disney studio by 1934 was such that it could easily support the kind of stories which involved more intricate and varied displays of emotion. Disney's artistic staff had grown considerably by 1934, and the overall artistic training and ability of his staff as a group was largely superior to the staffs elsewhere in the Hollywood animation industry. Furthermore, this higher level of technical artistry at Disney was a key element in its production of cartoons to which an audience could relate. Animators who were skilled artists – not just individuals who were skilled animators and draftsman – were a crucial factor in supporting larger, more complex animation projects. Furthermore, these higher levels of artistic training meant that new technical aspects, such as the experiments with full-colour animation, meant that even greater interest, depth, and complexity could be incorporated into their work. These factors, combined with the greater financial viability of feature-length productions over short subjects, were what led Walt Disney to the decision to attempt his next great cinematic experiment – feature-length animation.

Feature animation and spectatorship

When, in 1934, the Disney studio began work on what was to be its first animated feature film, *Snow White and the Seven Dwarfs*, Walt felt that his studio was ready, both financially and commercially, to undertake such a challenge, and that his animators were by now more than capable of meeting the technical and artistic demands such a project would involve. Moreover, it had become clear by 1933 that short subjects of all kinds were no longer as economically viable as they once had been. Not only were shorts expensive to make in terms of their length and sophistication (and indeed, Disney by this time was producing some of the most expensive shorts in the industry), but also the overall costs of promotion and distribution were such that shorts provided little or no profit to the studios producing them, many of whom – Disney included – were independent studios and, therefore, reliant on larger studios to distribute their films for them. Furthermore, a number of cinemas generally at this time – as a means of maintaining income during the Depression – were beginning to move away from promoting short subjects, choosing instead to emphasise feature-length entertainment, a circumstance which is evidenced in the era's trade press, which tried to persuade theatre owners and managers to show a variety of short subjects and feature films instead of simply showing double-features).[169]

In fact, short subjects had always been deemed by the Hollywood film industry as being less significant than feature films to the overall programme (indeed, even the term 'feature-length' being used as a name for films which averaged ninety minutes in length implies that, for Hollywood at least, not only bigger – but longer – was better).[170] For most studios, shorts were a testing ground for new actors, writers, and directors; the shorts themselves were seen as an important part of a balanced film exhibition program, but those involved in creating these shorts were often seen as less significant than those involved in feature production.[171] In order for the Disney studio to succeed as a company, it became clear that it needed to expand into feature films. Nonetheless, the decision to make such a film was very much a gamble, since although the Disneys – and others – had enjoyed great success with their short features, there was no real proof that audiences would be prepared not only to sit through a ninety-minute "cartoon feature", but also actually to enjoy it. The financial costs involved in making such a film were, moreover, enormous for the studio. Reputedly, Walt's initial estimate for making *Snow White* was somewhere between $250,000[172] – a figure which, supposedly, was arrived at because Walt estimated that a feature was roughly ten times as long as a short, and therefore would cost ten times as much to make[173] – and $500,000,[174] a figure almost twice the average cost of producing feature films in Hollywood at that time. In the end, production costs for *Snow White* would amount to approximately $2 million, a figure then unheard of by anyone in the animation industry, and an enormous amount to spend on a single feature film by any Hollywood standards. Detractors of the experiment took to calling the concept of an animated feature film "Disney's Folly", but the film's immediate success silenced such critics. Preceded and accompanied by an enormous merchandising and advertising campaign, *Snow White and the*

169 For an example of this sort of trade press, see "Shorts Audience Appetizer", in *The Hollywood Reporter*, 5 February 1931, pp. 1, 2.

170 Barrier, *Hollywood Cartoons*, p. 34. Barrier notes that Disney's success had the effect of elevating to some degree the status of animation. *Hollywood Cartoons*, p. 154.

171 For a more in-depth discussion of this, see Thomas Doherty, "This is Where We Came In: The Audible Screen and the Voluble Audience of Early Sound Cinema", in Melvyn Stokes and Richard Maltby, *American Movie Audiences: From the Turn of the Century to the Early Sound Era*, pp. 143–163, especially p. 153.

172 Barrier, *Hollywood Cartoons*, p. 125.

173 Frank Thomas and Ollie Johnston, *The Illusion of Life: Disney Animation* (New York: Hyperion, 1981), p. 90.

174 Bob Thomas, *Disney's Art of Animation: From Mickey Mouse to Hercules* (New York: Hyperion, 1997), p. 66.

Seven Dwarfs, when it was released on 21 December 1937, became a huge critical, popular and financial success for the Disney studio, and would earn $8 million by the end of its first run.[175] While there is no doubt that the merchandising which promoted *Snow White* throughout its initial run made a major contribution to the film's overall financial success, it is normally the case that no amount of advertising will urge people to see a film which is not supported by an excellent critical and word-of-mouth reputation. Urged on, therefore, by his correct reading both of the public's appetite for his studio's output and of the movie-going public's ability to appreciate feature-length animation, Disney continued to develop and release animated features as often as he could, despite the enormous amount of time and money these films cost, and even though they were not always as successful as *Snow White* had been.

In all, between 1937 – the year of *Snow White*'s release – and 1967 – shortly after Disney's death in December 1966 and therefore including *The Jungle Book* (1967), the last feature animation to be made during Walt Disney's lifetime, nineteen animated features[176] were released by the studio, to varying degrees of popular success. Of those, eight fall within the parameters of my study. They are *Snow White and the Seven Dwarfs* (1937), sections of *Melody Time* (1948), the second half of *The Adventures of Ichabod and Mr. Toad* (1949), *Cinderella* (1950), *Alice in Wonderland* (1951), *Peter Pan* (1953), *Sleeping Beauty* (1959), and *One-Hundred-and-One Dalmatians* (1961). The reason for choosing these eight films out of the nineteen possible to serve as my subjects for this study is that they all have as central characters humans (as opposed to animals, as are used in *Bambi* or *Dumbo*).

Because an appreciation of animated films implies an acceptance of (and even a sense of delight in) the basic unreality of animation, it is possible for the audience to empathise with a sympathetic, more developed character, no matter what its species. Certainly, the element of make-believe which is a normal part of childhood activity greatly assists in enabling a spectator to identify with any screen character who arouses the emotions, be that character a lion, a deer, or a princess. But identifying oneself with a lion, for example (such as Nala and Simba in *The Lion King*, 1994), may well take a slightly greater leap of the imagination than does identification with a human character. There is no need to

175 Thomas, *Disney's Art of Animation: From Mickey Mouse to Hercules*, p. 77.

176 These films were *Snow White and the Seven Dwarfs* (1937); *Pinocchio* (1940); *Fantasia* (1940); *Dumbo* (1941); *Bambi* (1942); *Saludos Amigos* (1943); *The Three Caballeros* (1945); *Make Mine Music* (1946); *Fun and Fancy Free* (1947); *Melody Time* (1948); *The Adventures of Ichabod and Mr. Toad* (1949); *Cinderella* (1950); *Alice in Wonderland* (1951); *Peter Pan* (1953); *Lady and the Tramp* (1955); *Sleeping Beauty* (1959); *101 Dalmatians* (1961); *The Sword in the Stone* (1963); *The Jungle Book* (1967).

try to imagine what it would be like to be a human, as there is with pretending to be another animal. The only imaginative leap required on the part of the spectator when it comes to identifying with a human character is imagining what it would be like to live in the same time and place as the character in question.

This idea of identification with another is supported by a wide range of opinion on the subject of female spectatorship. Specifically, a number of scholars have examined in detail the notion that audiences learn, over the course of their movie-going lives, how to identify with not just the character that is most like them (i.e. women identify with female characters, men with male characters),[177] but also with the protagonist of the film, regardless of his/her/its physical similarity to the spectator.[178] Research into notions of race and spectatorship, however, lend more credence to the idea that, although cinematically marginalised groups (i.e. all spectators who are not white middle-class heterosexual males) have learned to identify with the "other", they are happiest and most comfortable when identifying with a cinematic object which is most similar to themselves. These marginalised spectators have learned, as Hollinger puts it, "either to turn away from the … images they see on the screen or to recast these images in a more favorable light".[179]

Although, as yet, there is something of a gap in academic enquiry when it comes to the extent to which audiences identify with non-human cinematic characters, some cautious inferences can be made by examining the extensive and growing body of research into the ways that women and minority groups read mainstream Hollywood cinema. Certainly, the far-reaching success of films like *Dumbo* (1941), *One-hundred-and-One Dalmatians* (1961), *An American Tail* (Amblin Productions, 1986), and especially the phenomenal success of *The Lion King* (1994) suggest that the right combination of such factors as strong story, interesting and sympathetic characters, and what Walt himself called "heart" can produce a film with non-human characters that nonetheless possesses features which promote strong audience identification. It is, however, the current lack of definitive enquiry into this aspect of spectatorship and animated films which has led to the concentration in this book on animated films which have human characters in leading roles.

177 Karen Hollinger, *In the Company of Women: Contemporary Female Friendship Films* (Minneapolis: University of Minnesota Press, 1998), p. 21.

178 Hollinger, *In the Company of Women*, pp. 18, 19–20.

179 Hollinger, *In the Company of Women*, p. 187.

When examining Disney feature animation as a body of work, the image which comes through is one of fairy tale princesses and little girls on magical adventures. The usual perception of the Disney films of this era seems to be that these films were made up almost solely of not just fairy tale princesses, but specifically blonde-haired, blue-eyed, "all-American" types. As an article in *Look* magazine described Cinderella the heroine in a review of the film of the same name, "Like most Disney heroines, Cinderella is … 'the typical American girl'. She is cute, lively, of medium build, weighing about 120 pounds – and with a tender heart for boys and animals."[180] As can be seen in this quote, the perception is that Cinderella is a "typical" Disney heroine. Furthermore, it implies that there is such a thing as a "typical" American girl with "typical" – and very specific – traits. Indeed, not only this reputation that female characters outnumber the males, but also this supposed high propor-tion of princesses in Disney films, is misleading. Amongst those films which feature human female characters (such as the eight which are the focus of this chapter), a simple head-count sheds light on the true make-up of Disney movies. In the eight films concerned, there are sixteen major characters (not including the villains or any of the fairies) who can be deemed central to the story and are not in a supporting role. (This number rises to twenty-three if the seven dwarfs are counted as individuals, but here they are counted as a single character since they function within the story as a single unit.) Of this sixteen, eight are male and eight are female. Of the eight female characters, only three are princesses – and only two of those are princesses by birth; the third, Cinderella, becomes a princess, through marriage, in the last thirty seconds of the film. Of the other five female characters, two are little girls, two are young single women of marriageable age, and one is a newly-married young woman. Of the eight females, two are married at the end of their films, one is married early on, and two are shown to be extremely likely to marry at the films' ends. One of the women (Slue-foot Sue, from the "Pecos Bill" segment of *Melody Time*) attempts to marry, but her plans are thwarted by a horse and her subsequent, accidental "exile" onto the moon.

Of the eight male leading characters who appear in Disney animated films during the period covered by this chapter,

180 Anonymous, "Cinderella: The fairy princess comes gloriously to life in Walt Disney's newest feature-length film", *Look*, vol. 14, No. 3 (31 January 1950), p. 54.

three are little boys, five are young men of marriageable age (and of those, three are married during the film, one will obviously be married in the near future, and one (Pecos Bill) tries to get married, but, in connection with Slue-foot Sue (mentioned above), is thwarted by his horse). Only the seven dwarfs in *Snow White*, and Peter Pan, Michael, and John (all from *Peter Pan*) are never shown to be romantically attached to a woman (though several of the female characters in *Peter Pan* are depicted as being romantically interested in Peter, even if he is unaware of that fact). Although it is not discussed in detail due to its overwhelming emphasis on animal characters, it is nonetheless worth noting that even Mowgli, the boy in *The Jungle Book*, is finally persuaded to return to the Man Village by the sight of a girl, and as she is singing about the fact that she will marry one day. And as it is Mowgli's obvious attraction for her which encourages him to leave the jungle, one can assume that Mowgli will marry someday in the not-too-distant future, as soon as he is old enough to do so. So, in terms of marriage and romance, the boys are just as likely as the girls to seek out a marriage partner.

The real difference between the male and female characters, however, is not really elucidated by the head-count just presented, although it is nonetheless important to have in mind the "demographic make-up" of the characters as a group. The major difference between the two groups is not just the number of females versus males, but rather the level of agency demonstrated by each group's members.

Slue-foot Sue

As was said of the females, six are women, two are girls; three are married (Katrina van Tassel, Cinderella, and Anita), two could be described as being "engaged" to be married by the ends of their respective films (Snow White and Aurora), and one has tried to get married but been disappointed (Slue-foot Sue). More interestingly and significantly, of these eight females, only two – the little girls – go on sustained adventures in the course of each one's film. Five of the six women are framed within domestic settings throughout their films. Only Slue-foot Sue is living an active life outside the domestic sphere, though nothing of her life is shown prior to her meeting Pecos Bill (which, since he is the main

93

character of the segment, is not surprising); nonetheless, one can surmise from her description in the narration, and the way she is introduced in the film, that she has led an active, out-doorsy life before Bill meets her. Of the eight, seven are passive to varying degrees, but those who are passive at the start remain so (again, to varying degrees) throughout their stories. In other words, seven of the eight simply *react* to the things happening around them, and when events work out for them in the end, it is thanks to a combination of luck and someone else's (usually a man's) efforts. Only one, Slue-foot Sue, shows true agency. When she sees Pecos Bill for the first time, it is she who takes the lead in their relationship. Prior to their courtship, Sue is shown to be as fantastical (she makes her entrance riding a fish down a stream), athletic, and active as Bill – they are a match of equals in that sense. Perhaps comically, certainly revealingly, the song which accompanies Sue and Bill's courtship scene describes Bill as the active arranger of the situation and as the one doing the pursuing, yet the visual images are of Sue, not only encouraging Bill's few efforts, but also being the one who is taking the initiative in bringing everything together. It is Sue who takes Bill's hand when he turns away in shyness (and, when they are holding hands, Bill's face is bright red whereas Sue looks calm and comfortable). Then, when they kiss, it is Sue who places Bill's arms around her, then tilts his head up toward her and kisses him (he is sitting, she is kneeling, on a mesa in the desert). Their posture and position when they kiss show Sue in a dominant pose, and it is the first such instance of a "woman on top" in a Disney animated film (and the only such image that would appear until forty-seven years later, when Pocahontas leans over and kisses a wounded John Smith good-bye in the 1995 film). Up until Kida's and Milo's courtship in *Atlantis* in 2001, fifty-three years later, it was the only instance in a Disney animated film in which (1) an able-bodied man was in a sexually subordinate position and (2) the only instance when it was the female character who initiated the couple's first kiss.

Slue-foot Sue is also, interestingly, the only one of the eight women who can be said to be truly active or to show any agency within her story. Of the stories in which women are at any time portrayed as a bride (which is four), Slue-foot Sue is the only one who is shown to have more romantic experience than her intended mate. She is also the only one of the heroines of these stories to receive permanent punishment. Her punishment, however, is *not* linked to her romantic forwardness. Instead, it seems to be connected to two other aspects of her personality – her fondness for putting on feminine "airs" and her stubbornness. It is these two traits, demonstrated just prior to what would have been the commencement of the wedding ceremony, which serve as her undoing. Specifically, Sue requests two things for her wedding: she wants a bustle to wear under her wedding dress, and she wants to be married while sitting on Bill's horse, Widowmaker. Widowmaker, however, has hated Sue from the first moment he and Bill saw her (and, indeed, has reacted jealously to her "intrusion" into his and Bill's lives), and has to be tied down by a group of cowboys to hold him still long enough for Sue to mount him. As soon as the cowboys let Widowmaker go, he tries ferociously to throw her, but she initially has no problem holding on, with one of the cowboy narrators commenting admiringly that "No doubt about it, that there Sue was a regular female buckaroo". It is then, however, that Sue's undoing comes about. Her bustle (described in the narration as being a "fiendish contraption of steel and wire") begins to bounce, and it is the combination of Widowmaker's bucking and her bustle bouncing that finally defeats Sue: it is as if she is being punished for trying to be "girly" and exaggeratedly feminine, and, indeed, she is not the only character to be punished for wanting to dress up; Cinderella, the only other of these characters who chooses to "dress up" in the course of her story, suffers her first ball gown (the one made by the mice and birds) being torn to shreds by her step-sisters just before the royal ball. In Slue-foot Sue's case, she is thrown from Widowmaker's back and lands on her bustle, which causes her to bounce upward. Every time she lands, she lands bustle-first and so bounces even higher (Bill tries to lasso her but, unbeknownst to everyone but the film's audience, Widowmaker contrives to make Bill miss her). Eventually, Sue bounces so high that she lands on the moon, where she remains stranded forever.

Bill, who was raised by coyotes, takes to wailing at the moon because he misses her, and the coyotes howl with him sympathetically, and the story as a whole is an explanation of why coyotes howl at the moon. It is also mainly the story

95

of Pecos Bill, not Slue-foot Sue. The segment, which is the final section of *Melody Time*, lasts twenty-five minutes, and Sue makes her first appearance fifteen minutes into the segment. The first fifteen minutes are all about Pecos Bill, how he came to be raised by coyotes, and some of his major exploits. The story is narrated and sung by Roy Rogers and the Sons of the Pioneers, and the form the story takes is a typical example of an American tall tale, which exaggerates the abilities of the hero and attributes all sorts of incredible incidents to him (in this version, for example, Pecos Bill is credited with digging the Rio Grande, putting all of the water into the Gulf of Mexico, making Texas the Lone Star state, contributing to the formation of the painted desert, and putting gold in 'them thair hills').

The inclusion of the story of Slue-foot Sue, as well as the depiction of her which shows that she is more than a match for Pecos Bill, also fits the mould of the typical heroine/mate in a tall tale. One source defines the tall tale in this way:

> Tall tales, stories that the narrator does not believe but that are supposed to dupe the naïve listener, are particularly associated with the US frontier, although variants of such stories were well known in earlier times in Europe and Asia. In the United States, tall tales were presented to the city dweller as true pictures of life out West. They rely for their comic effect on the incongruity between sober narration and fantastic elements in the stories themselves.[181]

Where "Pecos Bill" as a story and its heroine differ from the other stories and leading figures within Disney films as a group, however, is that Slue-foot Sue is not typical of Disney heroines, and the legend of Pecos Bill – being a tall tale and not a fairly tale, folk tale, or book – is highly atypical of the usual Disney choice of story. Certainly, the style of this story is a substantial factor in why its characters – its female character in particular – differ so significantly from the other characters to be found in Disney films. Slue-foot Sue is not a fairy tale princess. She has no nemesis (apart from Widowmaker, of course), she is not oppressed or down-trodden, and she is not a shy, innocent maiden. The fact that she is a cowgirl even implies that she has a profession, and her wedding attire, which includes cowboy boots and a white cowboy hat (as well as her decision to be married while riding her husband-to-be's horse) further implies that she has no intention of not being a cowgirl after she is married.

181 "Tall tales", "Folktales" section, CD-ROM *Encarta Encyclopedia 99*.

The words used to describe Bill and Sue's meeting are not the usual optimistic, romantic sort normally heard, especially in a Disney film. Instead, the day they meet is referred to as "that fateful day", and references are made repeatedly to "Poor Bill" and "trouble". This doleful description of their romance is unique amongst Disney animated films. Sue's fate, however, is also unique. Her independence and activeness garner not happiness and eternal love, but instead permanent exile and bereavement. She is not the worst-behaved of the heroines of this period, but she is the most independent. The second most independent of the heroines is even more of a coquette than Slue-foot Sue and is shown to use and deceive men in order to gain the upper hand with them, but she does so within the domestic sphere. Although she does take something of a hand in shaping her future, she does so not by actively arranging events in her life, but instead passively, through the manipulation of others, getting them to take the action she wants them to take. She is the second American heroine to be encountered in Disney films, this time based on a story by Washington Irving.

Katrina van Tassell and Anita

Katrina van Tassel, the female lead in the "Legend of Sleepy Hollow" segment of *The Adventures of Ichabod and Mr. Toad*, is a notorious flirt, and the film even introduces her in these terms with a song which specifically states three times in a one-and-a-half minute-long song that she is a coquette. She, however, is in no way "punished" during the story, and at the end of the film marries Brom Bones, Ichabod Crane's rival for her hand. She is described in the narration as being "Plump as a partridge; ripe, melting, and rosy-cheeked", and her look in the film is a cross between a Dutch girl from a Delft painting and a Hollywood-style vamp. Wearing a white peaked cap over her blonde hair and clad in a wide-skirted pink dress, she spends the majority of the "Sleepy Hollow" segment engaged in such activities as fluttering her long black eyelashes, smiling coyly, puckering her very red lips, shopping, dancing, and manipulating her suitors. She is quite the local belle, and the narrator tells us that she has every man in the county – including Ichabod Crane, who is described by the narrator as always being possessed of "the most remarkable equanimity" – waiting on her hand and foot in an effort to gain her affection. In every situation, she remains calm and unflustered, and she is usually in control of the circumstances. She even seizes upon Ichabod's obvious interest in her so as to gain the upper hand with Brom Bones, who prior to Ichabod's arrival had enjoyed the advantage of having no serious rival for the position of Katrina's chief suitor, though only because all of the other local men were loath to challenge him, Brom being depicted as what would now be termed the "Alpha male" of the group.

If Brom was the alpha male in Sleepy Hollow prior to Ichabod's arrival, however, Ichabod – who is superior to Brom in a number of ways – offers a serious challenge to Brom's dominance in the area: the deciding factor in their rivalry will be who wins Katrina, the "alpha female" of the local society. Realising this, and obviously enjoying the sense of power it gives her (this is shown in several instances, such as when she is shown writing a special note on Ichabod's invitation to the Halloween dance), Katrina uses Ichabod, and plays Brom Bones and Ichabod off against one another, in a way which is made blatantly obvious to the audience, but which neither Brom nor Ichabod ever seems to appreciate. The interesting thing is that, although she obviously possesses a fair amount of intelligence and certainly has a high level of wealth and status within the community, she uses her intellect only for manipulation and game-playing, and in the end she happily settles for marriage with Brom Bones. Because all of her thoughts prior to the marriage are concentrated on flirting and coquetry, it is hard to imagine what sort of wife she will make. Certainly, in order to be a good wife, she will have to change considerably from what she was throughout the story, and this transformation in her life and character will be brought about through marriage. In the end, although she could have been more active within her story, she becomes the typical Disney heroine of her period, allowing others to act while, for the most part, she simply observes and/or reacts. Nonetheless, it must be noted that, as was the case with Slue-foot Sue and Pecos Bill, Katrina van Tassel and Brom Bones are very equally matched in a number of ways, and are a logical coupling, given the way the other men and women of their community are depicted. Since she is shown as bringing considerable wealth to the marriage, it is also implied that she will wield a certain degree of power and independence even within her marriage; this is foreshadowed in the final shot of Katrina and Brom when, just as they are married, it is Katrina who reaches up, pulls Brom down to where she can reach his face, and kisses him enthusiastically, much to his obvious surprise (and delight).

What sort of wives the heroines of Disney movies will actually make can only be guessed at, since their lives as married women are almost never explored. Only one married woman – Anita from *One-Hundred-and-One Dalmatians* – ever features as a major character in a Disney film. Forty years after her film appeared, Anita's marriage to Roger continues to be the only Disney treatment of life after the wedding. Very little of Roger's life before his marriage is revealed, and even less of Anita's life. All we know about her life before her marriage is that she was unfortunate enough, during her school days, to have captured the unwavering devotion (or, at least, the attention) of Cruella deVil. What we know about her life after her marriage is that she lives a quiet life in a little house near Regents Park in London with her husband, their two Dalmatians, and their maid, Nanny. She is shown to have spirit in the way she deals with Cruella and interacts with Roger, and there are even hints that she and Roger are, in their physical relationship at least, a typical young married couple (though this is never shown on-screen; to use live-action parlance, the camera pans away from them to another part of the room just after Roger approaches her in a playfully suggestive manner).

Granted, *One-Hundred-and-One Dalmatians* is primarily about Pongo, Perdita, their fifteen puppies, and eighty-four other Dalmatian puppies whom they rescue from Cruella deVil's clutches. But when concentrating upon Anita and Roger, we are nonetheless presented with a fairly positive image of married life. The two are obviously happy, obviously in love, very equally matched, and obviously quite contented with their life together. An examination of Anita, however, leaves us wondering how it is she manages to escape total boredom. Roger, a song writer, seems to be the only bread-winner (certainly, no career or job is ever mentioned in reference to Anita, so we have no idea whether she had a career before her marriage, much less afterward; a passing reference made by Cruella, however, suggests that Anita does not work). Nanny, the housekeeper, looks after Roger, Anita, and the dogs. Although the dogs have puppies, the humans make no mention of being about to have (or even that they are intending to have) children. Anita, therefore, seems to have very few activities or responsibilities with which to occupy herself. Nonetheless, bearing in mind that the married human couple is largely in the background when compared to the dogs' relationship and adventure, what we have is nonetheless a largely positive view of marriage. Although no suggestion is made that a married woman pursues any activity outside the home (and, indeed, may have precious little to do within her home), the image is at least that marriage can be a safe, happy, comforting institution, and affords both partners a good life.

Interestingly, there is little precedent in Hollywood cinema for focusing on a depiction of a happy couple and a happy, stable marriage. Jeanine Basinger points out that "The happy-marriage film most commonly presents a story in which the union is a background for another, broader story ...", and that, particularly in films aimed at women, marriages were rarely both the focus of a film and portrayed as being perfect. This, Basinger argues, was because "audiences knew what marriages were like and were familiar with the problems",[182] and therefore would be unlikely to accept an unrealistic portrayal. Since, in *One-Hundred-and-One Dalmatians*, the film's focus is on the kidnapping and rescue of the puppies, rather than Roger and Anita's relationship, it fits within the pattern, described by Basinger, in which happy marriages tend to serve as background for stories about other subjects. Describing this tendency as a part of the women's film genre,[183] such a parallel with a Disney film fits with Walt Disney's assertion, which will be discussed in-depth later in this chapter, that the audience for his films was predominantly women.[184]

Snow White, Cinderella and Aurora

That marriage is, at least sometimes, depicted as a seemingly blissful way to live must be good news for the three brides whose stories end either just before or just after their weddings. The three princesses of this era are Snow White (1937), Cinderella (1950), and Aurora/Brier Rose/Sleeping Beauty (1959). All three come from western European fairy tales, all three spend their early lives in reduced circumstances, and all three spend their childhood and youth under threat from an evil older woman who holds some kind of

182 Jeanine Basinger, *A Woman's View: How Hollywood Spoke to Women, 1930–1960* (London: University Press of New England, 1993), pp. 323, 322.

183 Basinger, *A Woman's View*, p. 322.

184 Robin Allan, *Walt Disney and Europe: European Influences on the Animated Feature Films of Walt Disney* (London: John Libbey, 1999), pp. 42–43.

authority over them. Appearing as their films do in three fairly distinct eras of the period being covered, one would normally expect three differing views about young woman-hood which reflected to some extent the year in which each was released. Any differences between them, however, are largely superficial, stylistic, and artistic. *Snow White and the Seven Dwarfs* is characterised very much by the sounds of Hollywood's golden era, and the look, while very much in keeping with the influences of various European children's book illustrators,[185] nonetheless possess touches which are unmistakably from 1930s Hollywood. Cinderella's look (especially when she is dressed for the ball and in her wedding dress) has a definite "Grace Kelly" quality. Princess Aurora epitomises Christian Dior's "New Look" with her tiny waist and her full-skirted, three-quarter length dress. Perhaps because the heroine spends a substantial section of the second half of the film in a trance, this is the first of the films featuring a princess in which her prince actually contributes a substantial portion of the film's action and dialogue. In terms of their personalities, the princesses are very much alike. All are very kind, graceful, good-natured, beautiful, musical, innocent young girls. Snow White and Cinderella both work, and indeed are shown performing quite hard physical labour (although, of course, their beauty and gentility shine through despite their rags). Aurora, however, never does any work of any kind throughout the film: she goes into the forest with the intention of picking berries, but never actually does, and after meeting the prince, is hurried off to the castle, pricks her finger, and then is reawakened by the prince at the end of the film. She then greets her parents before waltzing with the prince off into the clouds as the film ends.

Of the three, Aurora is the most passive when it comes to accepting her fate. Snow White at least flees from danger, and, once she finds the dwarfs' cottage, she takes an active role in earning her keep by doing housework for them. Cinderella is forced to work as a maid in her own home by her step-mother and seems to accept this role with a surprising amount of equanimity. However, during the course of the film, she works hard to try and earn permission to attend the royal ball, then, after her hard work is sabotaged, seizes the opportunity offered by her Fairy Godmother to be able to go to the ball. She is then locked away in her room to be

185 Allan, *Walt Disney and Europe*, pp. 37–40.

101

kept from trying on the slipper but, in the end, subverts her step-mother's attempt to keep her from trying on the glass slipper by getting help to escape her room from the mice with whom she has become allies, then shows the presence of mind to have held onto and protected proof that it was she with whom the prince fell in love: just as her step-mother thinks she has thwarted Cinderella's chances yet again, Cinderella subverts her by pulling from her pocket the mate of the broken glass slipper and sliding it onto her foot with ease. Even going to the ball, albeit with her Fairy Godmother's help, takes a certain degree of bravery on her part, since discovery by her step-mother would no doubt have resulted in Cinderella's public humiliation, or worse.

In general, Snow White, Cinderella, and Aurora are the three least active and least dynamic characters of the classic era. One thing that all three have in common is the fact that they either have a dead mother (Snow White and Cinderella) or a mother who, though alive, is powerless to protect them (Aurora). In fact, this is a common trend in Disney films, though – for the most part – this is because the weak or absent parent is a common theme within folk and fairy tales; it is the lack of a strong parent which forces the young hero(ine) to undertake the adventure/journey which leads to their maturing into strong, independent adults. However, there are instances (such as in *Snow White* and *Aladdin*) when the decision was made not to include a parent in the film. Given that film-makers have demonstrated throughout the history of cinema a willingness to alter source material to fit the constraints of cinema and/or to make the story more "meaningful" for its audience, however, the decision to add or keep a parent in the film is still significant, regardless of source material. When there is a mother alive and present in the film, she is rendered powerless. More often than not, she is either dead or completely out of the picture before the start of the film.[186] Out of the thirty-nine[187] animated films produced to date which have sustained plots, only ten of them feature mothers who are still alive (though one of them, Bambi's mother, is killed during the film), and none of them are capable of protecting their offspring from harm. Dumbo's mother is imprisoned; Wendy's mother is not aware that her daughter has been endangered until the danger is passed; Aurora's mother can only protect her daughter by giving her up to be raised by three fairies;

[186] For a discussion of mothers in Disney films, see Lynda Haas, "'Eighty-Six the Mother': Murder, Matricide, and Good Mothers", in Elizabeth Bell, Lynda Haas, and Laura Sells, (eds), *From Mouse to Mermaid: The Politics of Film, Gender, and Culture* (Indianapolis: Indiana University Press, 1995), pp. 193–211.

[187] This is not counting either *Fantasia* (1940) or *Fantasia 2000* (2000) Nor is it counting the package films *Saludos Amigos* (1943), *The Three Caballeros* (1945), *Make Mine Music* (1946), *Fun and Fancy Free* (1947), and *Melody Time* (1948), due to the format in which the stories within each film are told, since more often than not they are less story-oriented and more music-oriented. Officially, there are forty-six animated feature films which have been produced by Walt Disney Pictures.

Cody's mother (in *The Rescuers Down Under*) is so unimportant to the film that we never even see her face; Simba's mother (in *The Lion King*) does not know that her son is in danger, and when she learns of it she thinks that he is dead, so he grows up without her; Hercules' mother is a supportive character, but relegated to the background; Mulan's mother, also kindly and loving, can do nothing to protect Mulan once she learns her daughter has run away. Sarah Hawkins (in *Treasure Planet*) clearly loves her son, and is a hard-working, honest woman, but cannot control her son's wild ways and – ultimately – allows him to go on his journey to find Treasure Planet in the hope that the experiences of the journey will be good for him.

Instead, particularly in the cases of Snow White and Cinderella, what is left for the main character is a "maternal" figure in the form of a step-mother who is openly against the young girl in her care, doing everything she can to oppress the girl and keep her from finding love. In the section of *A Woman's View* in which Jeanine Basinger writes about the character of the "destructive mother" in the women's film genre, she describes this type of character:

> Mothers who are destructive are either interfering in their children's love lives or in their careers. Where love is concerned, they are always trying to stop it, and where career is concerned, they are always trying to push it ahead. This further endorses the idea that a woman's proper choice in life is love. If her mother blocks it, an audience can see she is destructive. If she is trying to push her daughter into a career, she is also blocking love. Bad mothers of men are always trying to block love, since a man is allowed a career, and his mother wants him to have one.[188]

In Disney, it is not so much the mothers themselves who are bad as it is the step-mothers. When the mother is alive and present, she is as good a mother as she possibly can be. However, she is powerless, for whatever reason, to really help her child, thus forcing the child to save him- or herself. Most often, however, she is not only dead, she is never even mentioned. Fathers are a little luckier in Disney. They are rarely killed, and whereas only a handful of Disney characters have mothers, many more – nineteen out of thirty-nine – have fathers. Granted, where there are fathers, they are often just as incapable of protecting their offspring as are the mothers (indeed, only Bambi's father, The Great King, and Pongo, the father of the Dalmatian puppies stolen by

188 Basinger, *A Woman's View*, p. 432.

Cruella deVil, and Buck Cluck, Chicken Little's father in *Chicken Little* (2005), are the only fathers who manage to save and/or protect their young; no human fathers show similar competence). But they nonetheless have an important presence in the films, and are there to offer advice, love, and support to their children.

In *Snow White* and *Cinderella*, there is much the same parent-child set-up: the heroines' natural parents are dead, and they have each been left in the care of an evil, domineering, jealous woman who has taken over the home and rights that should have been the heroines and usurped them for herself. Furthermore, the evil step-mother actively threatens and thwarts the heroine in her "care", and will stop at nothing to destroy the heroine and her chances for a happy, independent life. In *Sleeping Beauty*, the scenario is not quite the same, in that Aurora's nemesis is an evil fairy queen, and both of Aurora's parents are alive. However, they have no power or ability to protect Aurora themselves, and must give her up to the care of three elderly fairies who take the infant princess away and live hidden in the forest, letting Aurora grow up thinking she is an orphaned peasant.

Whether parents in a Disney film are alive or dead, they are powerless to protect their children. Granted, it is the parents' lack of aid to the children that allows the child the opportunity to live out the adventure of his or her story. Nonetheless, the reduced role of the parent in Disney films is important for the characterisations of the heroes/heroines. They may function in a naïve, innocent way throughout much of their stories, but as they have no one to teach them how to be good adults, then the fact that their first independent steps are rather wobbly and unsure is to be expected. For some of the characters, the journey to adulthood begins in their teens. For two of the characters in this first period of Disney films, however, those first steps are taken much sooner.

Alice and Wendy

In this period of Disney films, there are only two little girls who serve as central characters. Though both Alice, from *Alice in Wonderland* and Wendy, from *Peter Pan*, are voiced by British child actress Kathryn Beaumont, both are nonetheless very different characters. Alice's film does not seem to have been terribly interesting to those who made it,[189] nor does it seem to have garnered much critical respect. Wendy, too, although a character in a more critically and popularly successful film, never seemed completely to catch the attention of the public. And yet, interestingly, of all the female characters of this era, it is only Alice and Wendy who ever enjoy real adventures into new, strange worlds. Alice falls down a rabbit hole and wanders from one strange character and situation to the next before finally, in danger of being decapitated and fleeing from the insane Queen of Hearts, realises that she is dreaming and awakens to find herself safely in her garden at home. Although it is possible that Wendy dreamed her adventure as well, we are given strong reason to believe that she did in fact go to Neverland with Peter Pan and her brothers, and that she did meet mermaids and Indians and help to vanquish a band of evil pirates.

In both films, it is implied that only little girls (as opposed to grown women) go on adventures, and that little girls are still in possession of their imaginations. Alice is shown in the first and last scenes of the film with a woman (possibly her older sister, though in fact her identity is never stated), and this woman, although expressing the fact that there are many good books in this world without pictures, does not imply when saying so that she has an imagination capable of supplying the pictures. The only female characters Alice encounters while in Wonderland are a garden full of terribly snooty, mean-spirited flowers, and the Queen of Hearts, whose main pleasure in life seems to come from ordering executions and dominating her husband, the king.

Wendy is taken by Peter Pan to Neverland because she tells him that it is her last night in the nursery, saying with a sad little sniffle that, "I have to grow up tomorrow". Horrified at the prospect of her growing up, Peter whisks her away, but in the end her impulse to become an adult is such that it cannot be denied, and Peter eventually takes her home (in fact, when her parents see her, they tell her that she does not have to leave the nursery just yet, but she tells them that she *is* in fact now ready to grow up). While in Neverland, the female characters she encounters are Tinkerbell (who is very spiteful and jealous when it comes to Wendy's friendship with Peter), the mermaids (who are all very flirty with Peter and extremely catty towards Wendy), and Princess Tiger Lily (the daughter of the Indian chief), who is captured by

189 Leonard Maltin, *The Disney Films: From Snow White to Pocahontas* (New York: Hyperion Press (3rd edn, 1995), p. 103.

Captain Hook. Tiger Lily is also portrayed as a little girl, but this aspect of her representation is overshadowed by the common racial stereotype of the Native American, which casts her as proud, brave, and silent. While in the Indian camp, Wendy is ordered by an Indian woman (with an unusually masculine, "drag"-style comic voice), "Squaw, get some firewood", and Wendy is stopped from dancing in the celebration (Tiger Lily, however, is not). In fact, Tiger Lily is the only female whose participation in the celebration is allowed. When Wendy is initially stopped from dancing with the boys, it is when the old woman tells her, "Squaw no dance". The message is clear: girls may dance with the men and boys, but women have to work. Although Wendy initially complies, returning to the festivities with a bundle of sticks, the sight of Tiger Lily and Peter Pan rubbing noses (also known as an "Eskimo kiss") makes her drop her sticks in fury. Soon afterward, Wendy refuses to obey the woman's orders (shouting at the woman, "Squaw *no* get some firewood! Squaw go home!") and returns alone to Peter Pan's hide-out.

The message we get from Wendy and Alice is clear – little girls can go on adventures, but as soon as they start to approach womanhood, their adventures have to cease. Alice, still safely ensconced in the cocoon of girlhood, gives us the impression that she may well have another great adventure, even if only in a dream (her dreams, after all, are not of handsome princes and happily ever-afters, but of mad tea parties and talking caterpillars, and there is no sign that she will cease such dreaming anytime soon). Wendy, however, is shown to be very grown-up and responsible, and it is very much stressed throughout *Peter Pan* that she has "to grow up tomorrow". Although at the end of the film her father has relented in his insistence that this is to be her last night in the nursery, Wendy herself is quite happy and accepting of the fact that she needs to grow up, and that her trip to Neverland was the last adventure she needed. It is interesting that fathers are characterised in *Peter Pan* as such mean-spirited people. Wendy's father, in fact, bears a very striking resemblance to Captain Hook. Mr. Darling, the father, is heavier and has shorter hair, fitting the model of the Victorian/Edwardian gentleman. Captain Hook is thinner and has longer hair more suited to the classic representation of a pirate. Those are their only physical differences. Fathers –

patriarchy – are portrayed as the enemies of children's games and ways, and both Mr. Darling and Captain Hook (who have no first names – in what is an interesting and subtle acknowledgement of the formal politeness paid to patriarchy, it is only by their titles and surnames that they are known) seek to put an end to Peter's and Wendy's natural imaginativeness and inventiveness. *Alice in Wonderland* and *Peter Pan*, linked as they are by the use of Kathryn Beaumont's voice and their focus on girls and girlhood, share one very significant theme in common: only children can have fun.

Wicked women and evil fairies

Perhaps the most distinguishing feature of the villainesses in this era of Disney films is the much higher proportion of agency they show when compared to that of their victims. They change themselves into other things when functioning in their usual form is not working for them. They actively seek to control not only their lives but also their circumstances. They are strong, fearless, and often very creative. They are mature, powerful, and independent. In short, they are everything that their female victims are not. And, like Slue-foot Sue (the only active heroine in this body of films), they all suffer the same fate – destruction. Usually, this demise is brought on by their own actions. The evil Queen in *Snow White* falls off a cliff while being pursued by the seven dwarfs. Maleficent turns herself into a dragon (in a way which, despite all her evil actions before, is nonetheless even more intense and menacing) in order to destroy Prince Philip, which leaves her vulnerable to being struck down by his magical sword. Cinderella's wicked stepmother is not destroyed, of course, but she completely disappears from the story after her defeat, and the Queen of Hearts is vanquished by Alice simply because, as a figure in a dream, she ceases to be once Alice wakes up. Cruella deVil survives but is humiliated and – we are left in no doubt – will never bother anyone else again. The theme of these wicked women and their fates is not only that evil never goes unpunished, but also that it is the evil women – the bitches – who are the strong, active, no-nonsense people who stop at nothing to get things done. Of course, the things they want to "get done" are not very nice, and these women seem to be particularly sensitive and easily offended (Maleficent, for

107

example, is initially thrown into a fury against Princess Aurora and spends sixteen years trying to destroy the young princess because she was not invited to Aurora's christening, despite the fact that this is in no way Aurora's fault). They are evil, and goodness and happiness in the films are protected by the removal of these evil antagonists. But it is interesting that it is these evil women who are the active women in their films, and that their activity is forced upon them by their own jealousy and unhappiness. Goodness and happiness are not given only to the beautiful (after all, the evil Queen is second in beauty only to Snow White, and yet she is very unhappy and frustrated). Instead, real happiness seems to be linked to one trait alone – passivity. If you are willing to wait patiently for your happiness, it will surely come to you. Try to make it happen for yourself, and you will only end up defeated and alone.

In her book on representations and uses of the occult in cinema, *A Skin for Dancing In: Possession, Witchcraft, and Voodoo in Film*, Tanya Krzywinska discusses the idea that, in fairy tales and films based upon them, the idea of the evil stepmother is tied to teenage fantasies of the bad mother. As she describes it, it is during the teenage years that mothers and daughters (and, indeed, fathers and sons) enter into the most difficult period of their relationship. As a way of dealing with this, the mother has been split into two personas: the "good" mother (whose biological relationship to the daughter is maintained) and the "bad" mother, who is distanced, typically, from the heroine by making her a step-mother. As Krzywinska points out, in film, "… the stepmother, for modern audiences, may stand in for the real mother in her bad guise. It is used to articulate girls' unconscious and conscious fantasies about getting rid of the mother, albeit filtered through Hollywood's goal of addressing a broad audience".[190] Certainly in most of the Disney films which focus on a rivalry between an older woman and a younger heroine, these heroines are all depicted as teenagers, usually around sixteen years of age (certainly, in *Sleeping Beauty*, the curse on Aurora is set to take place "before the sun sets on her sixteenth birthday"), and there is some credence to Krzywinska's idea. What is interesting, however, is that, with only two exceptions, the Disney films which follow this pattern were made in this earlier era, and the most recent film following anything similar to this pattern was *The Little*

190 Tanya Krzywinska, *A Skin for Dancing In: Possession, Witchcraft, and Voodoo in Film* (Trowbridge, Wiltshire: Flicks Books, 2000), p. 137.

Mermaid, released in 1989. Not all of the evil women in Disney films are step-mothers: Maleficent is an evil fairy, for example (though one could argue that, as Aurora is raised by good fairies, an evil fairy would serve as a "bad" mother figure and, therefore, still fits this idea). Regardless of their connection to the heroine or their degree of magical ability (after all, not all of these characters have magic powers), the characteristic shared by these women are that they see something about the heroine as a threat which must be controlled – or removed. This, however, as Krzywinska shows, is not unique to Disney films: it is an archetypal use of the "good" and "bad" mother, and to be found in fairy tale and film alike. The common interpretation is that of the step-mother, who sees her step-daughter as a rival/threat.

Besides their evil natures, the other trait which links these evil women together is an obsessiveness akin to madness. The Evil Queen is not just jealous, she is *insanely* jealous, willing to murder Snow White for the sake of her own vanity. Cinderella's step-mother will stop at nothing to forward the interests of her own daughters, even though, as an intelligent woman, some part of her must acknowledge that her hopes for them are completely unrealistic (if this were not the case, she would not find Cinderella so threatening). Maleficent has such an inflated sense of herself that the smallest slight justifies – at least in her mind – her vindictive rage and her murderous plans. Cruella deVil will stop at nothing to satisfy her own selfish whims and vanities, again out of what is apparently a much-inflated ego. Evil in Disney is not just meanness – it is a symptom of madness, embodying as it does various levels of paranoia.[191]

Separating the men from the girls

191 For a discussion of themes of paranoia and their cinematic representations, see Michael Fleming and Roger Manvell, *Images of Madness: The Portrayal of Insanity in the Feature Film* (London: Associated University Press, 1985), pp. 147–158.

Putting aside such portrayals of insanity amongst strong female characters, the real difference between the male and female characters is their level of activity (as opposed to passivity) within their stories. Of the male characters, ten of the thirteen (which includes characters from films not analysed in this book) demonstrate a definite sense of agency: Pecos Bill is a highly athletic, energetic cowboy and "a western superman" (as he is described in the song which introduces him); the boy in the "Once Upon a Wintertime" segment of *Melody Time* (neither of the characters in this segment have names) goes to great lengths first to impress his girlfriend, then to save her when she is trapped on thin ice; Ichabod Crane and Brom Bones are heavily in competition for Katrina van Tassel; Johnny Appleseed plants apple trees all over North America; Peter Pan has one adventure after another, as do Michael and John (Wendy's brothers), who are visiting Neverland; Prince Philip (from *Sleeping Beauty*) is the brave hero who battles and finally defeats the Evil Maleficent before awakening Princess Aurora; the Seven Dwarfs are Snow White's protectors and, though they do not actually save Snow White, nonetheless are partially responsible for the death of the evil Queen.

To sum up, one of the eight females and six of the eight males are active participants within their own stories, and seven of the eight females and five of the eight males express romantic feelings during their films. One-third of the women are princesses, and nearly one-half of the men are boys. This is the overall composition of leading characters in the eight films being covered in this chapter. What does it tell us about Walt Disney's view of women and the perceived make-up of the audience for Disney films, and what do audience reactions to these films tell us about the success each of these films enjoyed?

Walt and women

It is known that Walt Disney saw his audience not so much in terms of adult versus child as he did male versus female, and that he himself recognised that his audience was primarily female. This analysis is supported by Walt's comment in the storyboard notes for *Snow White and the Seven Dwarfs* when, in discussing a dream sequence (which was later dropped from the film) on 8 December 1936, he stated that

> "I feel this sequence would be for the women. After all 80 per cent of our audience are women. If we get something they loved it would help because there is a lot of slapstick stuff that women don't like so well. If our characters are cute they'll like them. We don't cater to the child but to the child in the adult – what we all imagined as kids is what we'd like to see pictured."[192]

Walt Disney's attitudes towards women, however, can be understood from his films in only the most superficial way. After all, as is the case with most individuals, Walt's personal views and attitudes towards women – as both consciously

192 Allan, *Walt Disney and Europe*, pp. 42–43.

and unconsciously expressed by him – were complex and, in some cases, often contradictory. Little is known definitively about his early views on the matter, and that may be thanks to his lack of attention to this subject, his lack of experience with women in his early life, and, until recently, the lack of scholarly enquiry and interest in his childhood. His mother, Flora Call Disney, was a constant presence throughout Walt's childhood and youth, and Walt had a sister, Ruth (born 1903), who was only two years younger and very much a part of his early life. Particularly since the closest of Walt's brothers to him in age, Roy (born 1893), was eight years older, it was predominantly Walt and Ruth who grew up together, their three older brothers becoming somewhat distant figures throughout much of Walt and Ruth's later childhood years. Walt had a favourite aunt, Margaret, whom he remembered as being his main childhood supplier of paper and pencils for practising his art, and he had at least one school teacher, Daisy Beck, of whom he possessed fond memories throughout his life.[193] His romantic experience of women, however, seems to have been fairly limited. There are only two definite recorded instances of Walt having been attracted to women. The first was a girl from his high school in Chicago, with whom he corresponded throughout his time in the Red Cross and for whom he brought back a number of presents from France, only to discover upon his return that she had already married someone else. The second was his shy courtship of a young woman who worked as an ink-and-paint girl at the fledgling Disney Brothers studio. Her name was Lillian Bounds, and Walt married her in 1925, a few months prior to his twenty-fourth birthday. He and Lillian would go on to raise two daughters: Diane, whom Lillian gave birth to on 18 December 1933, and Sharon, whom the Disneys adopted in 1937.[194]

Although he would work with women to an extent in his studio, and though his home life was filled with women, particularly once marriage and fatherhood arrived, in reality Walt had a relatively limited amount of experience with women, and his attitude towards women as a group was characterised by a mixture of respect and suspicion. Steven Watts, one of the few scholars to offer a balanced, in-depth, account of Walt's childhood and early life, describes this contradictory attitude in these terms: "[Walt] associated

193 Bob Thomas, *Walt Disney: An American Original* (New York: Hyperion, 1994), p. 29; Steven Watts, *The Magic Kingdom: Walt Disney and the American Way of Life* (New York: Houghton Mifflin Company, 1997), 15.

194 Thomas, *Walt Disney: An American Original*, pp. 120, 145; Watts, *The Magic Kingdom*, p. 352.

women with security in a particularly intense fashion. ...
These [boyhood] experiences of female security, however,
gave way to resentment when the adolescent Walt saw his
ideal violated".[195] Watts mentions how Walt's mother was
seen by him as being "the one with the humor".[196] She was
beloved by her children because, together with standing up
to her husband's strictness towards the children, she would
also subvert his more Spartan demands upon his family, for
example, passing pieces of bread to her children with the
buttered side down so that Elias would be unaware that she
was being so "wasteful" with butter. His sister Ruth would
later recall the time in grammar school when Walt signed up
for a domestic science class. As the only boy in the class, Walt
seems to have enjoyed it, despite the teasing it incurred from
some of his friends, because "the girls were all making over
him something terrible".[197]

By late adolescence, Walt's idealised concept of women as
sources of attention and security was seemingly being chal-
lenged. He would later recall, upon arriving in France with
the Red Cross, how he and the other young men were
shown films about the dangers of venereal disease, saying of
this that "That's when you begin to hate women".[198] He
would then learn a few months later of the deception of his
high school "girlfriend", who married another man while
Walt was in France without informing him until after he had
returned. Throughout his life, Walt's views would vie between these two highly contradictory notions of Woman as
source of love and goodness, and Woman as source of danger
and duplicity. Certainly, this bi-polar view of women is to
be found throughout the animated features produced by the
Disney studio during Walt's lifetime. Furthermore, the fact
that the good women in Disney films, at least until the late
1950s, were younger women just on the verge of achieving
sexuality, largely fits in with Walt's experiences of women
during his own childhood and youth. To take this argument
a step further, however, and say that Walt was alone in these
views of women, or to argue that his simplifications of
women as a whole were not to be found within twentieth-
century American society as a whole, would be grossly
inaccurate.

Furthermore, it is difficult to argue that, when it came to his
employees, Walt's attitude towards women was either discriminatory or paternalistic. While it is true that the staff of

195 Watts, *The Magic Kingdom*, pp.14–15.

196 Watts, *The Magic Kingdom*, p. 14.

197 Watts, *The Magic Kingdom*, p. 15.

198 Watts, *The Magic Kingdom*, p. 15.

the ink-and-paint department – a department which was relatively low in status at both Disney and at other animation studios – was usually staffed entirely by women (or "girls", as they were referred to at the time), and while it is also true that the majority of the upper-level animators at Disney were men, this was apparently not because Walt was against the idea of women working in the higher ranks of his studio. In a speech given by Walt to his studio staff on 10 February 1941, he explicitly defended his decision to employ women in upper level positions: "The girl artists have the right to expect the same chances for advancement as men, and I honestly believe that they may eventually contribute something to this business that men never would or could".[199]

This belief on Walt's part – that it was women who would make a contribution to animation (and the film industry as a whole) which would take it above the level at which it functioned during that time and turn it into something more interesting and significant than had the men who had dominated it in its early years seems to have been a fairly consistent one. Years later, when he would hire writer Joan Scott to work on the screenplay for what would become the live-action bio-pic of the life of Beethoven, *The Magnificent Rebel* (1962), much the same ethos towards what he saw as women's unique contribution to entertainment would be demonstrated. In an article she wrote in 1987, Scott related that, when her agent was telling her of the Disney studio's interest in hiring her as a writer for the film, he revealed to her that it was because Walt had been quite specific in his requirements in a new writer: "[Walt] wanted a woman writer for the Beethoven story because he felt a woman would bring more heart to it".[200] This seems to have been Walt Disney's only specification. A definite note of paternalism, however, was to be found amongst his executive staff. Scott would later write of the obvious sexism of these executives, pointing out how they projected onto Walt their own conservative attitudes about women: "[T]he studio executives assigned the task of lining up the right woman", Scott remembered, "had made the point that a younger woman was preferred because Disney didn't like being contradicted … and it was feared that a more mature, better established writer might be tempted to argue with Disney about his approach to the material".[201] Likewise, the very fact that Walt found himself having to defend to his male

199 John Canemaker, *Before the Animation Begins: The Art and Loves of Disney Inspirational Sketch Artists* (New York: Hyperion Press, 1996), p. 112.

200 Joan Scott, 'Ordeal By Disney: Little Bit Goes a Long Way', *Film Comment*, vol. 23 n. 6 (November/December 1987), p. 52.

201 Scott, 'Ordeal By Disney', p. 52.

employees (and his employees as a whole) his decision to promote women in his company shows that there was a definite dislike by some at Disney of the idea of taking orders from a woman. Although it is clear that Walt saw men and women as being different from one another in certain very deep and profound ways (hence his argument that it would fall to women to add that something extra which animation lacked under the stewardship of men), it would seem that Walt himself was more than prepared to listen to women's opinions, work with them as artistic and intellectual equals, and accept that they had something worthwhile to contribute to a discussion.[202] This attitude is continually supported in accounts of those who worked with him and from his own known verbal and written comments on the issue.[203]

This is not to say, however, that Walt did not hold conservative opinions on a number of subjects. In the testimony he gave as a friendly witness before the House Committee on Un-American Activities in 1947, and in his co-operation with the FBI in the 1950s, he makes it clear that he is a fairly conservative individual, particularly when it comes to patriotism (he describes those who are not communist as being not only good, but also as "100 percent American"[204]). Some writers, however, have exaggerated both his conservatism and the specific nature of his commitment to anti-Communism. Marc Eliot, in his 1995 biography of Walt, claimed that "Uncle Walt", far from being the kindly, loveable figure he was portrayed as being, was in fact a spy for the FBI in Hollywood throughout the 1950s.[205] Steven Watts, however, characterises Walt's relationship with the FBI as being "cordial, if distant", and points out in his more scholarly biography that, rather than being a spy in Los Angeles for the FBI, Walt was in fact an "SAC contact", which is "a largely honorary designation given to friendly community leaders who are willing to talk with the agency's special agent in charge for their region".[206] For Watts, these charges that Walt was an FBI agent are "overheated accusations", and he argues that Walt's endorsement of the FBI's "broader agenda" during the Cold War was not any different from that of many other Americans.[207]

As for Walt's 1947 testimony, although he is thanked by the committee for his co-operation and described by them as being a "good witness" (he even "named names" in his testimony), he makes it clear that, while he is against

202 For more on Walt's working relationships with female employees in his studio, see Amy M. Davis, "The Dark Prince and Dream Women: Walt Disney and Mid-Twentieth Century American Feminism", in *Historical Journal of Film, Radio, and Television*, Vol. 25, No. 2 (June 2005), pp. 213–230.

203 Whether or not this acceptance of women as professional equals extended to the concept that they should be paid as equals, however, cannot be known at this time as this information does not seem to be available in the public domain and the closure to outsiders of the Disney Archives prevents investigation into this matter.

204 The Testimony of Walter E. Disney before the House Committee on Un-American Activities, 24 October 1947. See http://eserver.org/filmtv/disney-huac-testimony.txt

205 Marc Eliot, *Walt Disney: Hollywood's Dark Prince* (London: Andre Deutsch Limited, 1995), pp. 152–157, 230–245.

206 Watts, *The Magic Kingdom*, p. 349.

communism, he is not against the majority of unions or liberal causes. When asked by committee member H.A. Smith how he (Walt) thinks the communist "menace" should be attacked, Walt says that he thinks they should be kept out of the unions:

> I know that I have been handicapped out there in fighting it [the communist menace], because they have been hiding behind this labor set-up, they get themselves closely tied up in the labor thing, so that if you try to get rid of them they make a labor case out of it. We must keep the American labor unions clean. We have got to fight for them.[208]

Clearly, if Walt were truly anti-union, he would not be proposing to fight *for* them, however politically naïve his testimony on the subject may have shown him to have been. In his support both for cleaning up the unions *and* liberalism in general, Walt replies to Smith's question "What is your personal opinion of the Communist Party, Mr. Disney, as to whether or not it is a political party?" by saying that:

> Well, I don't believe it is a political party. I believe it is an un-American thing. The thing that I resent the most is that they are able to get into these unions, take them over, and represent to the world that a group of people that are in my plant, that I know are good, one-hundred-percent Americans, are trapped by this group, and they are represented to the world as supporting all of those ideologies, and it is not so, and I feel that they really ought to be smoked out and shown up for what they are, so that all of the good, free causes in this country, all the liberalisms that really are American, can go out without the taint of communism. That is my sincere feeling on it.[209]

Walt was anti-Communist (as his testimony clearly indicates), but he was not an FBI agent. Like many people, Walt held both conservative and liberal views on various subjects.

Although Walt himself has gained a reputation for profound chauvinism, possibly because of the ways in which women were portrayed by his studio on film, the evidence concerning Walt's views on women does not bear out this perception. While there can be no doubt that there was a definite air of paternalism to be found at Disney, it is equally true that Walt Disney saw women as being very different from men, but in a way which balanced men's concerns. More succinctly, the evidence suggests that Walt believed in the over-riding view of women in the 1940s and 1950s as characterised by such traits as emotionalism, domesticity,

207 Watts, *The Magic Kingdom*, p. 349.

208 Testimony of Walter E. Disney before the House Committee on Un-American Activities, 24 October 1947.

209 Testimony of Walter E. Disney before the House Committee on Un-American Activities, 24 October 1947.

maternal concerns, an over-all emphasis on beauty and romance (as opposed to more "practical" concerns). It was also widely considered at this time that women had a generally softer, quieter, more delicate approach to viewing the world. Walt did not, however, see these traits as being evidence of women's emotional or intellectual inferiority. Rather, he perceived them as serving the important function of balancing the needs, views, goals, and characteristics of men and masculinity, stressing that without one to support the other, the whole (be it the whole of society, a company, or an artistic project) would be left unbalanced and, therefore, wanting.

Changes in American society

A film reflects the society which produces it. During the nineteenth and twentieth centuries, American society showed a marked tendency to separate and define the sexes, doing so through economic, political, and cultural means, as well as by fostering the development of strict social roles and hierarchies. As women's functions within their communities moved from a contributory role in production (as was largely the case during the era prior to the Industrial Revolution) to the roles of housekeeper and consumer (a new role which emerged with the growth of the middle-class and the rise in the ideal of the male bread-winner supporting his wife and children), the ways in which a woman's worth and value were understood within society changed concurrently. The simultaneous rise of the authority of science in the nineteenth century would eventually find "evolutionary justifications" for this division of the sexes, but those who continued to favour the validity of religion over science were equally capable of finding tracts which legitimised the subordination of women. As middle-class women found themselves contributing less and less to their families' livelihoods and became increasingly financially dependent upon a male bread-winner (usually a husband or father), their worth – and the goals which became acceptable achievements for them – changed from what they could produce (as was more typically the case in pre-Industrial society) to what they could achieve in terms of their beauty, their "accomplishments" (i.e. music, painting, sketching, and dancing), and their appearances.[210] In other words, their acceptable goals became those which reinforced

210 Underlying and justifying this, the doctrine of "separate spheres" evolved. Men inhabited the "public" sphere of business and politics, women the "private" sphere of home and family. See Barbara Welter, "The Cult of True Womanhood", *American Quarterly*, 18 (1966), pp. 151–174.

their status as ornaments. According to Naomi Wolf, it was the simultaneous advent in the nineteenth century of the ability to mass-produce printed images of women and "beauty ideals" which lead to the sort of standardisation of fashion and beauty norms which we still find in fashion/beauty magazines throughout the twentieth century and continue to take for granted in the early twenty-first century.[211]

Although the twentieth century saw two major changes in women's power levels within society – the right to vote, achieved by American women in 1920, and the women's movement from the 1960s onward – the idea that a woman's major function within society was as a consumer and the notion that a woman could be judged (and, most crucially, judge herself), on the basis of her physical appearance, are two cultural constrictions which, according to Wolf, continued to reduce the other accomplishments to which women could aspire. There are, however, many examples of successful women who were subjected to Western society's sexist backlash in the late twentieth century, and who found their accomplishments within their professions being subordinated to society's evaluation of them as women, based upon their looks and how well (or, in the cases of many successful women, how poorly) they fit within the narrow limits of what society deems acceptable for women.

While it is true that the definitions of female beauty altered considerably over the course of the twentieth century, the fact is that the earlier ideals – first of corseted, "waspwaisted" women, then the boy-like Flappers of the 1920s, were just as unnatural for the majority of women's bodies as have been the ideals set forth by the fashion industry in the late twentieth/early twenty-first centuries of the waif, whose thin, underdeveloped body, typically found amongst pre- or early pubescent girls, is promoted as an ideal for adult women. As Wolf states, "The qualities that a given period calls beautiful in women are merely symbols of the female behavior that that period considers desirable: *The beauty myth is always actually prescribing behavior and not appearance*".[212] Certainly, when we consider the emphasis on Woman's role as wife/mother in the 1930–1960s, the images of women which show young, attractive women whose bodies are the softer, more curvaceous bodies of women in their twenties and thirties (typically, at least in the twentieth century, the

211 Naomi Wolf, *The Beauty Myth: How Images of Beauty are Used Against Women* (London: Vintage Books, 1991), pp. 11–15.

212 Wolf, *The Beauty Myth*, pp. 13–14.

period of women's lives when women tended to marry and/or reproduce). This fits perfectly with the idealisation of Woman's role as homemaker during this era (especially during the comparatively prosperous post-war era of the 1950s, as epitomised by such television characters as Lucy Ricardo (played by Lucille Ball) on *I Love Lucy* and by June Cleaver (played by Barbara Billingsly) on *Leave It to Beaver*).

Though the general perception of popular images of women during the decades covered by this chapter is that the "happy homemaker" is the image of the 1950s alone, the fact is that she was very much alive and well throughout the Depression years and the Second World War era as well. After all, it was the perceived ability of the good housewife to economise in terms both of money and material resources which was credited with helping stretch her family's income during the lean times of the Depression. To this duty as wife and mother, her patriotic duty to her country was added during the privations of the war years. In America, this image was a modernised version of the ideal of republican motherhood.[213] Even the "Rosie the Riveter" image was that of an obviously feminine woman; the change, however, simply showed her both strong and muscular (although not *too* muscular) so that she could shoulder the burden of traditionally male-associated labour in support of the war effort. Once the war had ended, however, these images of women with strong, developed muscles quickly gave way to images of women with soft, rounded arms and shoulders, and the fashion world responded to the return of peace and relative prosperity with the introduction of such fashions as were typified by Christian Dior's "New Look", introduced in 1947. The emphasis on beauty throughout the 1930s, 1940s, and 1950s was upon the soft, physically comforting, inviting (although not *too* inviting; anything too overtly sexual was hinting that a woman might be more sexually experienced than society's emphasis on female chastity outside of marriage would permit), mature body of a young woman. An attractive young wife and mother (or at least a woman who would achieve these feminine goals soon) was the image most seen in fashion and house-keeping magazines (and, later, in the television) of this era.

The images of women in popular magazines may have remained relatively similar throughout the earlier half of the twentieth century, but in Hollywood films a more notice-

213 On the original ideal of "republican motherhood", see Linda Kerber, *Women of the Republic: Intellect and Ideology in Revolutionary America* (Chapel Hill: University of North Carolina Press, 1980).

able change was occurring. While there were, of course, a number of film genres from this period which might be used to illustrate this point, the most obvious examples come from comparisons of women in screwball comedies and *film noir*. In fact, according to gender historians such as Lawrence S. Wittner, it was during the late 1950s and early 1960s in particular that gender roles began to shift noticeably as issues surrounding the Cold War and safety questions surrounding the building and testing of atomic and nuclear bombs came to the forefront of public awareness. In his article "Gender Roles and Nuclear Disarmament Activism, 1954–1965", Wittner writes that the anti-nuclear campaigns of the early Cold War years signalled a change in traditional gender roles, arguing that this change was necessitated by the patterns of protest which the anti-nuclear lobbies and groups adopted. As Wittner writes,

> "Women could no longer protect children by caring for them at home and men could no longer guarantee their safety by soldiering. Both female and male activists, of course, drew upon conventional values: women's role as mothers and men's role as participants in politics. Nevertheless, these women and men were also moving into new territory, shaking up not only the national security system but the gender system, as well."[214]

Although Wittner is careful to stress that the increased political activism amongst women during this period was not motivated by feminist concerns, he touches only briefly upon the idea that anti-nuclear campaigners found it necessary to couch their criticisms against the US government in carefully moralistic, patriotic terms in order to protect themselves and their organisations from being accused of anti-Communist sentiments (not to mention the possibility of being brought in front of HUAC). To protest against the nuclear arms race (and atmospheric nuclear tests in particular) as a mother or father worried about the effects of strontium-90 upon their children was a moral stance, whereas protesting against the nuclear arms race and testing with a stance on such issues as war and politics could have possibly tarred such protesters as being, at least, Communist sympathisers.

There is also the debate, which Wittner touches upon, as to whether this kind of maternalism – in which women in the cultural role of Mother (whether or not they themselves had

119

children) used their assumed moral position within society to protest political support for the arms race and nuclear testing – is a form of feminism. Wittner thinks not, and agrees with those feminists who point to the language used by the female anti-nuclear campaigners to describe themselves. As Wittner points out,

> Scholars are divided, however, as to whether maternalism constitutes a form of feminism. Proponents of this idea point to the fact that maternalism and feminism have sometimes overlapped within movements and individuals and that, at occasional junctures, maternalism has been used by women to advance their interests in society. Some also contend that the capacity to bear children unites women and, therefore, sharpens their conflict with patriarchal institutions. Opponents, however, have contended that maternalism reinforces the idea that the two genders have "separate spheres" and, therefore, has bolstered sexist efforts to limit opportunities for women. Indeed, they have argued, maternalism promotes a very limited notion of women's nature, while feminism is genuinely egalitarian, stressing equal abilities, rights, and opportunities.[215]

However, in the political climate in America in the 1950s and 1960s, it seems that perhaps the safest and most effective means of protest on this issue was through the use of traditional terms and descriptions. Women have traditionally adopted more conservative terms for themselves on an outward level when engaged in areas of public life which were usually seen as being male bastions of power and decision-making. A woman calling herself a "typical housewife" or a "concerned mother" is not as easily singled out for smear and ridicule by her opponents as a woman who wants to protest against the system as an outsider (which, as a self-described feminist in the 1950s, she would have been). Therefore, denying a feminist stance and adopting a traditional, maternal one, was a safe course of action during the Cold War. Confirming this notion is the fact that many male anti-nuclear campaigners likewise stressed their roles as fathers – the protectors of children through the protection of their society's safety (protecting them in the public sphere in the same way that mothers were protecting children within the domestic sphere) – in their protests. But, as with many political issues during the Cold War years, this sort of covert protest was safer than more overt expressions of dissent. In Hollywood, this sense of fear and paranoia would find vent in, amongst other genres, *film noir*, a mood which

215 Wittner, "Gender Roles and Nuclear Disarmament Activism", p. 205.

contrasted sharply with earlier genres such as the screwball comedy, but which would also echo in the women's melodrama, which had its heyday in the 1950s and early 1960s.

Women as characters in Hollywood films

It is important to examine the changes in portrayals of femininity in several genres spanning the 1930s to the 1960s in order to contrast what was taking place at Disney with the broader Hollywood scene. Within the three genres examined in this section, an important series of changes in these portrayals is in evidence. Those transformations, although to be found throughout mainstream Hollywood's live-action cinema, are only barely hinted at in Disney. This is an important point: although Disney is discussed in this book as a genre, the fact is that it is a genre which spans seven decades, and yet underwent almost no changes in the first four decades of its existence. By examining the defining traits of three other genres for evidence of the attitudes towards women which were most prevalent at the time, a greater understanding of Disney's largely static approach may be acquired.

In her introduction to *Women in Film Noir*, E. Ann Kaplan briefly compares women in Westerns to the women characters of *film noir*, pointing out that women stand out in *film noir* because, unlike the women in most Westerns, they are not merely "background for the ideological work of the film which is carried out through men".[216] The women characters in the *film noir* genre, which flourished in the 1940s and early 1950s,[217] are very much a part of the action of the story, but not necessarily in a straightforward, positive way. Still limited by their positions as sexual objects, and therefore as potentially threatening to the patriarchal order, "... the women function as the obstacle to the male quest".[218] As Kaplan states it, "The hero's success or not depends on the degree to which he can extricate himself from the woman's manipulations. Although the man is sometimes simply destroyed because he cannot resist the woman's lures (*Double Indemnity* is the best example), often the work of the film is the attempted restoration of order through the exposure and then destruction of the sexual, manipulating woman."[219]

This idea that the woman is not only a danger to the man's goal, but also to the man himself, is in direct contrast to the

216 E. Ann Kaplan, *Women in Film Noir* (London: BFI Publishing, 1980), p. 2.

217 Kaplan, *Women in Film Noir*, pp. 1–2.

218 Kaplan, *Women in Film Noir*, p. 3.

219 Kaplan, *Women in Film Noir*, p. 3.

ways in which women and men function together in the screwball comedy, a genre which, although it lasted well into the 1940s, saw its hey-day in the 1930s. While, in the screwball comedy, the woman often presents problems and/or distractions for the man, she never does so intentionally or maliciously, and once the pair have learned to work together as a team and have begun to communicate effectively (as well as having acknowledged their love for one another), they are finally able to surmount the various barriers in the plot and resolve their problems. Perhaps the best example of this is to be found in the 1938 film *Bringing Up Baby*, starring Cary Grant and Katharine Hepburn. Hepburn is an eccentric, scatter-brained young heiress who happens to meet and fall instantly for the quiet, staid palaeontologist played by Grant. Grant, however, already engaged, wants nothing to do with Hepburn, particularly since every time they meet some disaster occurs for which he is forced to suffer the consequences. The difficulties between them deepen further when they realise that they are in competition with one another for a large sum of money from Hepburn's wealthy aunt. The situation – and their problems – are finally resolved when they both acknowledge their love for one another, since by working together and learning to communicate they are able to find the missing bone Grant needs to finish a dinosaur skeleton he is shown working on at the film's beginning, and he and Hepburn are also able to share the fortune from her aunt, rather than having one benefit over the other.

Sexuality is very much a part of the story of *Bringing Up Baby* in that Hepburn immediately and openly falls in love with Grant and, indeed, pursues him (romantically, as well as literally in certain scenes) throughout the film. She serves as an obstacle to Grant and his work because of her accident-prone ways and eccentric behaviour. She is in competition with him over a large sum of money. Any of these elements could be translated into the world of *film noir*, in which a sexually-confident woman pursues the main male character of the film, causes problems and obstructions for him, and competes with him for a final, important goal. The difference, however, is that, in the earlier genre of screwball comedy, female sexuality is portrayed not as a weapon or a source of evil power or deception, but instead as a normal thing that happens when "boy meets girl". There is a sense of deception linked with sexuality in screwball comedy, but secrets are kept to protect and to secure love rather than to destroy the male love object. Irene Dunne in *My Favorite Wife* (starring Dunne and Cary Grant, 1940) hides her identity from Grant's new wife because the woman believes her to be dead (as did Grant at the start of the film) because she thinks that this deception will help to oust the new wife from the picture so that she and Grant can be re-married and live happily ever after. Likewise, in another Cary Grant film, *Mr. Blandings Builds His Dream House* (1948), Grant's wife, Myrna Loy, keeps secret from Grant the fact that she used to date Bill Cole (Melvyn Douglas), their friend and lawyer, knowing that it will only make him unnecessarily jealous. Screwball comedy and *film noir* are both peopled with strong, independent women, and problems in screwball comedies and *film noir* both have ties to miscommunications between the sexes. But in the screwball comedy, the problems are resolved when the man and woman learn to communicate and work together. In *film noir*, it is only when the man rejects the woman's "wicked wiles" (as Grumpy calls them in *Snow White and the Seven Dwarfs*) and reveals her deception that he – not they – is finally victorious in overcoming difficulties. In this sense, Screwball Comedy might be seen as representative of celebrating (at least on film) the emancipation of women for the first generation of American women to enjoy its fruits from the start of their adult lives. Coming later, after the arguments against women in the workplace from the Depression years (in which women were seen to be taking jobs away from men) and their further rejection from the workplace and the public sphere after the end of World War II, *film noir* could be seen as the first great anti-feminist backlash film movement of the twentieth century.

More significant for this book, however, is a brief examination of the ways women were portrayed in certain films of the huge cinematic genre loosely known as "Women's Films". Indeed, when the broadness of the category of Women's Films is considered alongside Walt Disney's statement late in 1936 that "80 per cent of our audience are women", then seeing the older Disney films in particular as having at least a strong connection with the Women's Film genre is not unreasonable. This is particularly true when several of the Disney films of this period – notably *Snow*

123

White, *Cinderella*, and *Sleeping Beauty* – are examined in the light of a type of Women's Film, produced mainly in the 1930s and 1940s (but not limited to those two decades) identified by Jeanine Basinger and Lucy Fischer as "female double films".[220] Although these two scholars read the impact of this type of film in very different ways, they agree on its definition as a sub-genre. The "female double film" is one of two kinds of Women's Films exploring women's relationships with each other, the other being the "Life Choices" sub-genre, which deals with the theme of how the overall quality of a woman's life is affected based upon the decision she makes in reaction to an event. The "female double film" sub-genre is characterised by its presentation of two women, usually sisters (often identical twins played in the film by the same actress) but otherwise generally bearing a strong physical resemblance to one another, one of whom is portrayed as "good" and the other as "evil". As Hollinger puts it, "the good woman's traits are aligned with conventional femininity (passivity, sweetness, emotionality, asexuality), and the bad one's personality is associated with masculinity (assertiveness, acerbity, intelligence, eroticism)".[221] She points out that, in these films, the distinction between the two women is further strengthened by the alignment of the good woman's character with something which is morally "right", and the identification of the evil woman's character as being "typically treacherous, deceptive, and jealous", as well as being involved with something immoral.[222]

The classic example of this type of film is *The Dark Mirror* (1946), starring Olivia de Havilland in the dual roles of twin sisters Ruth and Terry. The story of the film is that Terry, whose jealousy of her sister's beauty and attractiveness to men has driven her insane, commits a murder. The police, on the hunt for the murderer, narrow their suspects down to Ruth and Terry but, because they are identical, the police cannot arrest one of them until they can identify which is which. The evil Terry, however, has convinced the good Ruth that she is innocent, and persuades Ruth not to co-operate with the police. In the end, however, a psychologist is brought in, administers a lie detector test, and reveals Terry's insane jealousy and evil nature. Meanwhile, charmed by Ruth's goodness and beauty, the psychiatrist falls in love with her, and the film ends with Terry being

220 Hollinger, *In the Company of Women*, pp. 30–31.

221 Hollinger, *In the Company of Women*, p. 31.

222 Hollinger, *In the Company of Women*, p. 31.

found guilty of the murder and taken to a mental hospital while the psychologist declares his love and admiration for Ruth.

Particularly in the fairy tales which Disney brought to the screen between 1937 and 1967, these themes of insanity and jealousy versus sweetness and innocence, so much a part of the "Female Double Film" sub-genre, are very much present. In *Snow White*, in particular, there is a definite physical similarity between Snow White and the Evil Queen (albeit before the Queen disguises herself as a hag). Both women look alike, their few physical differences being attributable only to the age gap between them. Snow White can easily be defined by quoting Hollinger's description of the "good woman" as exhibiting "passivity, sweetness, emotionality, asexuality".[223] Snow White passively accepts her fate when she is forced to flee her castle; she remains sweet, kind, and loving to all she meets; she displays a tendency toward emotionalism during her flight through the forest; and her childish naïveté effectively renders her asexual. By contrast, the Queen can be defined as showing (in Hollinger's words) "assertiveness, acerbity, intelligence, eroticism".[224] She rules with an iron hand, forcing those beneath her to do her bidding no matter what their objections (such as her ordering the Huntsman to kill Snow White). She is bitter in her attitude toward life, and never smiles or demonstrates love. In her ability to use black magic, her constant scheming, and her manner of speaking, she shows herself to be keenly intelligent. In her jealous reaction to seeing the Prince woo Snow White, as well as in her obsession with her own and Snow White's beauty, she reveals her strongly sexual nature. In the end, the Queen is destroyed by her own wickedness, which is also a key element in the resolution of the "Female Double Film": once evil has been suppressed and the more "feminine" woman rewarded with love and happiness, the world is shown as having been righted and the film can end on a happy note.

This sort of plot structure can also be found in *Cinderella* and *Sleeping Beauty*, although perhaps not as fully as is the case with *Snow White*. Although Cinderella and her Step-Mother do not really look alike, there are nonetheless certain elements which link them. They are both technically the heads of the household, since the Step-Mother is the maternal head and the house is in fact Cinderella's, since she *should*

223 Hollinger, *In the Company of Women*, p. 31.

224 Hollinger, *In the Company of Women*, p. 31.

have inherited it from her father. Both take care of the running of the household, the Step-Mother in the social and financial sense (albeit not terribly well) and Cinderella in the care-taking sense (cleaning, feeding the animals, and so on). Apart from that, the similarity to the plot structure with the general thematic constructs of the "Female Double Films" is easily identifiable in the same way as demonstrated with *Snow White*. Likewise, in *Sleeping Beauty*, Aurora and Maleficent, despite having different colouring, have an overall physical similarity with each other in terms of their linear construction and glamorous beauty (although Maleficent's looks are more exaggerated and elongated in order to emphasise the fact that she is an evil fairy, not an evil human). They are also linked by Maleficent's obsessive pursuit of Aurora for sixteen years. Maleficent's destruction at the film's end further marks out *Sleeping Beauty* as fitting within the basic constructs of the "Female Double Film", since Maleficent is defeated by the hero, Prince Philip, who will take Aurora's hand in marriage, and is the romantic leading "man" of the film.

While these stories do not fit perfectly into the typical thematic construct of the "female double film" thanks to their fairy-tale elements, nonetheless their similarities to the "female double films" are obvious. The notion, however, that elements of such a Hollywood sub-genre could be linked with the Disney studio's output is not perhaps surprising, given the conservative representations of women offered by the "female double film" and the Disney studio's popular reputation as a purveyor of the more conservative cultural values of American society. As Walt himself – in his 1947 testimony to the House Committee on Un-American Activities – described his efforts to keep inoffensive material out of his studio's films,

> We watch so that nothing gets into the films that would be harmful in any way to any group or any country. We have large audiences of children and different groups, and we try to keep them as free from anything that would offend anybody as possible. We work hard to see that nothing of that sort creeps in.[225]

Analysis of screwball comedies, *film noir*, and "female double films" illustrates a very basic, but nonetheless important, screen-based metamorphosis in attitudes towards women's sexuality. Whereas women in screwball comedies are praised

225 Testimony of Walter E. Disney before the House Committee on Un-American Activities, 24 October 1947.

as the friend, helper, and partner of man, by the time *film noir* began to flower, the notion of woman as partner seems largely to have disappeared. Within the context of the "Female Double Film", the groundwork for turning American society away from the potentially progressive climate fostered by the necessity of women working in traditionally male areas during World War II was laid. Although the heyday of the "Female Double Film" overlaps the main eras both of Screwball Comedies and *film noir* (but is most closely aligned in terms of mood with *film noir*), its images of strong, forceful women were usually women who were evil and insane. This typing of "feminine" women as being passive, sweet, emotional, and asexual was maintained by the characterisations of women within both the "Female Double Film" (where examples of both "good" and "bad" women were shown, as was the potential duality of all women's natures) and in *film noir* (in the sense of demonstrating what was good by showing its opposite – and the consequences of being a "bad" woman). Of course, these themes do not present themselves only within these genres or periods: the women who populate the gangster films of the 1930s are both foils for and users of men. The women of the domestic and romantic comedies of the 1940s and 1950s are shown as being good, strong women who can achieve goals of their own but do not do so as a means of destroying men. As with every rule, there are always exceptions. But when a genre comes to characterise the film-making of a particular decade as much as screwball comedy does the 1930s and *film noir* does the 1940s, this suggests that a theme within the genre touches a nerve of some contemporary salience with audiences. The screwball comedy was predominately an escape from the harsh realities of the Depression, "Female Double Films" served as illustrations of both acceptable and unacceptable women's behaviour, and *film noir* was perhaps a way to understand post-war and Cold War fears and paranoia. But inherent in these particular genres are to be found sets of cultural norms that are assumed and even, at times, acknowledged.

Women as spectators of Hollywood films

Such norms may have been assumed by the film-makers working in Hollywood, but it is important to try and establish whether they were also held by audiences. Furthermore, the nature of the audiences of various films and film genres is itself a possible means of understanding the divide between the sexes. It is known that Hollywood saw certain films as being more appealing to one sex over the other, but the information upon which these assumptions were based was rather questionable. What is clear, however, is that the intended audience for the film was not necessarily the one with which a particular film (or even a particular genre) would eventually become identified. Of no Hollywood film-maker is this truer than Walt Disney. As cited earlier, Walt made the statement about the target audience for *Snow White* that "After all 80 per cent of our audience are women. … We don't cater to the child but to the child in the adult – what we all imagined as kids is what we'd like to see pictured". By the mid- to late Twentieth Century, however, Disney films were seen by many as being an essential part of childhood; since the 1980s, the predominant audience has been seen as being "the family".

But what was the female audience at which Disney (and other Hollywood studios) was aiming? Did Walt assume that this female audience was further subdivided into distinct categories with different viewing habits and interests? Were racial and class lines seen as factors in audience composition? The short answer to these questions is: probably not. Particularly in the first half of the Hollywood film industry's history, American society as a whole tended to assume that its members were white and middle-class, and while, of course, it was ostensibly recognised that there were individuals who were not white and/or middle-class, these divisions within the group were only peripherally considered. By and large, the in-put of these sub-groups seems to have been viewed as limited at best, and was not generally considered when it came to target audiences. In fact, the notion that an audience might be composed of various subgroups or special interest groups really seems only to have been considered in the most general of terms. According to Richard Maltby, the classifications of the audience which seem to have guided early classical Hollywood were "a series of overlapping binary distinctions between 'class' and 'mass', 'sophisticated' and 'unsophisticated', 'Broadway' and 'Main Street'".[226]

For women audiences, no divisions other than age seem to have been taken into account. Certainly, within the spec-

226 Richard Maltby, "Sticks, Hicks and Flaps: Classical Hollywood's generic conception of its audiences", in Melvyn Stokes and Richard Maltby (eds) *Identifying Hollywood's Audiences: Cultural Identity and the Movies* (London: BFI Publishing, 1999), p. 25.

trum of American politics, women's votes have traditionally been viewed as a block, with repeated references by politicians and political analysts to "the women's vote" or "the female vote", as if all women voted the same way and did so for the same reasons. Women were certainly referred to as a political interest group by Eisenhower during his 1952 presidential campaign,[227] and various political organisations, groups, and lobbies have used the notion of women's historical difference as a way of asserting what they saw as women's collective needs and goals, such as child care and equal rights. Even forty years later, in a book published in 1993 on voting trends in the United States, in a discussion of the so-called "gender gap" amongst the American electorate, the author, David McKay, specifically states that "Younger, single women are especially prone to vote Democratic, reflecting, perhaps, an antipathy towards the tendency for Republican candidates to be conservative on a range of issues affecting women (abortion, child care, the Equal Rights Amendment, affirmative action)".[228] The singling out of this particular group – young, single women – as being particularly affected by the above-named issues over any other group in American society shows a tendency to consider such ideas as being more a part of women's lives than of men's, despite the fact that all of the four issues listed by McKay as being women's issues also have a strong impact on men.

This assumption of female unanimity seems to hold true not only for studies of twentieth-century American politics, but also for Hollywood's target audience, particularly in the first half of the twentieth century. Walt's lack of definition for his own target audience, other than its being eighty percent women, does not specify what he saw as the "typical" woman. The context of the quote is from a story memo for a scene being considered for *Snow White* which was eventually not included in the film, a proposed dream sequence which would feature, amongst other things, a wedding amongst fluffy white clouds with an escort of babies.[229] Walt also stated that this scene would be a good inclusion for the film because, elsewhere in the film, "there is a lot of slapstick stuff that women don't like so well. If our characters are cute, they'll like them".[230]

An analysis of these ideas – that women *do* like babies and cute characters and that they *do not* like slapstick – shows

227 Sheila Rowbotham, *A Century of Women: The History of Women in Britain and the United States* (London: Penguin Books, 1999), p. 315.

228 David McKay, *American Politics and Society* (Oxford: Blackwell Publishers, 3rd edn, 1993), p. 125.

229 Allan, *Walt Disney and Europe*, p. 42.

230 Allan, *Walt Disney and Europe*, p. 42.

three major assumptions of women as an audience: (1) that physical comedy and "low" humour have no appeal for women; (2) that women's maternal instincts will result in them automatically enjoying (and perhaps even preferring) soft, rounded, child-like characters; (3) that all women will fit into these first two generalisations. The first two assumptions do fit well with the observations made earlier in this chapter relating to Walt's attitudes towards to women. Walt seems to have believed that women's natures were more emotional and nurturing than men's, and because of their maternal instincts and potentially higher levels of imagination, combined with their greater emotional depth, they were more capable of appreciating a baby parade (which seems to have been the basic format for the proposed scene), and were less likely to enjoy slapstick because of its lack of appeal to their specifically "feminine" instincts of maternalism and emotionalism.

Except for this set of assumptions on Walt's part, however, there does not seem to have been any consideration of further divisions in his perceived female audience: race, age, education levels, and economic circumstances seem not to have played a part. This may, perhaps, be explained to some extent by Walt's oft-repeated claim that he was seeking to appeal to the child in the adult, and seemed to view this aspect of human nature as a universal quality which anyone who was in touch with him- or herself would be able to express. As Walt himself once publicly observed,

> I go right straight out for the adult. As I say, for the honest adult. Not the sophisticates. Not these characters that think they know everything and you can't thrill them anymore. I go for those people that retain that something, you know, no matter how old they are: that little spirit of adventure, that appreciation of the world of fantasy and things like that, I go for them. I play to them. There's a lot of them, you know.[231]

On the face of it, Walt's perception that his films appealed to the "spirit of childhood" and his conviction that their audiences were eighty per cent female implies that he saw women as essentially child-like. In reality, however, he appears to have regarded women as possessing a unique quality that made it possible for them to *attune* themselves emotionally to the world of childhood without in themselves being child-like. It was this special emotional quality he had in mind when he predicted that women would at

231 Voice recording of Walt Disney, in "Library/Walt talks about appeal to adults", "Library" section of the CD-ROM *Walt Disney: An Intimate History of the Man and his Magic*.

some stage be able to contribute something to animation that men never could.

Despite this generally favourable impression of women, however, Walt also seems to have believed that they had a "dual nature", as evidenced in the contrast between his general conviction of women's greater emotional depth and his critical comment, in reference to the venereal disease films he saw while he was in the Red Cross, that "that's when you begin to hate women".[232] Whether he thought that every woman possessed this duality is hard to say, though the evidence of his respect for women (and for what he perceived as being "typically female") suggests otherwise. Nonetheless, this idea that Disney could believe in female duality is hinted at in his films. The idea that *Snow White* uses its female characters to showcase the notion of woman's dual nature can certainly be seen in at least one subsequent reading of the film, in this case within another Hollywood production. *Nine to Five* (1980), a film which Hollinger terms "the first contemporary female friendship film with an overtly political message",[233] tells the story of three secretaries (played by Lily Tomlin, Dolly Parton, and Jane Fonda) who take revenge on their boss for his sexist, paternalistic treatment of them and their co-workers.

Early in the film, as the three women are bonding and sharing their revenge fantasies with one another, Violet (Tomlin's character) says that her way of "doing the boss in" would have to be "… like a fairy tale. You know, something gruesome and horrible and real gory, but kinda cute". The scene then dissolves into Violet's fantasy, in which she is costumed head to toe in an interpretation of Snow White's look heavily inspired by (and in some aspects a complete copy of) the Disney film's depiction of her. She is surrounded by a variety of animated animals who are her friends and companions. Mr. Hart, the boss (played by Dabney Coleman), tells Violet to get him a cup of coffee (a task she finds demeaning in real life, given her position within the company). In the fantasy, her obvious sweetness, as personified by the assumption of a Snow White costume, is tinged with a number of Tomlin's trademarked mischievous sideways looks. In a true combination of Snow White's persona with that of the evil Queen, Violet/"Snow White", while making Mr. Hart's coffee, "sweetens" it with a dose of poison which, when he drinks the coffee, makes steam

232 Watts, *The Magic Kingdom*, p. 15.

233 Hollinger, *In the Company of Women*, p. 107.

come out of his ears and his head spin. Then, after revealing to him that she poisoned his coffee (speaking in the sort of syrupy, lisping tones of a perfect Snow White), she tells him why she poisoned him (because he is "a sexist, egotistical, lying, hypocritical bigot") and, using his executive chair as a catapult, she throws him out of the office window. We hear him fall and crash to the ground, and then the scene cuts to a shot of Violet, Dora Lee (Parton), and Judy (Fonda) dressed as fairy tale princesses (more in the *Sleeping Beauty* mode this time) waving to the cheering masses from a balcony of their castle (again, a very Disneyesque interpretation of a castle). The portrayal by Tomlin of a sweet, smiling Snow White with a malicious streak and a penchant for poisoning the boss is, at least covertly, a reading of *Snow White* which recognises the possibility of seeing the characters of Snow White and the Queen as being aspects of the same character, and shows that, in the years following *Snow White*'s original reception, the rise of feminism allowed the public, mainstream consumption of such an interpretation.

The female spectator as research subject

Within academia, there is a growing body of scholarship since the 1970s on the "female spectator". Rarely is special attention paid to the various "sub-groups" who fall within that overall heading, however, and the further into the past the scholar is looking, the less likely they are to look at (much less compare) various racial/ethnic/economic groups within the heading of "female spectator". Jacqueline Bobo has looked at black female audiences, but in relation to a modern film, *The Color Purple* (1985).[234] Others, such as Brigid Cherry, have examined the female fans of particular genres (such as, in Cherry's case, horror).[235] But, where there is acknowledgement that women are not one massive, homogenous group, attention is generally paid to audiences closer to the present day and to more modern films, rather than to, for example, black female audiences in the 1930s or lesbian audiences in relation to pre-Hays code talkies (just to name two rather random examples).

The major reason for this is largely pragmatic: little attention is now paid because little (if any) historical evidence exists of the movie-going habits and cinematically-related thoughts of such groups. The major, readily-available method of acquiring such information on the past is through

234 Jacqueline Bobo, "*The Color Purple*: Black Women as Cultural Readers", in E. Deidre Pribram. *Female Spectators: Looking at Film and Television* (London: Verso, 1988), pp. 90–109. Also, see Hollinger, *In the Company of Women*, pp. 179–206; bell hooks, "The Oppositional Gaze: Black Female Spectators", in Manthia Diawara (ed.), *Black American Cinema* (New York: Routledge, 1993), pp. 288–302.

235 Brigid Cherry, "Refusing to Refuse to Look: Female viewers of the horror film", in Stokes and Maltby (eds), *Identifying Hollywood's Audiences*, pp. 187–203.

present-day interviews, but the information to be gained in this way is very reliant on the vagaries of memory. Diaries and letters which mention such specific topics are rare (if at all existent) and not necessarily available. Furthermore, such aspects of audience composition were rarely taken into account in the early surveys of George Gallup and Leo Handel for the Hollywood film industry in the late 1930s and the 1940s. Gender distinctions were made (and an age difference within genders was sometimes acknowledged), but such racial distinctions as were made seem to have been acknowledged only in the context of distribution to segregated cinemas, and involved not so much a consideration of film making as film distribution.[236]

Certainly, there is some indication of what some women thought about the films they were watching. In 1967, for example, *McCall's* magazine conducted a survey in the form of a mail-in questionnaire which they distributed in the January 1967 issue. 12,000 women responded to the questionnaire. The article about the results of this survey appeared in May 1967, and was titled "What Women Think of the Movies". It showed a fairly wide range of attitudes amongst the self-selected respondents. Lenore Hershey, the article's author, says of the readers' response to the survey, that "Within one month, 12,000 questionnaires were returned, sometimes by airmail and special delivery, from every state in the US and as far off as Australia. Almost all of the answers were from women, nearly half in the 18- to 34-year-old brackets. … To weigh the response, a cross-section of questionnaires was tabulated by a research organization, and other answers were studied by McCall's editors and consultants".[237] Interestingly, in this article, which demonstrates the fact that the majority of the respondents were genuinely concerned about the growing levels of sex and violence in Hollywood films (and the subsequent effects of this upon young people, not to mention the embarrassment which such subjects tended to cause many of the respondents themselves), only one established film-maker is mentioned by name: Walt Disney (who had died in late 1966, just five months before the article was published, and just weeks after the questionnaire was distributed). Specifically, mention comes from the batch of letters which accompanied the questionnaires upon their return. In reference to the growing levels of sex and violence in movies, Hershey

236 For further discussion of how Hollywood understood the nature of its audience divisions, see Maltby, "Sticks, Hicks and Flaps", specifically p. 34 for the context of Hollywood's understanding of its segregated theatre trade.

237 Lenore Hershey, "What Women Think of the Movies", *McCall's* (May 1967), pp. 28, 124.

wrote that the question appeared "… over and over again: 'What's going to happen now that Walt Disney is dead?'"[238] The implication is that Disney was seen, at least by the 1967-era readers of the housewife-oriented *McCall's*, as being synonymous with safe, family entertainment and, in particular, as being suitable for younger viewers.

Disney may have seen his audience as being women or as the "honest adult"/spirit of childhood (rather than as children specifically), but it seems clear from the context of this article in *McCall's* that, however Disney saw his audience, they saw him as being not just for "honest adults" but for "the family". And, in this sense, there is substantial evidence that the kind of films Disney was producing were, by and large, what a substantial cross-section of the American movie-going public wanted to see on their local cinema screens. Over and over again in the *McCall's* article, references are made to the discomfort, shock, anger, and even embarrassment which movie-goers felt when viewing much of Hollywood's output at that time. When stars are mentioned by name in the article as being beloved, the tendency is toward the old stars (Cary Grant, Bette Davis, Irene Dunne, Clark Gable, Ginger Rogers, and Fred Astaire were amongst those mentioned, though Paul Newman was also named as a favourite) and praise is predominately aimed at older films (according to Hershey, *Gone With the Wind*, 1939, was repeatedly mentioned).[239]

Such surveys have appeared from time to time in family and in women's housekeeping-oriented magazines, as have books on particular films, such as the numerous books for and about fans of *Gone With the Wind*. Yet with few exceptions, such popular expressions of interest in (and opinions on) Hollywood's output have paid little thought to the racial, ethnic, or socio-economic class of the spectators. Although Hershey, in describing the respondents to the *McCall's* article, mentions that most of the respondents were women, that they came from all fifty US states as well as at least one other country (Australia is specifically mentioned, but the impression given is that it was not alone in the list of foreign respondents), and that nearly half were aged 18–34, no mention is made of the racial, religious, ethnic, educational, or economic profiles of those participating in the survey. There is not even an acknowledgement that such information was of interest to those who wrote, tabulated,

238 Hershey, "What Women Think of the Movies", p. 28.

239 Hershey, "What Women Think of the Movies", p. 124.

or analysed the survey. The women's ages and geographic locations are reported next to quotes from their letters, but no mention is made as to any other information about the women. As with Hollywood film-makers and distributors in the early days of classical Hollywood cinema, the only differentiations made within its female audience were those of age and geography. No other factors seem to have been considered influential.

Conclusion

Although there are a number of changes in the portrayals of women in Hollywood cinema as a whole between 1937 and 1967, this constant shifting of roles is not in evidence within Disney's animated movies. There are bright spots in terms of positive images of female strength – Slue-foot Sue springs to mind, and possibly Anita from *One-Hundred-and-One Dalmatians*. But otherwise the image of women in Disney's animated films from this period is one of strong women being evil and virtue being synonymous with passivity and pre-marital chastity. Although there is the message – positive in its realism – that virtue, goodness, and beauty do not protect from harm and unfairness, there is nonetheless the unrealistic – and more heavily emphasised – message in these films that remaining the naïve and gently passive heroine throughout one's struggles will secure the reward of a happy ending. Throughout this era, however, as is evidenced by the *McCall's* survey conducted (coincidentally) only one month after Disney's death, there seems to have been no objection raised to the way in which Disney's films portrayed women. In fact, the opposite is true, as is evidenced by the worry, which is demonstrated in the *McCall's* survey, about what would happen to the availability of family movies after Walt's death.

The fact is, however, that Walt's own interest in his animated films had begun to decline sometime in the late 1940s, once the studio began to produce live-action features as a way of utilising the blocked funds earned by Disney from the distribution of its films in Britain during and after World War II. Although Walt had done some live-action work in the 1920s during the production of the *Alice Comedies*, he had eventually all but phased out the live-action work involved in order to concentrate on the animation aspects of the series. A few live-action segments had been created to link the animation segments of *Fantasia* (1940), and a fairly fictionalised tour of the Disney studio (which was nonetheless filmed on location and did include some of the real artists amongst the actors) was a major aspect of the studio's first true combination film, *The Reluctant Dragon* (1941). After World War II, the Disney studio had begun to edge its way into live-action films through such combination films as *Song of the South* (1946) and *So Dear to My Heart* (1949). One of the Disney animators from the 1940s reputedly noted, years later, that "We realised that as soon as Walt rode on a camera crane that we were going to lose him".[240] Walt's interest in live-action films itself, however, eventually gave way to other, less cinematically-related projects. Certainly by the time Walt became active in planning and constructing Disneyland (which opened to the public on 17 July 1955), his interest in film production had begun to wane.[241] Nine years after the opening of Disneyland and during the time when "the Florida Project" (as the Disney theme park in Florida was referred to in the studio at that time) was beginning, Walt's interest in his theme parks still remained strong. In 1964, he described his zeal for Disneyland to a reporter for *Look* in this way: "Since Disneyland opened, I've poured another $25 million into it. ... That place is my baby, and I would prostitute myself for it".[242] Despite this increasing interest in projects other than films, however, the animation and live-action film units at the Disney studio would always insist that, throughout this period, Walt was still available for story ideas and still had the final say over not only what went into production but also what was included within the final versions of the films which carried his name.[243]

But despite Walt's reduced presence at his studio in the last ten years of his life, his death – and the vacuum it created in terms of a focal point and idea source – threw the studio itself into turmoil and nearly saw its collapse, despite the presence of a high degree of talent and ability amongst the studio's employees. This lack of direction was further increased by the retirement between 1967 and 1989 of many of Disney's key animators, artists, directors, and producers. Occurring as it did at a time of unprecedented social change within the United States, the Disney studio – and its film output – was about to move in a new, not entirely successful, direction.

240 "Library/Live Action slideshow", "Library" section of the CD-ROM *Walt Disney: An Intimate History of the Man and His Magic.*

241 For more on this trend, see Chapter 9, "The Disney Diaspora, 1942–1950" (pp. 367–402), in Barrier's *Hollywood Cartoons.*

242 Gereon Zimmerman, "Walt Disney, Giant at the Fair", *Look* (11 February 1964), p. 32.

243 Barrier, *Hollywood Cartoons,* pp. 552–553.

136

5

Disney Films 1967–1988: The "Middle" Era

etween 1937 and 1967, the Disney studio's representations of women remained largely static. With
the notable exception of Slue-Foot Sue and the
somewhat lesser exception of Katrina van Tassel, the heroines of the animated films made by the Disney studio during
much of Walt Disney's lifetime were primarily weak, passive, virginal, and virtuous. The villainesses (and, apart from
Captain Hook in *Peter Pan*, all of the evil human characters
were female[244]) were invariably strong, older, dominating
women, usually skilled in black magic and possessed of an
all-consuming obsession with destroying their young rivals
for personal reasons of jealousy and vengeance. Out of the
ten films made between 1937 and 1967 which fit the criteria
of this study, only *One-Hundred-and-One Dalmatians* can be
seen to have a woman character (Anita) with no direct threat
from an evil other. And in her case, the story's villainess,
Cruella deVil, is still linked with Anita in numerous ways
(mainly through their having been at school together, but
also through the Dalmatian puppies which Anita owns and
Cruella covets).

244 The other major
villain in this era
was a panther,
Shere Kahn, in *The
Jungle Book*.

By the late 1960s, and continuing into the 1970s, changes
were occurring in the character of the Disney studio's overall plots for its animated films. In the earlier period, the
studio released nineteen films altogether. Of those, six were

137

package films and one (*Fantasia*, 1940) was an avant-garde experiment which, nonetheless, bore certain hallmarks of the package films which would come after it. Therefore, discounting these, the studio produced twelve films each based on a single story. Of these, four were based on European fairy tales, four on nineteenth-century children's book classics, and four on popular children's books written between 1900 and 1940. In other words, the majority of these films' sources were considered to be classic children's fare that had become an established part of the repertoire of children's reading lists by the beginning of the twentieth century. These stories were also hand-picked by Walt Disney as suitable sources for his films, and were generally either favourites from his own childhood or were introduced to him as an adult (usually through friends, co-workers, or from reading to his own children). Although he continued to be the only person in the Disney studio who could give the green light to any project, Walt Disney's own personal involvement in the animation department gradually waned over the course of his career. It was thanks to Walt's desire to take his studio into different areas of the entertainment industry that the studio branched out first into live-action films, then into television, and eventually into theme parks. A workaholic who sought new projects for his company in order to keep himself from becoming bored with his work, Walt became increasingly uninvolved in the animated films that his studio produced simply because he had grown tired of such work.[245]

This does not mean, however, during this time that Walt ceased entirely to pay attention to the animation department itself. No project was begun without first consulting him, and nothing left the studio without his final approval. Furthermore, Walt always made himself available for consultation by his animators, and was involved in some manner at almost every stage of a project's production.[246] After all, it was through animation that the Disney studio became known in the beginning, and it was with animated films that the Disney studio continued to be principally identified. Nonetheless, in his later years, Walt became increasingly involved in the creation of Disneyland (in Anaheim), the contribution of several exhibits for the 1964–65 World's Fair,[247] "the Florida Project" (as Walt Disney World was called during the early stages of its planning), and a proposed

245 Michael Barrier, *Hollywood Cartoons: American Animation in its Golden Age* (New York: Oxford University Press, 1999), pp. 552–553.

246 Barrier, *Hollywood Cartoons*, pp. 552–553.

247 These exhibits, which included such attractions as "The Tiki Room" and "It's a Small World", would later be transformed into amusements for the Disney theme parks.

ski-resort and recreation park at Mineral King, California.[248] During this period, he left others to do the day-to-day work involved in running the animation, live-action film, television, merchandising, and various other departments of his studio. Meanwhile, his brother Roy continued to oversee the finances of both the studio and Walt's own various companies.

Therefore, when Walt died on 15 December 1966, much of the everyday running of the studio was already in the hands of Disney studio employees. Walt, suffering from lung cancer, had undergone the removal of a lung just weeks before his death at the age of sixty-five. The fact that Walt had kept his illness largely hidden from others (particularly those outside his family) made his passing seemed sudden to those outside his immediate family and came as a shock to both the film industry and the public. As newspapers around the world reported Walt's death in sentimental terms, news anchor Eric Sevareid soliloquised on *CBS Evening News* that "He was a happy accident; one of the happiest this century has experienced; and judging by the way it's been behaving in spite of all Disney tried to tell it about laughter, love, children, puppies and sunrises, the century hardly deserved him".[249] Roy Disney stressed his brother's importance to the company which bore his name in the press statement announcing his death, saying simply that, although the company would go on, "There is no replacing Walt Disney".[250]

Without Walt?

Although Roy Disney's view that his brother's creative abilities and instinctive knowledge of the entertainment industry were irreplaceable seems to have been shared by everyone at the studio, it was nonetheless the initial goal, in the first few years following his death, to find a way to replace Walt with someone who could function approximately in the same way. Following the immediate shock of Walt's death, and evidenced in financial articles about it, initial nervousness about his company's ability to survive him was soon calmed. But within the studio, Walt's absence began to become increasingly noticeable.

Immediately after Walt's death, his brother Roy, then aged seventy-three, took over the running of the entire studio, WED Enterprises (which controlled Disneyland),[251] and the

248 Mineral King, as the project was called by Disney, was an elaborate ski resort in which Disney became interested in 1958, during production on the film *Third Man on the Mountain* (1959). Planning for the project, which was very detailed, called for, amongst other things, the building of such facilities as 10 square miles of skiing areas, numerous restaurants, lodges, and shops, and was expected to cost $35 million upon completion. Although a great deal of time and money would go into planning Mineral King, after Walt's death the studio lost interest in pursuing the project both for financial reasons and because it was plagued by law suits filed against it on environmental grounds. To date, the project has not been revived by any of the Disney companies. See Steven Watts, *The Magic Kingdom: Walt Disney and the American Way of Life* (New York: Houghton Mifflin Company, 1997), pp. 418–419, and the essay "The Final Vision" by Paul F. Anderson, in "Library/Expert Essays/Final Vision" of the CD-ROM other projects begun by Walt in his last years. According to Bob Thomas, Roy found himself working harder than ever after Walt's death, but seems to have felt there was little choice in the matter. One objective upon which Roy Disney focused his attention in these years was the building of the Florida theme park. Statutes were passed in the spring of 1967 allowing the building of the park to proceed, and Roy announced that the park, originally to have been called simply "Disney World", would now bear the official name of Walt Disney World, in memory of Walt Disney. As well as overseeing the project as he believed his brother would have done, Roy also carried on with what would have been his normal responsibility, namely overseeing the financing of the entire project. On 23 October 1971, Walt Disney World was opened by the then seventy-eight year old Roy Disney. Upon the completion of Disney World, it was his intention to start allowing others to take over the reins of responsibility within the Disney organisation, and he began the slow process of reducing his responsibilities. On 19 December 1971, however, his wife came home to find him collapsed on the floor, and he died in hospital of a brain haemorrhage the next day, 20 December.[252]

Before his death, Roy Disney had established a committee which was meant to deal with the studio's film production. The committee included Ron Miller, Roy E. Disney (Roy, Sr.'s son and Walt Disney's nephew), Winston Hibler, Jim Algar, Bill Anderson, Bill Walsh, Card Walker, and Harry Tytle. It was consequently made up of individuals who had worked closely with Walt Disney and were considered to be the most likely to know Walt's approaches to, and theories of, film production. According to Walt's biographer Bob Thomas, it was recognised that a committee was probably not the best way forward, but such a solution, which seems to have been viewed as strictly temporary, was seen as a way to smooth the transition which would occur between Walt Disney's leadership and that of whomever would eventually replace him.[253]

Under new management

Eventually, it was Ron Miller, Walt Disney's son-in-law (Miller had married Walt's daughter, Diane, in 1954), who emerged as the head of film production at Disney, as

(contd)*Walt Disney: An Intimate History of the Man and His Magic* (Santa Monica, CA: Pantheon Productions, 1998).

249 Text of this speech quoted in Bob Thomas, *Walt Disney: A Biography* (London: W.H. Allen, 1981), p. 383.

250 "December 21, 1966; After First Shock of Disney's Demise Spotlight Shifts to Brother & Staff", *Variety Obituaries*, vol. 6, 1964–1968 (New York: Garland Publishing, 1988).

251 WED were Disney's initials (standing for Walter Elias Disney). WED Enterprises was the company which Disney founded to finance and oversee Disneyland when, it is said, the board of directors of the Disney studio refused to help him finance the theme park with studio money, and prohibited him further from using the name Disney in the name of the company, since Walt Disney Productions owned the copyright for the name Walt Disney.

252 Thomas, *Walt Disney: An American Original* (New York: Hyperion, 1994), pp. 357–58.

president and Corporate Operations Officer of Walt Disney Productions, while Card Walker became the company's chairman of the board.[254] Miller had worked with Walt Disney since around the time of his marriage to Diane, but otherwise had no background in film-making. Certainly, he did not have the sort of experience it took to run film production at the studio, and although he managed during the time he had charge of the studio to score a few successes with films such as *The Love Bug* (1969) and one of its sequels, *Herbie Rides Again* (1974), overall his stewardship of the Disney studio was disastrous. As Douglas Gomery described the situation, "Miller left theme park operations to others, and with that, guaranteed that the company would continue to make money. He concentrated on reviving the moribund film division, properly reasoning that the long-run corporate future lay in generating new material."[255]

As Gomery points out, however, despite Miller's recognition of the importance of the film side of the Disney corporation's output, his choice of film projects was, by and large, proof of his inability to gauge the interests and sensibilities of the movie-going public. Gomery attributes this misunderstanding in the main to Miller's failure to grasp the changes in both Hollywood films and audience expectations after the releases of such films as *Jaws* (1975) and *Star Wars* (1977). Such Disney/Miller productions as *The Black Hole* (1979) and *Tron* (1982) were box office failures despite their high budgets, big-name stars, widespread advertising campaigns, and release in active seasons. *The Watcher in the Woods* (1980) brought such universal condemnation from both the public and the critics that the presence (and presumable box-office appeal) in the film of screen legend Bette Davis was not enough to save it. In the end, it did so badly that Miller quickly removed it from cinematic distribution and replaced it with a re-release of the more popular *Mary Poppins*,[256] thereby giving the studio time to change the ending and cut a scene before re-releasing it in 1981.[257]

Thanks to such disastrous box-office returns, Disney films had, by the early 1980s, dropped to a share of less than four per cent of the market as a whole. Things fared no better for the Disney television series, which had run, in various forms, since Walt Disney had introduced the series *Disneyland* on ABC in 1954, moving it in 1961 to NBC as *Disney's Wonderful World of Color*. For much of its history, the Disney

253 Thomas, *Walt Disney, A Biography*, p. 385.

254 Card Walker, a UCLA graduate, started in the traffic department at the Disney studio in 1938 before moving up the ranks in the 1950s to marketing, where he became a vice-president. He was made president of the company after Roy Disney's death in 1971. In 1980, he became chairman of the board.

255 Douglas Gomery, "Disney's Business History: A Reinterpretation", in Eric Smoodin (ed.), *Disney Discourse: Producing the Magic Kingdom* (London: Routledge, 1994), p. 78.

256 Gomery, "Disney's Business History", p. 78.

257 Leonard Maltin, *Leonard Maltin's 2000 Movie and Video Guide* (New York: Signet Reference Books, 1999), p. 1519.

television hour had been a success, as a show for the network and a source of advertisement for the Disney films and parks, as well as for the Disney name and the image of "Uncle Walt" as a corporate symbol for the Disney "product".[258] By spring 1981, however, ratings for the show had dropped so significantly that NBC decided to cancel it. Indeed, although the Disney corporation as a whole continued to make money at this time, it was marked by an ever-decreasing profit margin. It survived almost entirely thanks to the theme parks' revenue, which basically subsidised the costs being incurred by the film production units of the studio.[259]

As Jon Lewis pointed out, "Miller had vision but little ability to run the company. Roy Jr. was a far better businessman, and with Hollywood's move into the Reaganomic eighties, his way of doing business tended to carry the day".[260] In support of his claims for Miller as a visionary, Lewis points to the fact that it was during the short spell when Miller served as Disney's chief executive that such ideas as the launching of Touchstone Pictures and The Disney Channel were first introduced, the film *Splash!* (1984) was produced, the rights to *Who Framed Roger Rabbit?* (1988) were acquired, and the idea was put forward to tap the studio's backlog of films for release on video cassettes.[261] But Lewis also points to Miller's naïveté when it came to decision-making, a trait supported by comments made later by Michael Eisner.

In his book *Work in Progress*, Eisner recalled a meeting he had had with Ron Miller in 1982, when Eisner was himself an executive at Paramount. He says that he agreed with Miller's idea to expand the company's target audience beyond that of families with young children, as well as encouraging Miller's idea to launch a second, non-Disney-labelled film division which would make films aimed at a more adult audience. However, he also noted in his descriptions of his meetings with Miller between 1982 and 1983 that Miller, although interested in the advice of those more successful in running film studios (such as Eisner himself), rarely followed it, instead making choices detrimental to the Disney studio.[262] Eisner mentions how Miller "asked what I thought about some other candidates he was considering to run the studio. I strongly recommended against the ones he mentioned. Within weeks, he went ahead and hired them anyway."[263] Although Eisner's account of this period is no

258 Watts, *The Magic Kingdom*, p. 370.

259 Douglas Gomery, "Disney's Business History", p. 79.

260 Jon Lewis, "Disney after Disney: Family Business and the Business of Family", in Smoodin (ed.), *Disney Discourse*, p. 105.

261 Lewis, "Disney after Disney", pp. 104–105.

262 Michael Eisner, with Tony Schwartz, *Work in Progress* (New York: Random House, 1998), pp. 113–114.

263 Eisner, *Work in Progress*, p. 114.

doubt biased toward his own point of view, nonetheless Miller's track-record from this era shows that the way he ran the studio, both financially and artistically, bears out much of Eisner's assessment. Further justification for this assessment is to be found in numerous sources about the studio's financial and artistic reputation at that time, as well as from the fact that the Disney Company nearly fell victim to a series of hostile take-over attempts which, had they succeeded, would have seen the studio's effective demise. Indeed, it was thanks to the number of bad choices Miller made – both in terms of new studio employees and film projects – that Disney chairman Card Walker became worried about Miller's ability to perform both in his current position and, eventually, as chairman when Walker decided to retire.[264]

In 1982, a series of events occurred with very mixed effects on the company as a whole. Touchstone Pictures, the proposed non-Disney-labelled studio which would make fewer family-oriented films, was launched by Miller. However, thanks to the cost overruns that had occurred during the building of EPCOT (or Experimental Prototype Community of Tomorrow, the second theme park to be built at Walt Disney World), the company was forced to take on enormous levels of debt and, as a result, its earnings fell by nineteen per cent for 1982.[265] Moreover, Disney had only a few features in development, and the cancellation of the company's long-running network television show meant that it was no longer involved in television production.[266]

In fact, the Disney television hour, in its various incarnations as it moved between networks, had been running for thirty-four seasons (making it the longest-running US television show in history) and had had an enormous effect on the company's ability to generate revenue. As Walt Disney had recognised when he began it, the show served the company as a weekly hour-long advertisement for its latest projects, and had been launched both to produce interest in and revenue for Disneyland. Throughout his lifetime, Walt Disney had always managed to keep the show interesting, fresh, and innovative. As further proof of Miller's apparent lack of business sense, however, the Disney television show ceased to communicate a sense of the Disney Company being up with the times, and soon began to look as out of touch as many of the company's other projects. Allowing the

264 Eisner, *Work in Progress*, p. 116.

265 Eisner, *Work in Progress*, p. 118.

266 Eisner, *Work in Progress*, p. 114.

143

show's style and reputation to become outmoded is further proof that Miller failed to see just how valuable such television exposure was to the company. Although he apparently felt that his plans to launch an all-Disney cable channel on US television made the network show unnecessary, once again Miller failed to see that it was important that the Disney name be brought into *all* American homes with televisions (whether they happened to have cable or not), and also showed that he failed to understand the difference between the cable and network television markets.

By 1983, Disney's earnings had fallen a further seven per cent, in part thanks to the costs involved in setting up The Disney Channel, but also because of the fact that film production was suffering so badly.[267] Card Walker officially retired in the autumn of that year, naming Ray Watson as chairman of the company mainly, at least according to Eisner, to make up for Miller's lack of business experience.[268] It was obvious to outside investors that Disney was a perfect target for take-over. Its stock values were depressed, causing the company's market valuation to be listed at $2 billion, yet the fact that it was in debt on only a minor scale and possessed such assets as a highly valuable film library and theme parks that generated revenues of around $1 billion per annum meant that, when viewed in terms of the value of its parts instead of as a whole, it was worth considerably more than $2 billion. To someone interested in making a quick, large-scale profit, an obvious way to make money out of Disney shares would be to buy up a controlling interest in the company, then break it up and sell the various parts of the company. By mid-March of 1984, that was exactly the course of action initiated by Saul Steinberg, who began buying up all the available Disney shares he could. In mid-April, advised by another of its stock-holders, Sid Bass, to take on extra debt (thereby making itself less attractive to take-overs), Disney purchased from Bass the Arvida Real Estate company. Although Disney's fortunes might have seemed to be improving thanks to the release (on 9 March 1984) of Touchstone's first film, *Splash!*, the company's position was hurt when Roy E. Disney resigned from the board of directors over his disgust at the way the company was being run (he had already, in 1977, resigned from his job with the studio, citing his opinion that the company's creative spirit had become "stagnant"[269]), and

267 Eisner, *Work in Progress*, p. 118.

268 Eisner, *Work in Progress*, p. 116.

269 The full quote reads: "The creative atmosphere for which the company has so long been famous and on which it prides itself has, in my opinion, become stagnant". From Roy E. Disney's resignation letter to Card Walker, quoted in Eisner, *Work in Progress*, p. 116.

Disney's overall bargaining position as a company was further weakened.

By early June, Steinberg had acquired nearly ten per cent of Disney's outstanding shares and tendered an offer for the rest.[270] On 9 June 1984, ninety days after Steinberg began buying up their stocks, Disney agreed to pay Steinberg "greenmail", which meant buying back Steinberg's holdings at a premium of $7.50 per share over their market price at that time, netting Steinberg a profit of almost $32 million.[271] Although this action saved the company from Steinberg's take-over attempt, such dealings only showed other traders the attractive possibilities of trying to grab Disney for themselves. Indeed, by 20 June, Disney stock hit a low of $46 per share. At this point, however, Roy E. Disney, himself now a major stockholder, backed by the other three largest shareholders in the company (Sid Bass, Irwin Jacobs, and Ivan Boesky), decided to use his leverage in the company to take drastic measures. He urged the board, amongst other things, to give him three seats on the board (one for himself, one for his brother-in-law Peter Daily, and one for Dan Gold, a well-known Hollywood entertainment lawyer), and also managed to force the board to demand both Ron Miller's and Ray Watson's resignations.[272]

On 19 August 1984, the board discussed replacing Miller, and formed a special committee to review Miller's performance. That same day, Frank Wells, who had great expertise in management within the movie industry and had also caught the attention of those in charge at Disney, called Michael Eisner and arranged a meeting with him for later that day. That evening, he informed Eisner that Miller was expected to be asked to leave within weeks and that the board was already looking for Miller's replacement, implying that he and others felt that Eisner had a strong case to make to the board, because of his proven track records both at Paramount, where he was working at the time[273] and at ABC, where he had worked previously. By 6 September, the board had voted unanimously to demand Miller's resignation, and on 7 September they ratified his resignation. Soon afterward, they began actively searching for Miller's replacement, and, after a complicated series of campaigns and deal-making, on 22 September 1984, the board voted unanimously to hire Michael Eisner as Chairman and chief executive officer and Frank Wells as president and chief

270 Eisner, *Work in Progress*, p. 119.

271 Eisner, *Work in Progress*, p. 119.

272 Lewis, "Disney after Disney", p. 103.

273 In Chapter five of his book, however, Eisner describes at some length the state to which his situation at Paramount had deteriorated, despite his outstanding accomplishments there, because of personal conflicts with Marty Davis, the chairman at the time. See Eisner, *Work in Progress*, pp. 110–131.

operating officer. The pair officially began work at the studio on 24 September, with Jeffrey Katzenberg joining them later in the year. It would take Eisner, Wells, and Katzenberg a few years to shore-up the studio's financial situation, revive its film and television production, and stabilise and re-build its position within the Hollywood entertainment industry, but until 1989, at least in the animation department, the effects of Card Walker's and Ron Miller's uncertain leadership would continue to be felt.

The trend away from animation

Certainly in terms of animated film production, the number of films showed a marked decrease. Between 1937 and 1967, a thirty-year period, Walt Disney Pictures released a total of nineteen animated feature films in addition to their production of shorts, documentaries, and television specials. Between 1968 and 1988, only eight animated features were made: *The Aristocats* (1970), *Robin Hood* (1973), *The Many Adventures of Winnie the Pooh* (1977), *The Rescuers* (1977), *The Fox and the Hound* (1981), *The Black Cauldron* (1985), *The Great Mouse Detective* (1986), and *Oliver and Company* (1988). Unlike the types of stories chosen for the studio's animated film output between 1937 and 1967, only one of these stories, that of Robin Hood, was based on a classic legend. *The Great Mouse Detective* and *Oliver and Company* were both re-tellings of other stories rather than straightforward adaptations (*The Great Mouse Detective* was a re-working of the Sherlock Holmes genre, based on a children's book, *Basil of Baker Street* by Eve Titus; *Oliver and Company* was an updated, anthropomorphised version of Charles Dickens' *Oliver Twist*). *The Many Adventures of Winnie the Pooh* and *The Black Cauldron* were both heavily abbreviated versions of two popular series of books. Of these eight films, only three fit within the perimeters of my study: *The Rescuers*, *The Fox and the Hound*, and *The Black Cauldron*. While it is true that *Winnie the Pooh* and *Oliver and Company* both have highly visible human characters, none of these plays a central role in the story. Christopher Robin in *Winnie the Pooh* serves as a companion and a helper to the animals of the Hundred Acre Wood, but in most cases could easily have been cut from the story without much affecting the plot. Of the two, only Jenny, the little girl in *Oliver and Company*, plays anything close to a pivotal role in the film since it is she who takes in the orphaned Oliver and gives him a home and love. Later in the film, she is kidnapped by Sykes, the villain, an action which forces all of the cats and dogs to work together to save her. Otherwise, it is the animal characters, not the humans, who fulfil the vital positions of the plots, and therefore those films do not fit within the criteria for this study.

Penny and Madame Medusa (and Miss Bianca)

The first film made in this period which does have major human female characters in it is *The Rescuers*, based on the novels *The Rescuers* and *Miss Bianca* by Margery Sharpe. Made on a lower budget than most of the animated films traditionally produced by the Disney studio, it is characterised by a quality of animation which is noticeably inferior when compared to such films as *Snow White*, and even when compared to the animation in films such as *The Adventures of Ichabod and Mr. Toad* and *Fun and Fancy Free* (1947), which Walt Disney himself saw as low-budget alternatives to single-story feature animation. Nonetheless, what *The Rescuers* lacks in animation technique it makes up for in the charm of its story and in the sympathetic natures of its leading characters. The story is concerned with a mouse society called the Rescue Aid Society, the headquarters of which are in the United Nations Building in New York. A bottle with a message from a little orphan girl who has been kidnapped is presented to the society, and two of the mice, Bernard (voiced by Bob Newhart) and Miss Bianca (voiced by Eva Gabor) volunteer to go to her rescue. The little girl, Penny, has been kidnapped by a madwoman, Madame Medusa, and sent to Devil's Bayou to find a diamond called the Devil's Eye. In the end, Bernard, Bianca, and Penny are able to escape Medusa's clutches, the diamond is given to the Smithsonian Institute, and Penny's dream of being adopted by a loving family finally comes true.

Although a large proportion of screen time is devoted to Bernard and Bianca, nonetheless the human characters, Medusa, Penny, and Medusa's partner, Mr. Snoops, are also central to the story. As this is one of the very few Disney animated features in which animals and humans are actually able to speak to each other,[274] and because the character of

274 Cinderella's mice speak a kind of gibberish which she can understand, and Mowgli can talk with the animals of the jungle because he was raised by them. In the sequel to *The Rescuers*, *The Rescuers Down Under* (1990), Bianca and Bernard are again able to communicate with the child they are rescuing, this time a little boy, and in *Tarzan* (1999), Tarzan can of course communicate with the gorilla family who raised him. In this case, however, he cannot speak any human languages and must be taught by Jane and her father. But this accounts for only five films out of forty-six, belying the popular conception that humans and animals can always speak with one another in Disney films.

147

Miss Bianca is heavily humanised (she is bi-pedal, works for a living as a Hungarian delegate to the Rescue Aid Society, wears clothes and is very glamorous and fashion-conscious) in this instance only in this book will a discussion of a non-human character as if she were human be included. As Bianca, Bernard, and the other mice of the Rescue Aid Society are unusually highly anthropomorphised, indeed, they can justifiably be included.

Miss Bianca is, in every respect, characterised as a lady, and even as an extremely attractive lady with a good deal of glamorous sex appeal. When Bianca makes her appearance in the film, she is arriving – fashionably late – at the Rescue Aid Society meeting. She pauses before entering the meeting room, spritzes herself with perfume, and walks with a sassy confidence to her seat at the front of the room. As she passes, all of the males (that is, the majority of the delegates) watch her in a way which is impressed and approving and, at the same time, mildly lascivious. It is evident from her behaviour that she is both used to this sort of looking and rather fond of it, but she also demonstrates, in the way that she volunteers to go on the mission to rescue Penny, that she has a plucky spirit and a strong sense of courage and adventure. She is much braver than Bernard, the Rescue Aid Society's janitor whom Bianca "volunteers" to accompany her. Bernard is superstitious, particularly of the number thirteen. He is nervous, suggesting, for instance, that they would be better off taking the train rather than flying down to Devil's Bayou on Air Albatross (which is actually simply an albatross named Orville), but Bianca jauntily overturns this suggestion. During take-off, when it looks as though Orville is going to crash, Bernard is obviously terrified, whereas all Bianca can say, as she smoothes her hat and coat, is "I just *love* take-offs!" Although she and Bernard are always shown to work together as a team (and indeed, as romance develops between them, they are shown to make a very good team indeed), it is obvious in every situation that Bianca is braver and more adventurous than Bernard.

Bianca and Bernard as a couple make an interesting comparison with the only other couple whose relationship is portrayed in *The Rescuers*: that of Madame Medusa and Mr. Snoops. Medusa, as her name would suggest, is a madwoman. She is everything Miss Bianca is not: ugly, slovenly, mean, evil, obsessive, angry, and brassy. She wears elaborate eye make-up and false eyelashes, and her clothes and jewellery are loud, tacky, ill-fitting, and more in keeping with the clothes of a low-class prostitute. Medusa's companion, Mr. Snoops, is a fat, short, wheedley, snivelling, weak little man who is bullied and bossed by Medusa. It is Medusa who orders him to do various tasks, but, when he is unable to complete them successfully, she spends a lot of time screaming at him for being an incapable idiot. He is, in turns, flattering and fearful in his behaviour toward her. Even Penny, whom he is supposed to have helped kidnap, is not at all fearful of him, but stands up to him successfully when he tries to yell at her for attempting to escape. Whereas Bianca and Bernard are a loving couple and a good team, Medusa and Snoops are a nightmare pair who can accomplish nothing, either alone or together. In the end, it is their selfishness and inability to function as a couple which doom them to failure.

The most interesting comparison, however, is between Medusa and Penny. It is important to note, initially, that the two look nothing like each other. Penny is blonde, with rounded, soft, child-like features and large, sad brown eyes; Medusa is tall, manages to be both fat and angular (she has large, heavy breasts which hang nearly to her waist, flabby thighs and upper arms, bony lower legs and arms, strange, yellow-green eyes, a long, pointy nose, and slightly pointy teeth). And yet, despite the fact that they are portrayed as physically different, it is shown that, in their own ways, they understand how to manipulate each other. Medusa belittles and gains control of Penny by playing upon Penny's fear that she is not pretty enough ever to be adopted, and, in another scene, Penny does an imitation of Medusa for the amusement of Bernard, Bianca, and herself, and then devises a plan to get away from Medusa by using her knowledge of Medusa's habits as a means of subverting her control. The film goes to some lengths to create a comparison between the two: both are shown as women trying to achieve goals despite what might be considered a lack of adequate help. In a quick succession of shots, Penny and Medusa are both shown to be getting ready for bed, struggling into their night-gowns at the same time. Penny's imitation of Medusa's mannerisms is an obvious signal for comparing the two. Both are shown to view Mr. Snoops as sad and inadequate, and neither shows any fear of Medusa's two giant pet alligators, Brutes and Nero. Penny even mentions that she has always wanted to drive Medusa's "swamp-mobile" (a car-like contraption Medusa uses to drive in the swamp waters surrounding the beached riverboat on which they live), and at the end, when she drives away to safety with Bernard, Bianca, and some of the local swamp animals, Penny drives the swamp-mobile as naturally and competently as Medusa is shown to earlier in the film.

Why these parallels exist between Penny and Medusa is never made clear. Indeed, in her alliance by choice with Miss Bianca and her forced alliance with Madame Medusa, it is as if the film is demonstrating how Penny has these two very different examples of feminine adulthood as alternatives between which she can choose. It is the defeat of Medusa and the return to New York with Bianca and Bernard which shows that Penny, who the film underlines in many ways is an ordinary little girl, has chosen someday to be a lady like Miss Bianca when she grows up. This is further demonstrated by the fact that, although Penny is able to escape Devil's Bayou with the "Devil's Eye" (the diamond that Madame Medusa has been after for most of the film and which she has been sending Penny into an old well to search for), she takes the diamond with her only by accident because Medusa hides the diamond inside the stuffing of Penny's teddy bear. Moreover, once Penny has returned to the New York orphanage from which she was kidnapped, she gives away the diamond, causing it to be donated to the Smithsonian. Her reward, however, is not the millions of dollars that Madame Medusa sought or the adventure and excitement which Miss Bianca loved, but instead being adopted by a kindly, loving, ordinary-looking couple. Penny is still, however, only a child, and as an orphan has (presumably) not known much in the way of affection or stability. The film does not tell us what becomes of Penny as an adult, but, judging from her beginnings, we can only assume, once she has learned to feel the sort of safety and security which Miss Bianca takes for granted, that she will grow up to live a life in which she fearlessly rights wrongs – just like Miss Bianca

In certain respects, the film's characterisations of the relationships between Penny and Medusa (which is adversarial) and Penny and Bianca (which is symbiotic) serve as a kind of transition-stage film in the three main phases of the

Disney studio's portrayals of female connections. In the earlier Disney films, women are shown to be almost exclusively in competition with one another. The only women who are not in an adversarial relationship with other women are those few female characters who are surrounded exclusively by men (such as Slue-Foot Sue, in the "Pecos Bill" segment of *Melody Time* or Katrina van Tassel in the "Sleepy Hollow" segment of *The Adventure of Ichabod and Mr. Toad*). By the 1970s, however, the rise of women's history as an academic discipline, coupled with the women's movements of the late 1960s and 1970s (including the ultimately unsuccessful campaign for an Equal Rights Amendment[275] and the more successful one for abortion rights[276]), had begun to support feminist interpretations of such ideas as "sisterhood" and the supposedly unnatural competition between women that was fostered by the forces of male-domination as a way of maintaining their hegemony, in what was apparently believed to be a society-wide application of the theory of "divide and conquer".

As if it is trying to foster a type of compromise between these old notions of women in competition and women as allies in the struggle against male society's oppression, *The Rescuers* offers both sorts of relationships. Both kinds involve the character Penny, thereby emphasising her centrality to the plot and, in their own way, perhaps symbolising the traditional notion of woman's duality. When looked at in terms of the rise of feminist interpretations during the mid-1970s, the female relationships in *The Rescuers* become decidedly complex. Indeed, Bianca's plucky spirit, love of adventure, insistence on shaping her own life, and maintenance of a romantic relationship in which she is at least her partner's equal, if not his superior, show her to be the sort of figure of which most feminists of this period would be proud. Crucially, even in terms of the characterisation of the traditionally lady-like, even somewhat coquettish Miss Bianca as the most independent, balanced adult character in the film, it must be remembered that Bianca is trying to accomplish her goals as a mouse in a human world – a world which was not designed with her in mind, and which forces her to work harder as a mouse to achieve goals which would be much easier for her to accomplish were she human. At one point, Bianca herself declares in frustration "Oh, if I was only a ten-foot mouse, I'd show her!", putting in physical terms

275 The Equal Rights Amendment approved by Congress in 1972 had been ratified in thirty-five states by 1979, yet the final three ratifications required by the Constitution never materialised. To date, a movement in Congress or in the United States as a whole for a new Equal Rights Amendment has not occurred.

276 This led to a political climate which would result in the *Roe vs. Wade* decision, handed down by the Supreme Court in 1973, which allowed a woman to request a legal abortion from a doctor within the first trimester of a pregnancy.

her aggravation at being thwarted only by her physical state (her "mousehood") in her attempts to do something she sees as important. It should also be pointed out that there is no human woman in *The Rescuers* who is as strong, accomplished, and noble as Bianca. In such a politically volatile time as the 1970s, however, perhaps it was thought by Disney animators that portraying such a pro-feminist character in the form of a tiny mouse would soften it and make it more acceptable – by making it less noticeable – to a mainstream American middle-class audience.

Widow Tweed

The next woman to feature in a film from this period of the Disney studio's history is the character of Widow Tweed, the old woman who adopts Tod the fox in *The Fox and the Hound*. The only human female in the film, she is portrayed as an old woman, living alone. She is shown to have a grandmotherly demeanour and comforting aspect. She makes her living as a farmer, and one of the ways she is seen to make money is to sell milk (something which is itself associated with mothers, nourishment, and comfort). Widow Tweed functions as a source of safety, protection, and love for Tod (indeed, she adopts Tod as a baby fox when his mother is shot by a hunter and he is left alone in the woods). Although the film's predominant focus is on the animals (in particular on Tod and Copper, the fox and the hound, respectively, of the title) and not on their human counterparts, the humans in this story nonetheless play an important role in the film, and are on the screen for a large proportion of its running time.

In saying that Widow Tweed is a farmer associated with the fox (whom she loves and keeps as a pet) and Amos Slade is a hunter associated with the hound (whom he is training to be a hunting dog), one could easily spin out various arguments about the association of women with the natural order, pacifism, and maternalism, and the symbolic value of making the man an aggressive, non-nurturing hunter who advocates violence and the subverting of the natural order. The fact is that Widow Tweed's basic function in the plot – her adoption of Tod and her keeping and loving him as a pet – could have been assigned to a male character as easily as a female. Likewise, Tod's care could have as easily been taken up by Big Mama, the old owl who leads Widow Tweed to Tod after his mother is killed, and who remains a friend and confidante to Tod throughout the film. The fact that Widow Tweed is a woman, and that she was given a very definitely adversarial relationship with Amos (who spends much of the film trying to shoot Tod and who trains Copper to hate Tod – and all foxes – and to hunt them), exercises a distinctly symbolic function within the plot, whether the Disney story department, animation directors, or artists put it there intentionally or otherwise. Widow Tweed's affiliation with the natural world is cemented when, in an ultimate act of love, she takes the then-adult Tod to an animal sanctuary and leaves him there (despite the obvious pain and sorrow it causes her to give him up) because she is afraid that, if he stays with her, Tod will be killed by Amos.

At the end of the film, Amos is eventually made to see that he has been wrong to try to kill Tod (this happens when he sees Tod risk his life to protect Copper from an angry bear, and is confirmed when Copper, in memory of his childhood friendship with Tod and because he is now indebted to Tod for his life, puts himself between his friend and Amos' gun to prevent Amos from finally having the chance to shoot Tod). A shaky truce is further declared between Amos and Widow Tweed: she helps to bandage Amos's foot and shows him, both by helping him and through her wry comments to him, that as long as he recognises the wrong he has done in the past and gives up his adversarial, selfish, unnatural ways, she will be happy to be his friend.

But, in an unusual twist for a Disney film, Tod and Copper are not reunited at the film's end as friends. Although they now both know that each will always remember the other with affection (as is born out in a series of shots in which the adult characters remember their promising to each other as puppies that they will always be best friends), they are nonetheless forced to recognise the fact that they belong to two separate worlds which their friendship, no matter how old or how deeply felt, will never be able to bridge. It is this pessimistic finality and bleakness which is the end note for the film, and in many ways cancels out the hope which is presented by Amos Slade and Widow Tweed's truce.

The fact is that the late 1970s and early 1980s, the period during which *The Fox and the Hound* was under production,

153

was also a bleak period in the studio's history, and it was this mood amongst the Disney artists which was perhaps most reflected in the film. This attitude seems to have affected animator Don Bluth, who at the time was, despite being one of the younger animators, nonetheless something of a veteran within the studio. Late in 1979, during production on *The Fox and the Hound*, Bluth led away a small number of other animators, declaring that by so doing they intended to revive the glory of old-style Disney animation techniques and ideas. According to Leonard Maltin, Bluth described the situation in the studio in these terms: "We felt like we were animating the same picture over and over again with just the faces changed a little".[277]

Indeed, according to Maltin and other scholars who have examined this period of the Disney studio's history, the late 1970s and early 1980s, which saw a number of highly momentous changes in the ways in which nearly every aspect of the studio was run, were a very difficult phase of Disney's history. As Maltin writes, "The decision to rerecord the soundtrack to *Fantasia*, and cut both Leopold Stokowski and commentator Deems Taylor out of the film, was greeted with cries of horror from Disney buffs and purists. Other observers were amazed that the studio allowed a mediocre, low-budget short subject, *Winnie the Pooh and a Day for Eeyore* (1983), to go into theatrical release bearing the Disney name, even though it had been made by an outside production company."[278] Nonetheless, some experimentation was encouraged amongst some of the studio's younger talent, notably the decision to allow the (then) young Disney animator Tim Burton to create a stop-motion animated short called *Vincent*, which was about a young boy's obsession with B-horror film legend Vincent Price. It seems as though it was this spirit of experimentation, and of letting the younger animators stretch their wings a bit, which led to the decision to produce the next film, both for the studio and for this study: *The Black Cauldron*.

Eilonwy

Although ideas, sketches, and other preliminary planning for a film based on the children's books known collectively as "The Prydain Chronicles" had been around at least since 1975, the decision was finally made to go ahead with *The*

277 Leonard Maltin, *Of Mice and Magic: A History of American Animated Cartoons* (New York: McGraw-Hill, 1987), p. 78.

278 Maltin, *Of Mice and Magic*, p. 78.

Black Cauldron in the early 1980s. At the unusually high cost (at least for that time at Disney) of $25 million, *The Black Cauldron* became, according to Leonard Maltin, the studio's most ambitious feature-length animated film.[279] As Maltin writes, "It was released in 70mm and stereophonic sound, and boasted computer-generated animation effects – another first for a Disney cartoon feature (not to mention its PG rating). Basically a quest story, it presented a classical battle of good versus evil, with a young boy taking on the formidable challenge of wresting an all-powerful cauldron (which enables its owner to rule the universe) from the villainous Horned King who has gained control of it."[280]

By and large, *The Black Cauldron* suffers from its lack of balance between the strongly sympathetic side-kick, Gurgi, and the likeable but largely uninteresting heroes, Taran and Eilonwy. It is, however, well-animated and displays some technically innovative artistry. As already mentioned, this was the first Disney film to rely upon computers to achieve some of its animation effects, a technique which would be used with increasing frequency and skill by the studio in its subsequent films. But, despite such innovations, the film's appeal was not sufficient to draw in audiences. Maltin points out the warnings given to parents by some critics that the film might not be suitable for their younger children (as was confirmed by its PG rating[281]) as being a possible reason for its lack of success at the box office. Its source material, however, may also have been a factor. There is no evidence to suggest that the Disney studio was attempting to use *The Black Cauldron* and its PG rating to signal a change in its target audience. The animated films which were to follow, after all, would all receive G ratings, and with its emphasis on both Taran and Eilonwy, the film was clearly intended for a child audience, despite containing story and characterisation elements that were somewhat darker than usual for Disney. This film was very much an experiment for the animation department, and the suggestion was that it was very much the young artists within the animation department who were ultimately responsible for persuading the studio as a whole to take on the project.[282] In terms of its technical animation achievements, the film was very much a success, yet this success was tempered by its unbalanced story-line, uneven characterisations, and lack of box-office appeal.

279 Maltin, *Of Mice and Magic,* pp. 79–80.

280 Maltin, *Of Mice and Magic,* p. 80.

281 PG is the US rating meaning "Parental Guidance" is advised, implying that the film may not be suitable for some young children.

282 Maltin, *Of Mice and Magic,* pp. 79–80.

The *Prydain Chronicles*, by children's book author Lloyd Alexander, are a series of five books which tell the stories of Taran, the assistant pig-keeper who becomes a great warrior and then a king, and of Eilonwy, the wry, witty princess with magical powers who grows up to become a powerful sorceress and Taran's queen. The series, which began with the publication of *The Book of Three* in 1964 (*The Black Cauldron*, the series' second book, was released the following year, and was followed over the next three years by the publication of the last three books in the series), became a favourite with young readers. *The Black Cauldron* was made a Newbery Honor Book and *The High King*, the last volume of the series, won the prestigious children's book award, the Newbery Medal.

Although the books are adventurous, gripping tales full of fantasy and, thanks to the presences of both a strong hero and a strong heroine, offer something for both boys and girls, the fact is that *The Prydain Chronicles*, which cover a span of approximately ten years in the lives of their main characters and recount a number of their adventures, are greatly shortened by the film (which concerns itself only with the first of their adventures, namely the rescue of Henwen the Pig and the destruction of the Black Cauldron), and the personalities of the main characters (with the exceptions of Gurgi and, to an extent, Fflewddur Fflam) are much watered-down. These aspects of the film may have kept away those sections of the audience who were devotees of the books. The blandness of the characters also offered very little to those who might have been unfamiliar with the books but would perhaps have enjoyed the film as an example of the fantasy genre to which it clearly belongs. In fact, there was little about the film's characters or pace which would have appealed to either fans of fantasy or of Lloyd Alexander's books. Its lack of traditional "Disney" elements (such as a brighter, more up-beat story-line, strong leading characters, and more of a "fairy tale" aura, as opposed to the more gothic/fantasy feel of *The Black Cauldron*), furthermore, gave the majority of Disney fans little source of enthusiasm. Its only possible appeal would have been to animation fans, thanks to the inclusion in *The Black Cauldron* of various technological innovations.

As mentioned already, *The Black Cauldron* had several Disney firsts: the PG rating, the use of computers to enhance its animation, and its unprecedented (at least for a Disney film) high budget. But one significant first which seems to have been overlooked by those who have written on *The Black Cauldron* is the nature of its heroine, Princess Eilonwy. Eilonwy is the fourth Disney heroine to be a princess, and, with her blonde, flowing hair and Medieval-style clothing (in many physical respects, in fact, she could be Princess Aurora's little sister), she certainly looks the part. But it is with her physical appearance that Eilonwy's similarity to her predecessors at Disney ends: she is strong, feisty, wilful, adventurous, and independent. She is also the first of Disney's heroines to possess magical powers. In the Lloyd Alexander books, Eilonwy is descended from a long line of powerful and respected sorceresses, and, though this is never mentioned in the film, the presence of her magic bauble, which follows her everywhere and seems to possess an intelligence of its own, certainly hints that Eilonwy has superhuman abilities. Yet this aspect of Eilonwy that she herself will, upon reaching womanhood, be possessed of great magical powers – is never described in the film, despite there being opportunities to do so. Instead, those unfamiliar with the Alexander books would know only that Eilonwy was a bright, cheerful, spirited little girl who happens to have a magic bauble. In the context of a fantasy world in which an ordinary boy is caretaker to an oracular pig, ownership of a magic bauble does not in and of itself set Eilonwy apart from those around her.

What does set Eilonwy apart, however, is her girlhood. In the film, there are a total of six female characters: Eilonwy, Henwen the pig, the three witches who have the Black Cauldron, and an unnamed, unfeatured character who is shown in the initial scenes of the Horned King's castle: she is a fat, lascivious dancing girl whose sole function is to entertain the Horned King's human lackeys. Eilonwy is the only female character in *The Black Cauldron* whose personality is at all explored, and she is certainly the only one of the main adventurers of the story who is female. This is also true in the books, with the difference that, in the books, Eilonwy makes repeated mentions of her mother, who is dead, and of her aunt, who is a great sorceress, and of the fact that all of the women she is descended from were powerful sorceresses and leaders. In the film, we are given no indication at all of Eilonwy's heritage or background,

157

and, in contrast to the book, no hint that she has a number of strong female role models to whom she can look for guidance.

In the film, when Taran first meets Eilonwy in the dungeon of the Horned King's castle, she seems somewhat disappointed to learn that Taran is not a lord or a warrior since she was "so hoping for someone who could help me escape". Her tone, however, is never desperate. At worst, it is mildly disappointed, but otherwise remains cheery and conversational. Indeed, it would seem that Eilonwy truly does need only someone's *help* to escape, rather than to be rescued. Having apparently been held prisoner for some time, she has spent many hours exploring the castle's huge dungeon and clearly knows her way around much of its system of tunnels and warrens. In fact, the only thing which seems to be keeping Eilonwy from escaping is her lack of a weapon. Although there is nothing in the film to indicate this, those familiar with the book would know that Eilonwy's magical abilities had not yet developed because of her youth. In the film, Eilonwy's advantage comes solely from the knowledge she has gained in her explorations of the dungeon, and she serves as a guide to Taran, warning him to stay close to her so he will not get lost. Soon after Taran joins Eilonwy, he discovers – and takes – a sword he has found in a hidden tomb, and it is Taran's possession of this sword (which turns out to have magical powers), along with Eilonwy's calmness and her knowledge of the dungeon, which helps them both to escape (as well as to rescue the minstrel Fflewddur Fflam). Neither rescues the other, but both have the complementary tools which they are able to utilise through teamwork. In fact, in the final moments of their escape, it is Eilonwy who must remind Taran to use the sword to cut through a chain which will lower the drawbridge. In the scene which shows Taran and Eilonwy after their escape, however, they argue with one another about whose role in their rescue has been more important, but in the end they resolve this argument with an acknowledgement that it does not matter who gets the credit for their escape, since it was only through working together that they were able to escape the castle, and only through working together will they be able to succeed in finding Taran's oracular pig, Henwen.

Although *The Black Cauldron* has many of the typical portrayals of women which follow on from earlier Disney films, it nonetheless shows numerous aspects in its portrayals of Eilonwy and the three witches that possess a more egalitarian approach to the roles of the sexes. The three witches from whom Taran obtains the black cauldron are portrayed as sexually-frustrated, deceptive, ugly old women, but the witches in this film are not evil, nor do they obsessively seek to destroy the heroes of the film. They do trick Taran into trading his sword for the cauldron without telling him that it is impossible to destroy the cauldron's evil powers without bringing about someone's death. They do not, however, do so out of evil revenge, and they are at least ostensibly honest in their bargain with Taran (as they say in response to Eilonwy's protest that the witches had said that she and Taran could have the cauldron, "Of course we said you could have the cauldron – it's not our fault you can't do anything with it!"). In the end, the witches prove that they are not evil when, in a bargain with Taran, they restore Gurgi to life in exchange for the now powerless cauldron.

Eilonwy, as already said, is also very much a departure from previous Disney heroines (Disney princesses in particular) in that she has motivations other than romance and love, and that she has enough spirit and self-confidence to argue and to stand up for herself and her perceived rights. What makes her portrayal fit the mould of previous Disney heroines, however, is her youth. As was pointed out in Chapter four, Disney heroines of the past were generally given much more freedom to be adventurous and argumentative when they were pre-pubescent, and Eilonwy, although she seems to be close to reaching puberty, is nonetheless still a girl. The fact that she is a princess seems to be largely insignificant in her overall portrayal.

Where this use of girlhood as an excuse for vivaciousness seems to lose credence as an argument about Eilonwy's portrayal, however, comes in the final part of the film. At the ends of both *Alice in Wonderland* and *Peter Pan*, both Alice and Wendy are shown to accept that, once they are no longer girls and must make the transition to adulthood, their ability to escape from reality and go on grand, exotic adventures will cease. This point is made most poignantly by Wendy in *Peter Pan*, when she tells her parents of her adventure in rapturous tones, but then quickly regains her composure to announce to them that she is ready to make this her last night in the nursery and to "grow up". She is further allied with

159

the world of adulthood in the film's final shot of her, when she stands, framed in the window of her nursery, accompanied by her parents and by the grandmotherly, responsible figure of Nana, the family's Saint Bernard, who serves as the Darling children's nursemaid. Wendy's two younger brothers, thoroughly allied with childhood throughout the film, are shown just prior to this final shot to be sound asleep in their beds. Although she has had a wonderful adventure which she will remember the rest of her life, Wendy's own adventures are clearly over as she begins her transition into adulthood. Even more recently, in the portrayal of Penny in *The Rescuers*, although it is obvious that Penny still has several years of her girlhood remaining, her joining of the mainstream world via her being adopted hints that, although she will have a much happier, joyful life from now on, it will also be without the excitement she had previously known.

This is not the case with Eilonwy, however. Although the idea that Eilonwy is not far from womanhood is hinted at in the increased emphasis at the film's end on her growing romantic attachment to Taran (and his to her), there is no concurrent hint that, with the coming of womanhood, Eilonwy's adventures will be at an end. On the contrary, the final shot we have in *The Black Cauldron* of Eilonwy is of her striding happily and confidently away into the horizon, hand-in-hand with Taran, Gurgi, and Fflewddur Fflam, ostensibly on their way home but, presumably and more likely (as is implied by the triumphal music accompanying the shot) off toward their next adventure. That this shot comes only seconds after her kiss with Taran shows this link between the coming of maturity and the continuing of adventure.

Throughout the course of the film, it is clear that a romantic attachment is developing between Taran and Eilonwy, a factor which is typical of the plots of Disney films (and is, indeed, a story line which is also to be found in Alexander's books). Yet, unlike preceding Disney films, the heroine does not sit passively pining for her lover to find and rescue her, and the hero is not an all-conquering warrior or romantic dream-prince. In this relationship at least, the boy and girl are equally matched, have strengths which balance the weaknesses of the other, and are motivated in their quest – and their interactions with one another – by factors other than romantic longings (although, in truth, this shying away from a greater emphasis upon romantic themes may have been influenced by the very obvious youth of Taran and Eilonwy; as it is, the idea that Taran and Eilonwy may be destined for each other is only hinted at, and never emphasised by the film until the end, when Gurgi contrives for Eilonwy and Taran to kiss).

Instead, the focus of the film is upon adventure and team work, and the theme of romance seems present more as a way to add an interesting undertone and as an acknowledgement of Taran and Eilonwy's future relationship than as a goal, or even as a source of motivation. Indeed, in an era in the United States when the notion that men and women – and certainly boys and girls – could work together on equal terms was finally entering into mainstream thinking, certainly the portrayal of a girl working equally with a boy would have been seen as both positive to children and non-threatening to the status quo in ways in which a portrayal of Taran and Eilonwy as older – perhaps as older teenagers or young adults – would not have been. Safely ensconced as they both still are in childhood, they are portrayed as old enough to allow for a romantic undercurrent, yet not old enough actually to do more than imply the possibility of a future romance. However, as with the portrayal in *The Rescuers* of a pro-feminist mouse, a feminist notion of equality was neutralised and made more readily digestible – both to the conservative elements of middle-class American audiences and to the conservative middle-class Americans running the Disney studio in this era.

283 This is in fact a misnomer, since no bras (or anything else) were burned by the women during their protest. Nonetheless, the notion has stuck and has formed a historical myth around the episode. For more on this point, see Sheila Rowbotham, *A Century of Women: The History of Women in Britain and the United States* (London: Penguin Books, 1999), pp. 378–379.

Start the (sexual) revolution without me

It was only two years after Walt's death that the famous 1968 protest at the Miss America Beauty Pageant saw women throwing such items as make-up and high-heeled shoes – things the women involved in the protest characterised as symbols of the repression of women – into a large rubbish bin and being labelled as "bra-burners".[283] During this era, the United States experienced one of the greatest social upheavals in its history. However, even though a number of radical and progressive ideas were put forward – and deemed acceptable – by the intellectual and liberal elements of American society by the 1970s, these ideas would largely fail

161

to enter into mainstream consciousness for some time, and at best trickled down in highly simplified, watered-down forms. Although, by the end of the 1980s, certain aspects of feminism were coming to be accepted by a majority of Americans, ideas such as child-care facilities, equal pay for equal work, women working in leadership positions, and the importance of women's contributions both to the work-place and American life as a whole were slow to enter into the social and cultural lexicon, and did not become a secure part of the majority's accepted value system until, arguably, the mid- to late-1990s.

In the years prior to World War II, little had changed regarding women's perceived roles in society. According to Maldwyn Jones, "In 1940 only 25 per cent of women over fourteen were at work, almost exactly the same proportion as in 1910 and a much smaller proportion than in other industrial countries".[284] By 1970, however, this percentage of the US female population at work had risen to 47 per cent, which comprised 42.8 per cent of the total work force and was made up of 31.6 million women.[285] As Jones writes, "Married women workers now outnumbered single ones, a large proportion of working women were over thirty-five, and the greatest growth in the female labor force was taking place among well-educated, middle-class wives".[286] Yet, as Jones quickly points out, such figures belie the reality of women's position as a group in the workplace. Over half of the jobs of the thirty-two million working women in the United States were either clerical or service-oriented, and in almost all cases – whether low- or high-prestige positions – women were paid less than men for doing the same work. Jones even states that "in respect of earned income women were worse off *vis-à-vis* men than blacks *vis-à-vis* whites".[287] Nor did the situation improve in this era, as in the 1970s the disparity between men's and women's wages on the whole actually increased, rather than declining.[288] Furthermore, the 1970s and early 1980s also saw the failure to ratify the Equal Rights Amendment which had passed through Congress in 1972 but, by the end of June 1982, had lapsed as it had failed to be ratified by the required thirty-eight states. Likewise, a programme concerned with introducing child-care facilities to the United States on a wide scale was passed by Congress in 1972 but was vetoed by President Nixon as being anti-family.[289]

284 Maldwyn A. Jones, *The Limits of Liberty: American History 1607–1992* (Oxford: Oxford University Press, 2nd edn, 1995), p. 584.

285 Jones, *The Limits of Liberty*, p. 584.

286 Jones, *The Limits of Liberty*, p. 584.

287 Jones, *The Limits of Liberty*, p. 585.

288 Jones, *The Limits of Liberty*, p. 585.

289 Jones, *The Limits of Liberty*, p. 586.

Margaret Ripley Wolfe explains this failure to ratify the ERA as the result of the failure of its supporters to mobilise grass-roots support for it in the Southern states.[290] More likely or, perhaps, more symptomatically, this failure to ratify the ERA happened because American society as a whole was not yet ready to challenge the traditional male hegemony. Evidence that this may have been the case can be found in Molly Haskell's accounts in *From Reverence to Rape* of the reactions she noted during some of her lecture tours in the 1970s, particularly as concerned women's reactions to the films *Alice Doesn't Live Here Anymore* (1974), *A Woman Under the Influence* (1974), and *An Unmarried Woman* (1978). Citing the various flaws these films possess, in particular their dubious feminism, Haskell admits that, "housewives responded intensely to these characters [in *Alice Doesn't Live Here Anymore* and *A Woman Under the Influence*], identified with their superiority to their boorish and blue-collar husbands, even felt that Ellen Burstyn [in *Alice*] had suffered so grandly that she deserved (and they could overlook the improbability of her receiving) the ultimate in Hollywood having-it-all fantasy".[291]

Haskell's own interpretation of *Alice Doesn't Live Here Anymore* and *A Woman Under the Influence*, perhaps reflective of the intellectual community in America in the 1970s, was that "both [films] lapse into a shrill, accusatory tone, turning Burstyn and [Gena] Rowlands [in *A Woman*] into fashionably helpless symbols of martyrdom that deny the spunk and resourcefulness they radiate as women".[292] The way she saw these same housewives reacting to the decision of Jill Clayburgh's character in *An Unmarried Woman*, however, is perhaps more indicative of the prevalent mainstream attitude towards women's autonomy at that time. Likewise, Haskell's comments on the reactions of those "housewives" she encountered on her lecture tours go far toward illustrating the disparity between mainstream views of women's "natural" position within society and how intellectuals had come to see women's roles:

Women reacted less charitably toward … *An Unmarried Woman*, both toward Jill Clayburgh herself as an Upper East Side housewife left in the lurch by her philandering husband, and to her decision to forgo a trip to Vermont with irresistible Alan Bates in order to stick by her new job in an art gallery. Actually, as the sort of upper middle class woman who was

290 Wolfe gives credit to early twentieth century suffragists' mobilisation of Southern grass-roots support for passing the Nineteenth Amendment. Margaret Ripley Wolfe, *Daughters of Canaan: A Saga of Southern Women* (Lexington: University of Kentucky Press, 1995), p. 143.

291 Molly Haskell, *From Reverence to Rape: The Treatment of Women in the Movies* (Chicago: University of Chicago Press, 2nd edn, 1987), pp. 378–379.

292 Haskell, *From Reverence to Rape*, pp. 378–379.

163

raised on fifties notions of fidelity and the indissolubility of marriage, and who is thrown back on the minimal resources which upper-crust schooling and a taste for the arts have provided her, Clayburgh would seem more in need of compassion than women who have proved themselves professionally, who have a job and a modicum of self-esteem to fall back on. But somehow – was it the apartment overlooking the East River? Clayburgh's skinny thighs? or her relative stoicism? – women didn't seem to feel that Clayburgh suffered enough and refused her their sympathy. Nor would they buy her turning down the impossibly attractive Alan Bates, witty, gorgeous and successful, whose work was hanging in the Museum of Modern Art! Women were of fiercely mixed minds: on the one hand, she didn't deserve him; on the other hand, as long as he was there she'd jolly well better snap him up! How dare she pass up a trip to Vermont with the guy just to consolidate her position at that paltry art gallery. The very same women who had issued manifestos on the need for self-reliance and an independent income to face those statistically probable years of solitude found themselves gnashing their teeth at Clayburgh's missed opportunity. (And missed Mazursky's most telling revelation, when Bates tells Clayburgh he "approves" of her working, thus summing up centuries of condescension whereby men have whipped women's self-confidence more effectively than if they had beaten them.)[293]

Clearly, Haskell was troubled by her observations of women's reactions to these films. Yet American society's rejection of the ERA and of film characters such as Jill Clayburgh's in *An Unmarried Woman* reflected a definite conservatism when it came to challenging what was seen as the traditional role of women within society. Some women may have characterised themselves as "bra-burners" in their protests against such glorifications of female objectification as beauty pageants, but there were also numerous women lining up to enter those pageants, and millions more cheering them on from the audience. It may have become more acceptable for women (married women in particular) to work outside the home, but the jobs most women were limited to (thanks to what they had been limited to as women in terms of education and/or opportunity) – as well as the socially and legally condoned treatment of these women – helped relegate most of them to support roles which, in their own way, mirrored the role of woman as subordinated helpmate to her husband and supported the current hegemony.

[293] Haskell, *From Reverence to Rape*, pp. 379–380.

Conclusion

Although a rising feminist consciousness can be seen throughout the period 1967–1989, this changing perception of the roles women should play in American society was slow in disseminating throughout mainstream American society. In the 1970s, in particular, there was little change, perhaps in part due to the economic recession experienced by the United States at that time. Beginning in 1980, however, the success of films such as *Nine to Five* and *Private Benjamin* (both 1980) served as parables for the evolution of women's (if not society's) consciousness on the issue of women's independence. In *Private Benjamin*, in particular, what women traditionally have been conditioned to see as being right for themselves is strongly fore-grounded. Early on in the film, after her husband's death just six hours into their marriage, while indulging in (somewhat under-standable) self-pity, Judy Benjamin (played by Goldie Hawn), talking on a call-in radio show, says to the show's host, "If I'm not gonna be married, I don't know what I'm supposed to do with myself. Did you happen to see that movie *Unmarried Woman*? Well, I didn't get it! I mean, I would've been Mrs. Alan Bates *so fast* that guy wouldn't've known what hit him!" By the end of the film, however, Judy punches the face of her manipulative, condescending, chauvinistic fiancé and triumphantly walks out on her own wedding. Then, wearing her wedding dress and to the accompaniment of a triumphant march, she walks confidently – and alone – down a country lane, looking like a fairy tale heroine who has overcome her foe and is striding happily into the sunset. Likewise, *Nine to Five* shows three archetypal women characters defeating their equally archetypal evil boss and establishing a reconstructed workplace which is also archetypically feminist in its goals and ideals (providing its employees with a comfortable, supportive environment, equal pay, and a recognition of employees' special needs, outside commitments, and responsibilities, catering to disabilities, families, and children). Yet, as Hollinger points out, these feminist messages were still avant-garde enough that they had to be safely contained within more comic themes.[294]

Likewise, in the animated films produced by the Disney studio in this era, any feminist themes which crept into their characterisations of women had to be carefully contained

294 Hollinger, *In the Company of Women*, p. 109.

within more conservative forms. When women are shown to be defiant and independent (as is Widow Tweed in *The Fox and the Hound*), they are also carefully characterised as being nurturing, grandmotherly, forgiving individuals. When women are shown to be capable of working equally in partnership with men, they are either safely ensconced within the realm of childhood (i.e. Eilonwy in *The Black Cauldron*) or shrunk down from human women into three-inch tall mice (namely Bianca, or "Miss Bianca", as she is more often called, in *The Rescuers*). Of the Disney animated films of this era, only two adult human women are shown: Widow Tweed and Madame Medusa. One is a safe, grandmotherly, settled old woman; the other is a maniacal, raving, threatening, frustrated middle-aged woman who tears about America on her own and seeks out riches and fortune for herself. Few positive feminist role models are available in these films, and none – apart from Miss Bianca – are shown as being younger women in their more active years.

Although it could be argued that this lack of feminist portrayals was the result of troubles and confusion within the Disney studio itself, in fact this pattern of slow acknowledgement of feminist ideology as championed by the elite elements of American culture is mirrored throughout Hollywood in this era. Peter Krämer has argued that this shift in Hollywood away from films targeted at women and women's concerns is indicative of the notion amongst many Hollywood studio executives that men were deciding what films to see and that women were more likely to watch male-oriented films than vice-versa.[295] What seems more likely, however, is that, as feminist ideology slowly entered the mainstream, the threat this change implied to the established male hegemony was perhaps dealt with by the move by Hollywood away from more female-oriented cinema. When women offered less of a perceived, organised "threat" to the status quo, making films which looked at the difficult aspects of women's lives and supported strong, independent female characters would have been seen by male-dominated Hollywood studios as providing women with safe fantasy material. After all, for much of the first half of the twentieth century, the percentage of women in the workplace was seen as being lower than that of men, and since women would presumably have time to go alone to the cinema during the weekday, when their husbands were at work and their

295 Peter Krämer, "A Powerful Cinema-going Force? Hollywood and Female Audiences since the 1960s", in Melvyn Stokes and Richard Maltby, *Identifying Hollywood's Audiences: Cultural Identity and the Movies* (London: British Film Institute, 1999), pp. 93–108.

children at school, they made a perfect target audience. By showing sympathy and understanding for possible causes of discontent in women's lives and at least offering them a cathartic moment in a darkened cinema, as well as by offering solutions for their problems which were by and large beyond the reach of most women, such films seemed to lend women empathy but in fact helped firmly to enforce the status quo.

In most of Hollywood's films and throughout much of American popular culture as a whole in the 1970s and 1980s, this softening of feminist trends and implicit support of traditional female roles would continue. Particularly in a company such as Disney, for so long seen as a bastion of safe, family-oriented entertainment, the espousing of feminist ideals would come slowly, largely echoing (and responding to) the sentiments of its largely middle-class audience.

6

Disney Films 1989–2005: The "Eisner" Era

296 On women's magazines and related issues of consumerism, see Kathy Peiss, "Making Up, Making Over: Cosmetics, Consumer Culture, and Women's Identity", in Victoria De Grazia with Ellen Furlough (eds). *The Sex of Things: Gender and Consumption in Historical Perspective* (Berkeley: University of California Press, 1996), pp. 311–336. In the same book, Rachel Bowlby's piece "Soft Sell: Marketing Rhetoric in Feminist Criticism", pp. 381–387, also contributes to the discussion of marketing aimed at women.

Throughout popular culture in America in the 1970s and 1980s, changes in the ways in which women were portrayed began to appear. The images of the happy home-maker and contented wife and mother did not disappear, but neither did they remain the only acceptable alternative shown to be available to "respectable" women. Furthermore, the definition of a "respectable" woman was beginning to broaden throughout this time, encompassing not just the housewife, but also the single career woman, the working wife and mother, the single mother, and various permutations of these identities. Women's magazines expanded from covering only such topics as fashion, recipes, and maintaining a youthful appearance, and began including articles about the ways a woman could "have it all": being a wife, mother, and career woman all at the same time, and finding equal fulfilment in her work both inside and outside her home.[296]

Going also (though not completely gone) was the image of a woman whose goodness was exemplified by her being innocent and asexual, and beginning to emerge in this period was the woman who was kind, virtuous, good, and aware of (as well as able to enjoy) her own sexuality. Television, in particular, began to feature shows about strong,

169

capable women – referred to by some as "superwomen" – who were successful – and balanced – in their careers, with their families, with their love lives, and in any other areas of their lives.[297] A successful woman was one who was shown as either having it all or – if she had suffered a setback of some sort – was getting it back together and would, eventually, "have it all". Women characters such as Claire Huxtable of *The Cosby Show* were presented as positive role models for America's women, and the heroines of shows such as *Kate and Allie* and *Alice* served as role models for those women who were trying to sort out their lives.[298] In Hollywood's movie industry as well, examples were emerging of women who, instead of being on the hunt for a husband, were on the hunt for everything else, and when (because, in most of these films, a man eventually did come along and sweep the heroine off her feet) she fell in love, finding a husband and starting a family were often portrayed as being not her goal, but rather the last pieces of her life falling into place.

During this time period, the overall make-up of the Disney studio itself shifted from one of male-dominance to, if not full equality, at least a greater presence of women in leadership roles. A number of changes in the 1990s affected its animation department. Younger talent at Disney and an increase in the number of women in higher-ranking positions (such as writers Susannah Grant and Irene Mecchi, lead animators Nancy Beiman and Ellen Woodbury, cleanup artist Nancy Kniep, supervisors Janet Bruce, Karen Comella, and Hortensia Casagran, and producer Alice Dewey) undoubtedly influenced not only the kinds of female characters the studio chose to portray, but also the way these portrayals were shaped.

Another significant change was the number of celebrities being used to provide the voices for animated characters, helping to bring in the stars' fans as well as providing a depth to the portrayals of various characters which was not often to be found in earlier films, where unknown actors tended to be used. (Though, now and then, famous radio and film stars were brought in to provide voices. They were not, however, usually blockbuster stars such as Demi Moore, Mel Gibson, Minnie Driver, Glenn Close, David Spade, and Michael J. Fox, all of whom have lent their voices to recent Disney films).

297 For an examination of some of US television's more popular series, see Susan Sackett, *Prime-Time Hits: Television's Most Popular Network Programs, 1950 to the Present* (New York: Billboard Books, 1993).

298 For more on this see Sackett, *Prime-Time Hits*.

Animated films 1989 to 2005

A number of significant changes are to be found in the way such themes as love, independence, duty, goodness, and evil were portrayed in the Disney Studio's animated films between 1989 and 2005, sometimes reflecting current trends in Hollywood, more often echoing ideas of arguably the most pervasive discursive influence of the 1990s – political correctness.[299] It is in the eighteen films produced by the Studio during this period, and particularly in the twelve films covered in this study, that themes of multi-culturalism and tolerance of those who are different were depicted by Disney for the first time, and in which ideas about equality, integrity, honour, and spirit take on a greater significance and depth. Unlike the earlier films, in which the heroine's honour was depicted and proven simply through her goodness and acquiescence, the heroines of Disney's animated films of this period show their integrity through their actions, rather than through their inaction. Furthermore, the level of action and independence demonstrated by these heroines grew exponentially with each film, and could still readily be seen even when the main character of the film was male and the leading female character was in a more supporting role.

The twelve Disney films released between 1989 and 2005 that fit the criteria of this study are *The Little Mermaid* (1989), *Beauty and the Beast* (1991), *Aladdin* (1992), *Pocahontas* (1995), *The Hunchback of Notre Dame* (1996), *Hercules* (1997), *Mulan* (1998), *Tarzan* (1999), *The Emperor's New Groove* (2000), *Atlantis* (2001), *Lilo and Stitch* (2002), and *Treasure Planet* (2003). Only six Disney animated features, *The Rescuers Down Under* (1990), *The Lion King* (1994), *Fantasia 2000* (2000), *Home on the Range* (2004), *Brother Bear* (2004), and *Chicken Little* (2005) are not included. *The Lion King, Home on the Range, Brother Bear*, and *Chicken Little* are not included because they have no human characters in leading roles. *The Rescuers Down Under* has only one human female, and her role in the film is so small as to define marginal. Miss Bianca, the mouse featured in *The Rescuers* (1977) and examined in detail in the preceding chapter, does appear again in *The Rescuers Down Under*. However, as little change is made in her presentation, and furthermore as she does not interact in this film with any human female characters (as she did with Penny in *The Rescuers*), there is no reason to repeat a

299 "Politically correct (or incorrect)" is defined by *The Oxford English Reference Dictionary* as "conforming (or not conforming) to a prevailing body of liberal opinion, esp. in avoiding (or not avoiding) language, behaviour, etc., which might conceivably be regarded as discriminatory or pejorative to racial or cultural minorities or as reflecting undesirable implicit assumptions". (Oxford: Oxford University Press, 1996), p. 1121.

discussion of her here. *Fantasia 2000* is not discussed because, although there are some human female characters, the emphasis of this film is not character, but music, technological innovation, and visual spectacle in much the same vein as surrounded the original *Fantasia* (1940).

This tendency at Disney in this era to concentrate on stories about humans was, in fact, a change from the Studio's earlier history. Of the first nineteen films produced at Disney during Walt Disney's lifetime, only seven can be said to be solely about humans. Four of the earlier films were either package films or, in the case of *Fantasia*, similar enough to the package film format as to be broadly included in the category. Six are films in which both human and animal characters are emphasised, and only two films – *Dumbo* and *Bambi* – can be said to be concerned wholly with animals. Divided into two categories – only humans and animals/humans – the older films break down into seven films about humans and twelve which also emphasise/anthropomorphise animals. During what this study defines as the "middle period" of the Disney Studio's history, only one of the eight films focuses solely on humans, and the rest are either mixed humans and animals or else are heavily anthropomorphised animals (as in *Robin Hood*, 1973, or *The Great Mouse Detective*, 1986).

Why the Disney studio moved toward working more on stories about humans had many possible reasons, some of which may have been connected to the fact that technical and artistic advances in animation made it easier for animators to create more convincing and realistic human characters than was possible in the past. Another likelihood is that a relaxation of attitudes towards such topics as sexuality has allowed the animators to explore these issues more completely with human characters than was possible before. In earlier films, stories about animal characters have a greater emphasis on the characters' sensuality and sexuality than do stories about humans. The idea of a fairy tale princess sauntering up to her intended, preening, hips swaying, and flirting, is impossible to imagine in the earlier Disney films. The only human characters who do such things are generally depicted as being not very nice, and in fact as being vain and over-sexed (as is the case with the ugly step-sisters, Anastasia and Drusela, in *Cinderella*). Yet in *Bambi*, a girl rabbit behaves in a manner which is exactly as described above, and, though the scene serves as a source of comedy, never is the rabbit's integrity or morality called into question.

In these earlier films, in particular amongst the animal characters, the idea that the characters could experience sexual attraction is seen as being normal – perhaps as a source of comedy as well, but nonetheless as being a natural development in their lives. The girl rabbit who so sassily and sensually seduces Thumper in *Bambi* is, more so than perhaps any other Disney character in the fifty years between *Bambi*'s release and that of *Aladdin* in 1992, truly sexy, and even a bit of a vamp. Peg, a dog that Lady meets in the pound in *Lady and the Tramp*, sashays around her pen, fluffing her fur, and singing a song about how desirable Tramp is. When one takes into account the fact that Peg is voiced by jazz/soul legend Peggy Lee, it becomes readily apparent that this sensuality is very much intentional. The closest any of the humans get to a performance of that calibre is Briar Rose in *Sleeping Beauty* when she sings "Once Upon a Dream". As the title of the song implies, however, the man she sings about is a dream, not flesh and blood, and her movement to the song, while mildly flirtatious, does not exude the confident sexuality of characters such as Peg or the unnamed rabbit in *Bambi*. Indeed, once Briar Rose is confronted (during the singing of "Once Upon a Dream") by her "dream prince" (Prince Philip), her flirtatious demeanour immediately dissolves and she is shown to be shy, awkward, and inexperienced.

By the 1990s, however, the notion that a woman could be both good and sexy had ceased to be such an unimaginable concept in representations of femininity in much of America's popular culture. Within Hollywood cinema, women characters were beginning to exude a confident sexuality which in no way detracted from their portrayals as good, honourable individuals. Perhaps the ultimate example of this would be the character Vivian (played by Julia Roberts) in Touchstone's *Pretty Woman* (1990). Vivian is a prostitute in Los Angeles, and, as she reveals in the film, has ended up in that situation through what amounts to a series of bad choices and naïveté. She is shown to be unhappy in her current life, but is entirely unapologetic about what she does. And yet, despite her lifestyle and profession, Vivian is shown to be an extremely kind, thoughtful, loving person,

173

and her goodness and integrity are never brought into question. Indeed, in choosing to continue working as a prostitute rather than give up her independence by becoming a kept woman, she is venerated by the film, which celebrates her refusal. What is interesting is that she puts her rejection of Edward (Richard Gere)'s offer in the form of her belief that fairy tales come true:

> When I was a little girl, my mama used to lock me in the attic when I was bad, which was pretty often. And I would … I would pretend I was a princess trapped in a tower by a wicked queen. And then suddenly this knight on a white horse, with his colors flying, would come charging up, and draw his sword. And I would wave, and he would climb up the tower, and rescue me. But never, in all the times that I had this dream, did the knight say to me, "Come on baby, I'll put you up in a great condo".

Vivian is rewarded at the film's end – both for her refusal to become a kept woman and (apparently) for her faith in fairy tales – by finding true love with Edward, who realises both her goodness and her true worth and finds that he is in love with her. Although *Pretty Woman* was criticised by some for glamorising prostitution through such an ending,[300] and though some scholars have further criticised the fact that the film ignores race in its gender/class equation,[301] its success with the public was undeniable. It turned Julia Roberts into a star, and became Disney's highest grossing film for 1990.[302] In fact, the success of *Pretty Woman* was so great that, eight years after its release when Disney chairman Michael Eisner published his book about his work at Disney, he still listed the film as the company's most successful live-action film they had produced to date.[303]

Clearly, such film portrayals – as well as the phenomenal success of *Pretty Woman* (both at the box office and in subsequent video sales) – demonstrate that the mainstream American audience was more than capable of accepting that open sexuality and sex – even a career as a prostitute (albeit an unusually clean-cut one) – did not make a woman immoral. The very fact that *Pretty Woman* was produced by Touchstone Pictures shows that the Disney Company itself was also not against such notions. It should be noted, however, that Eisner later claimed that, in a memo to Jeffrey Katzenberg, he had instructed those working on the film to

300 For some examples of reviews which criticise the portrayal of prostitution in *Pretty Woman*, see Mary Maddin, "'Pretty Woman': Disney Turns Out Cinderella", *WHISPER: Women Hurt in Systems of Prostitution Engaged in Revolt*, vol. 4, no. 2 (Fall 1990), pp. 1, 4–5; Harvey Roy Greenberg, "Rescrewed: *Pretty Woman*'s Co-opted Feminism", *Journal of Popular Film and Television*, vol. 19, no. 1 (Spring 1991), pp. 9–13; Madonne Miner, "No Matter What They Say, It's All About Money", *Journal of Popular Film and Television*, vol. 20, no. 1 (Spring 1992), pp. 8–14.

301 For a discussion of the lack of racial themes in *Pretty Woman*, see D. Soyini Madison, "*Pretty Woman* through the Triple Lens of Black Feminist Spectatorship", in Elizabeth Bell, Lynda Haas, and Laura Sells, (eds). *From Mouse to Mermaid: The Politics of Film, Gender, and Culture* (Indianapolis: Indiana University Press, 1995), pp. 224–235.

302 Michael Eisner, with Tony Schwartz, *Work in Progress* (New

make Vivian "the only virgin woman-of-the-night in Hollywood", stressing that the film needed to be "a modern Doris Day movie".[304] Although no one could argue against the idea that *Pretty Woman* is a highly sanitised film about prostitution, nonetheless the fact that a prostitute could not only escape punishment, but actually be rewarded for her integrity by the film's end, is evidence of a changed attitude towards images of women's sexuality in mainstream American films. After all, sanitised though this portrayal may be, Vivian does make reference, in a conversation with Edward, to not only her first time as a prostitute (during which she says she "cried the whole time",) to her going on to say that, as she "started to get a few regulars", her situation became easier to live with. In other words, Eisner may have wanted her to be a "virgin woman of the night", but her being an experienced prostitute with numerous clients is highlighted throughout the film. However, the fact that there was no real public criticism of the film's portrayal of prostitution serves as an indicator that Americans were becoming more open-minded about what behaviours constituted morality or immorality. Certainly, as the ten animated films produced by Disney between 1989 and 2001 are analysed, this changing attitude towards what characterises a "good" woman, and what makes an individual "evil" or "bad", becomes increasingly apparent.

It is not just the ways the stories are told in these films, however, but also that the stories themselves, containing as they all do strong, independent, intelligent female characters, are potentially indicative of just how much feminist ideology had entered into mainstream American middle-class values. By the 1990s, three basic categories had become apparent amongst the Disney animated heroines: Princess, which was of course the oldest but which, in the 1990s, underwent a fundamental shift in its nature; the Good Daughter, a new category for Disney but a fairly common theme in fairy tales; the "Tough Gal", which was a particularly radical departure from more traditional characterisations of women at Disney. While further sub-divisions and variations can be made in such categories, they are nonetheless the major divisions into which these characters fit, and are the headings to be used in defining and discussing them.

York: Random House, 1998), p. 162.

303 Although he does not give the film's gross, he does say that it did better than the studio's next biggest hit, *The Santa Clause*, which he asserts grossed $20 million in its first weekend at the box office and "eventually became our second biggest live action movie, after *Pretty Woman*." Eisner, *Work in Progress*, p. 341.

304 Eisner, *Work in Progress*, p. 163.

The Princesses – Ariel, Jasmine, Pocahontas and Kida

There are four Disney films in this period in which the heroines are princesses: *The Little Mermaid*, *Aladdin*, *Pocahontas*, and *Atlantis*. The category of "princess" is fairly easy to define: a princess is a woman who is the daughter of a ruler or the wife of a prince. In all four examples in the period under discussion, the characters are princesses through birth, and all four are presented as having no mother, only a father (and it is the father who is the ruler; none of them have a mother who rules in her own right). Furthermore, all but Ariel in *The Little Mermaid* are shown as being only children (and indeed, Ariel's six sisters play such a minor role in the film that Ariel herself largely functions as an only child). In presenting them as having little or no parental guidance, the Studio continued the tradition within Disney films of "orphaning" main characters.

Other than this, however, the Disney heroines of the latest period have little in common with their predecessors. Their independence, strength of will, determination to engineer their own fates, and insistence on being true to themselves are unquestionably their strongest traits (both individually and as a group). With the progression of time, in fact, the choices made available to these four, as well as the decisions they make over the course of the films and the final solutions they reach, grow exponentially with each film. For Ariel the mermaid, her determination to live in the human world and to marry the human prince with whom she has fallen in love mean that she must overcome enormous obstacles, including growing legs, learning to walk, coming to understand and adjust to a whole new way of life, and living in a world in which she (literally) has no voice. For Jasmine in *Aladdin* (1992), as a princess who is trapped within her father's palace, she has no say in which princes come to court her (although, in the beginning, it does appear that she has final say over whether or not she will marry them), and yet her determination to know a life outside of the palace leads her to disguise herself as a commoner. It is during the course of her adventure in the city that she first meets Aladdin, whom she will eventually help to overthrow the evil Jafar and save the life and the kingdom of her father, the kindly but bumbling Sultan. Pocahontas (in the 1995 film of the same name) takes this determination to overthrow evil and be true

176

to herself even further when, behind her father's back, she meets John Smith and helps not only to stop a war between her people and Smith's, but even helps to establish communication and respect between the two groups by the film's end. Kida, who has been cut-off from the outside world within the remains of Atlantis, sees that her civilisation is dying but is initially unable to prevent its decline because her father, the king, refuses to acknowledge it (and, in fact, is portrayed within the film as an elderly blind man). By joining forces with scholar and dead language expert Milo Thatch, the film's main character, she is able not only to save her civilisation from the mercenaries who have come to steal its power source, but also is able to restore her world to prosperity and, because of her father's death, is able to assume the role of queen (in fact, Kida is the first Disney princess to succeed to the throne within the course of a film). In all four films, the heroines are initially shown to be adventurous, curious young women who are stuck within very definite boundaries which seem, at first, to be insurmountable; yet over the course of the film, through strength of will and hard work, all three go on to discover their rightful places in life.

Although, from the start of this period of Disney animation, major changes in how women are portrayed were in evidence, it should nonetheless be emphasised that this transformation did not occur overnight. In the characterisation of Eilonwy in *The Black Cauldron* (1985), discussed in the previous chapter, the beginnings of this transformation may be discerned. Feisty and adventurous, Eilonwy's strength and spirit set a new benchmark for what comprised the personality of a Disney heroine. The fact that Eilonwy was still a pre-pubescent girl, however, allied her characterisation with earlier Disney patterns of reserving such traits as wilfulness and determination either for the Studio's youngest heroines or for its villainesses.

By 1989, however, a definite shift had occurred at Disney when it came to handing out pluck to its leading ladies. At sixteen-years-old,[305] Ariel is assuredly old enough to be aware of herself as a sexual being, although her confidence in her maturity and her feeling it necessary to declare that she is "not a child" demonstrate that, in many ways, she is still a girl. Nonetheless, from the first time we see her, Ariel is clearly differentiated from earlier Disney princesses.

[305] Ariel very firmly reminds her father "I'm sixteen! I'm not a child!", thereby allowing us (both as scholars and as members of the audience) to define her as being an adult, at least in a physical sense. Her very shapely, feminine figure serves to confirm this.

Unlike Snow White, Cinderella, Sleeping Beauty, and even Eilonwy, Ariel actively seeks adventure and works hard to achieve goals she has set for herself, rather than simply responding to the crises with which she is presented. Even the fact that the film's first shot of Ariel is on her own, away from home, in the midst of an adventure, serves as a marked contrast to the initial shots of earlier Disney princesses, who are first seen either within their homes or within the grounds of their homes (or, in Eilonwy's case, in the dungeon in which she is being held prisoner). More than simply reflecting a longing for excitement and adventure for their own sake, however, Ariel's true quest seems to be to discover a place where she can find enrichment. In what serves as one of the set-pieces of the film as a whole, Ariel, surrounded by all of the human "treasures" she has collected in her explorations, sings of wanting more than a life filled with possessions, dreaming instead of living in a world where she is not just accepted, but valued. While the whole of the song is about her thirst for knowledge, it is this desire to be esteemed which comes through in such lines as:

> Bet ya on land, they understand
> Bet they don't reprimand their daughters.
> Bright young women, sick of swimmin', ready to stand!

Furthermore, despite the urging she receives from other characters to see that her life is "good enough" and to accept the world into which she was born (and in marked contrast to earlier Disney princesses, who accept far worse existences with cheerful smiles and infinite patience), Ariel cannot. Instead, she feels stifled and discontented, thwarted in her quest to fill what she considers to be an empty, meaningless life, and, defying her father's orders, continually goes to the surface of the sea to learn all she can about the forbidden, mysterious world of humans.

Yet all is not as positive in Ariel's portrayal as it initially seems. Unfortunately for her, she is (unknowingly) working with a heavy amount of misinformation and is depending primarily upon a well-meaning but nonetheless highly unreliable source (Scuttle, the seagull). The explanations which Scuttle gives Ariel of the various human artefacts she finds are so wrong as to serve as a source of comedy for the film (such as when he tells her that one item she has found, a fork, is called a "dinglehopper" and is used by humans to straighten their hair). Of course, once Ariel is living as a human in the prince's castle and sees the humans' bewilderment at her using the "dinglehopper" to comb her hair, it would seem that she must realise that perhaps other information Scuttle has given her might not have been accurate. In a later scene, however, as she is getting ready for bed, Ariel is shown again using the "dinglehopper" to comb her hair, despite overwhelming evidence that her earlier information was very flawed.

Ariel's other source of information on how to live as a human – one which should have seemed to her to be even less trustworthy than the bumbling but good-hearted Scuttle – is Ursula, the sea-witch to whom Ariel trades her voice for a pair of legs. In a song she sings to Ariel while persuading her to make the trade, Ursula tells her that:

> The men up there don't like a lot of blather,
> They think a girl who gossips is a bore.
> Yes, on land it's much preferred for ladies not to say a word –
> And after all, dear, what is idle prattle for!
> Come on, they're not all that impressed with conversation –
> True gentleman avoid it when they can.
> But they don't as soon inform on a lady that's withdrawn –
> It's she who holds her tongue who gets a man.

Such a performance points out that there are elements in both the human and "mer" worlds which trivialise the importance of a woman's voice, and that such attitudes can be used and played upon by the woman who is willing to make the temporary sacrifice of her voice (as, indeed, Ariel is). Nonetheless, what makes Ursula's advice particularly flawed is that it is Ariel's voice which Eric most clearly remembers from his encounter with her, and it is to her beautiful voice – a voice he clearly values very highly – that he makes repeated reference throughout the film. Indeed, it is not until Ariel regains her voice that Eric recognises her as the "woman" he loves.

Such a reading contradicts analysis such as that of Laura Sells, who sees the film as being a limited celebration of women's potential upward mobility and as a highly sanitised version of "bourgeois feminism".[306] For feminist interpretations of the film, such a comparison between the tale's older class associations and the film's gender-based interpretations are important. After all, in a society in which a number of gender distinctions take the form of economic and political discrimination, then the notion of moving

306 Laura Sells, "Where Do the Mermaids Stand?": Voice and Body in *The Little Mermaid*", in Bell, Haas, and Sells (eds), *From Mouse to Mermaid*, p. 177.

from a position of female "inferiority" to an alliance with "male" power has a similar aspect to the kind of social mobility one thinks of in terms of moving to a higher class. In Ariel's undersea world, her voice has a very real power: it is praised by all for its beauty, and even takes on a kind of monetary power when she trades it to Ursula. Yet the undersea world is, in the Disney interpretation of the story, given many elements which link it with disenfranchised groups in American society: women, non-white ethnic groups,[307] and third world nations.[308] The human world, by contrast, is shown as being thoroughly white, well-ordered, and predominantly male. The only human woman featured is Carlotta, the housekeeper in Eric's castle, and the only other human women who speak in the film are washer women working behind the castle. Therefore, when Ariel enters this world, she is the only "woman" shown on an equal footing with Eric and his advisor, Grimsby. Yet Ariel has no voice, and her attempts to communicate are not always understood. The trappings now surrounding her are strange to her, and she does not always know their proper uses. Furthermore, Ariel is only tentatively a part of the human world, and must accomplish a great task – win the prince's true love – or she will cease to be human and will have lost her soul to Ursula. In her reading of the film, Sells points out that, in contrast to the class themes found in Hans Christian Anderson's 1837 version of the tale, "… Disney's contemporary version has shifted colors from class to gender privilege", and argues that "… the Disney version, along with its ritual affirmation of women's coming of age, invites a reading of this film as a parable of bourgeois feminism".[309] The fact that, ultimately, Ariel does both form an alliance with the human world *and* regain her voice is the hopeful stance of the film at its conclusion, but as the film ends at this point, with no allusion to what is to come, no more can be surmised as to either what the results of Ariel's triumph will mean to her – or the true extent of the film's promotion of late 1980s/early 1990s feminism.

However, while many aspects of Ariel's portrayal are ultimately positive, there are nonetheless a number of troubling elements. Her seeming inability to detect unreliable advice (even when there is substantial evidence that she should be wary), and her willingness to risk her life over the possibility that she *might* find true love show a tendency toward

307 Patrick D. Murphy, "'The Whole Wide World Was Scrubbed Clean': The Androcentric Animation of Denatured Disney", in Bell, Haas, and Sells, *From Mouse to Mermaid*, p. 132.

308 Murphy, "The Whole Wide World Was Scrubbed Clean", p. 132, and Sells, "Where Do the Mermaids Stand?", p. 178.

309 Sells, "Where Do the Mermaids Stand?", p. 177.

portraying Ariel as being the victimised innocent princess found in earlier Disney films. Yet her willingness to gamble, her determination to make her own choices, and her tenacity in working toward what she wants out of life are all highly positive. Although her ultimate wish – to marry Price Eric and live as a human – are on the surface very traditional, symbolically this action can be seen as her ultimate assertion of herself thanks to the fact that it actualises goals she set for herself. She has now achieved full status as a human, has learned how to function within that world, and has even regained her voice, thereby giving her a say over what happens in her new environment. Therefore, while it cannot be denied that, as a "feminist" film, *The Little Mermaid* has a number of flaws, nonetheless it does mark – at least within Disney animation – a move away from praising traditional solutions for women's unhappiness and hints at offering them choices beyond simple contentment with the role into which they were born.

Someone else who is not satisfied with the world as she has found it is Jasmine, the princess of Agraba with whom Aladdin falls in love in *Aladdin*. It is as if the point of *Aladdin* is to shatter the idea that being a princess is something to strive for, since all being a princess means to Jasmine's life is that she has no personal freedom. The film begins this examination of the image and stereotypes of royalty with the traditional view of what it means to be a prince or princess, having Aladdin, as a believer in the traditional image, say that his hope is that, "Some day, Abu,[310] things are gonna change. We'll be rich, live in a palace, and never have any problems at all." This scene ends with him gazing with wonder and admiration at the distant, romantically moonlit palace, but in the next scene, with the palace now shown in the light of day, we see Jasmine's impression of what it is like to be a princess and live in a palace, and that it is not the perfect life which Aladdin envisions.

As the daughter of the sultan, Jasmine leads a very quiet, sheltered existence. Far from making her contented, however, she feels stifled, restless, and cut off from life. In the first scene in which we see her, Jasmine is complaining to her father that she does not want to marry because the laws of their kingdom say she must: "*If* I do marry, I want it to be for love!" She goes on to complain that she has never done anything on her own, never been outside the palace walls,

310 Abu is Aladdin's monkey side-kick who helps him and is his constant companion.

181

and has never had any real friends except her pet tiger, Raja. When her father reminds her that she is a princess (implying that this is the life a princess must lead), Jasmine retorts "Maybe I don't want to be a princess anymore!" When her father stomps off in frustration, Jasmine walks to a cage of birds and opens the doors to give them freedom, then stands, longingly, watching them fly away. In a slightly later scene, when she and Aladdin first discuss their impressions of what it must be like (or, in her case, what it *is* like) to live in the palace, her description is that it means "people who tell you where to go and how to dress", and that "you're not free to make your own choices … you're just *trapped*".

Despite this feeling of confinement, however, Jasmine refuses to allow herself to be controlled. We are given the impression that she has rejected numerous suitors because they were not so much interested in her as they were in the kingdom, power, and wealth which came with her. Early on in the film, Jasmine disguises herself as a peasant and climbs over the palace wall in order to see what life is like outside, and, despite her lack of knowledge and the danger she finds herself in (from which she is saved by Aladdin, which is how they first meet), she quickly learns how to take care of herself, impressing Aladdin with her intelligence and quick wit. Throughout the film, Jasmine is presented as a strong, intelligent, well-balanced individual who can instantly and accurately judge character. She is also fiercely independent, and, in the end, when Aladdin has proved his worthiness for her, she actively – and verbally – chooses him to be her husband. Whereas her past suitors failed because they tried to impress her with their power and wealth, Aladdin succeeds because he appeals to her intelligence, curiosity, and sense of adventure.

Jasmine is not on-screen as much as Aladdin since the film is primarily about his adventures and his quest to earn Jasmine's heart and win her hand. Nonetheless, far from being a secondary character, it is her presence in the film which allows Aladdin to grow and discover his true worth. It is, in fact, only the second Disney film in which one character is shown contributing to another character's self-understanding, the first being *Beauty and the Beast*, released only one year earlier. This would be a major theme in subsequent films during this period. In *Aladdin*, this theme of one character discovering his own worth is, indeed, the basis of the film as a whole. Aladdin is described at the start of the film – before we even see him – as being comparable to the magic lamp: "A young man who, like this lamp, was more than what he seemed – a diamond in the rough". We are also reminded at the start of the film, "Do not be fooled by its [the lamp's] common-place appearance. Like so many things, it is not what is outside, but what is inside that counts." Aladdin's subsequent adventures, conversations with Genie, and courtship of Jasmine are all centred around his learning to be honest about himself and to realise that his poverty does not mean he is less worthy than those rich and powerful individuals who suddenly enter his life. By the film's end it is Aladdin the "street rat", not Aladdin in his disguise of "Prince Ali-Ababua", who is found to be the one most worthy of the spirited, intelligent, beautiful princess and all that comes with her.

As a character, Jasmine changes very little over the course of the film. From the start, she is shown to be very bright, aware of those around her, and a very good, likeable person. If she has one major flaw, it is her innocence of the world outside the palace, and by the end of the film her adventures with Aladdin have helped her to overcome at least some of this innocence, which was the natural result of her having led such a sheltered life. Overall, the way Jasmine is portrayed is positive, and her message seems to be that being a princess does not mean happiness, and that far from being a goal, such status – and the things attendant upon it – are obstacles to be overcome. In a sense, Jasmine, who as a princess has been placed on a pedestal all her life, shows the dangers and difficulties inherent in this idealisation of women, since it robs them of their freedom and keeps them from where they can do the most good – the public sphere.

One character who is most definitely to be found in the public sphere of her world, however, is Pocahontas, the third princess to be examined in this chapter. As a Disney princess, the character of Pocahontas is one of the most interesting, unusual, and, in a number of respects, one of the most positive. Like a number of other Disney heroines, Pocahontas is a princess, but, unlike most of them, she thinks for herself, controls her own destiny, and is motivated in her actions not so much by romantic love as she is by the greater wisdom which she possesses. She is the only Disney princess (or, at least, the only grown-up Disney princess) who does not find romantic fulfilment by the film's end. Instead, although the choice is available to her, Pocahontas rejects love – which would mean leaving behind her people and her function as a leader – and chooses to devote herself to her people. No ceremonial princess, she is as much a leader of her people as her father, their chief, and in many ways her leadership is even more valuable for her tribe, since she has at her disposal the gift of female intuition. Indeed, it is this female intuition and wisdom which is credited by the film with preventing war and uniting peoples. This is shown as being more than simply an example of woman as nurturer and moral guide, however, through its portrayal of Pocahontas as a skilled diplomat and a careful decision-maker.

It is interesting to compare Pocahontas with the first of the Disney princesses, Snow White. In one sense, there is no comparing the two: Snow White's main goal is finding her prince. Even with her life constantly endangered by the evil Queen, self-protection is Snow White's secondary consideration. When given the chance (so she thinks) to make a wish for anything she wants in the world through the "magic wishing apple" (really a poisoned apple) which the Queen, in disguise, gives to her, Snow White's wish is not that she be kept safe from harm, or that her kingdom be saved from the evil woman who controls it, but that her prince find her and marry her. For Pocahontas, however, finding romantic love comes a distant second to her desire to find herself and identify her true path in life. Although she does find true love, in the end she chooses to stay behind with her people (rather than to journey to England with John Smith) and work to bridge the gap between the British and the Algonquins. Although it is made clear that Pocahontas truly loves John Smith and will miss him terribly, it is also made abundantly clear that she does not need him in order to be complete, or to fulfil her role with her people. In a more modern acceptance of feminine sexuality, and unlike Disney's earlier heroines, Disney's Pocahontas has more in common with Jasmine than she does with earlier Disney princesses in that she does not need a man either for identification or fulfilment, and it is, in fact, through association with her that her partner will gain both social and political status. Unlike Jasmine, however, Pocahontas will gain her power and authority totally through her own skill and determination, and not because she has married (for Jasmine, although she will inherit a degree of power from her father, most of that power will go to her husband, and it will be Jasmine's *husband* – not Jasmine – who will be sultan after her father).

In another departure from earlier princesses, though again like Jasmine, Pocahontas has a mature, confident sexuality which she expresses comfortably. She does not act demure or shy about her feelings for John Smith or his feelings for her, but reacts confidently, and in some cases even takes the lead. This ability to express her romantic and sexual feelings, however, is never over-emphasised, but is shown as being part of her wisdom and self-awareness, just as with Jasmine it is part of her self-confidence and strength. Unlike any of their predecessors (except perhaps for Slue-foot Sue, the cowgirl from the story of Pecos Bill, discussed in Chapter four), this new breed of Disney heroine is able to express with confidence both love and attraction as a part of expressing her true self, but is not seeking love as the ultimate goal of her life. Instead, she is more interested in finding herself and her destiny, whatever that may include. For Jasmine, this includes love, but, more importantly, it includes respect. Jasmine must marry: it is the law of her land, and she must obey it no matter what. She puts off this marriage, however, saying that she wants to marry for love. In reality, what Jasmine clearly means by love – as can be judged in the way she speaks of and deals with suitors – is respect for her, and for her to be able to respect and trust her potential husband. Pocahontas does not have to marry, although her father encourages her to find a suitable husband. She has no intention of rejecting love, but her first and foremost concern is following her destiny. Within the story presented in the film, being able to hold onto love is not shown as being part of her destiny, and so, painful though it may be to her, she is nonetheless strong and confident enough to say good-bye to it and follow her destiny.

Although Pocahontas may have little in common with most of her Disney predecessors, she has much in common with her most recent successor, Kida, the heir to the throne of Atlantis in the film of the same name. Although it is Milo Thatch – a scholar, linguist, cartographer, and misunderstood intellectual (voiced by Michael J. Fox) who is the main character of the film – Kida, by becoming Milo's guide, friend, and love-interest – is portrayed as one of the most vital characters in the film. Indeed, it is to her that we are introduced first, when we are shown how Atlantis came to be destroyed when Kida was a small child. When we next see Kida, shortly after Milo and the band of "explorers" (who turn out to be mercenaries, though all but two will have a change of heart) arrive on the edge of Atlantis, she is a beautiful young woman at the peak of health and vitality (despite the fact, as we soon learn, that she is around 8,800 years old). Most interestingly, she is portrayed as being a warrior, wearing a large mask (large enough to serve as a shield), wielding a spear, and leading a small group of similarly-clad warriors. When she first encounters Milo, he has been wounded, and she uses a crystal – which she and all Atlantians wear as necklaces – to heal his wound. Initially, she and the other warriors run off (with Milo running after them trying to find out who they are), but she and the other four warriors quickly corner the explorers on the edge of a cliff. She speaks to them in Atlantian, Milo begins trying to communicate, and it is soon discovered that the Atlantians have the ability to speak any language they wish (the only explanation for this coming from Milo, who theorises that their language must be a root language for other modern languages, including English).

Once communication has been established between the two groups, Kida quickly welcomes the explorers and leads them to Atlantis, saying that Milo must speak with her father, the King. King Nedakh, however, does not trust the outsiders, and once they are gone chides Kida that, a thousand years ago, she would have slain them on sight. She points out that, a thousand years ago, their people were better off, and that she believes that these outsiders might possess knowledge which might help Atlantis. She voices her opinion that she fears Atlantis' civilisation is dying, and she demonstrates that she wants to do all she can to save it. Her father, however, disagrees that these outsiders can bring them any knowledge worth having.

Determined, however, to find out all she can, Kida goes out on her own, seeks out Milo (who was also trying to find her), and together the two of them begin to unravel part of the mystery of why Atlantis has been hidden beneath the sea. Milo quickly learns that the Atlantians have lost the knowledge of writing and reading, and so he is able to help Kida, initially, simply by reading to her what various murals and inscriptions say. It quickly becomes apparent, however, that the other explorers are still intent on finding treasure, and the presence of a living civilisation is not going to deter them from trying to steal what they call "The Heart of Atlantis". At least half of the film involves Milo's – and eventually most of the other explorers' – attempts to stop this theft, which would, if successful, lead to the final destruction of Atlantis and its people. At one point, Kida becomes joined with the Heart of Atlantis, and is transformed into a figure of light (and looks as though she is made of light and crystal), and the king, just before his death, warns Milo that if she stays joined to the Heart too long, she will be lost to it forever (which, incidentally, was her mother's fate at the time of the initial cataclysm that caused Atlantis to be shut off from the world). Several of the final scenes of the film – and some of its most climactic moments – are about the rescue of Kida before she is taken too far from Atlantis.

Interestingly, although Kida is shown as a very attractive young woman – and it is quickly established that Milo is very attracted to her (though he is too shy and awkward to act on his feelings) – there is precious little romance in this film. This is an important departure from other Disney films portraying a heroine of marriageable age. Everyone recognises that an attachment has been formed between Milo and Kida during their attempts to solve the riddle of the Heart of Atlantis, but almost no comment on this is made. There is also no splashy, romantic climax in this film: there is an instance in which Milo and Kida reach for each other's hands at an emotional moment for the group; during their efforts to rescue Kida when she has become joined with the Heart of Atlantis, it is obvious that at least part of Milo's impetus to save her comes from his growing love for her, though there is nothing to imply that it is his only reason. With or without his feelings for Kida, Milo's noble character, as well as his interest in ancient civilisations, would have compelled him to do all he could to save Atlantis from destruction. But when Kida finally separates from the Heart of Atlantis and returns to the city in mortal form – descending dramatically into Milo's arms, the pair embrace, but do not kiss. When the surviving explorers return to the surface world, Milo remains behind. Although he explains this by saying that he has heard that "they need someone down here who's an expert in Gibberish", it is obvious that the main reason he is staying is Kida. It is another interesting departure from earlier Disney films – and an interesting comparison to the end of *Pocahontas* – that there is never any question that Kida might consider leaving her people to be with Milo. With the king's death, Kida has become queen, so naturally she would stay in Atlantis. But a very similar scenario does not bring about a similar mind-set in *Pocahontas*: although Pocahontas is portrayed as being her father's heir, and although she decides to remain with her people, the possibility that she might give everything up to go to England with John Smith is very much a part of the final scene, implying that it would be natural for her to give up her place amongst her people in order to stay with the man she loves. Concurrently, there is never the suggestion that it would be feasible for John Smith to stay with Pocahontas (she asks him, but it has already been stated – in a way which defies all rational thought and historical accuracy beyond anything else in the film) – John Smith must return to England or he will die. Kida, however, is not the one who is expected to chose between Milo and Atlantis: she is a leader, so she remains with her people. It is Milo who must decide, and it is Milo who chooses love over returning to the surface and becoming the hero who discovered Atlantis. To the very final moment of the film, however, Milo and Kida are never shown kissing. He is shown at her side, dressed as an Atlantian, finishing the carving on an image of the late king's face (so that his image may join the images of the kings of Atlantis' past), and they race to the top of a mountain to watch the carving rise up to the sky (where it will revolve with the other carvings around the Heart of Atlantis). But that is the full extent of the romance in this film. Also in a departure from other Disney films, there are no animal sidekicks for any of the characters. *Atlantis* is also only the second of the Disney animated films (the first was *The Black Cauldron*, 1985) produced between 1937 and 2005 which does not contain at least one featured song. None of the characters sing, and the only music the film contains is the background score. *Atlantis* is an action/adventure film beyond any other Disney animated features, and stands as a definite – and intentional – departure from traditional Disney animation.[311] This choice to focus on the adventure – rather than the romance – is perhaps part of why Milo and

311 In the audio/visual commentary on the DVD release of *Atlantis*, producer Donn Hahn and co-directors Gary Trousdale and Kirk Wise discuss how they wanted to make this film different, saying that they had initially intended on there being a rat in the boiler room for Milo to talk to, but that it slowed the action too much, that they felt it was better to let Milo tell his own story, and that it was as if they were providing Milo with an animal side-kick "out of habit". "We were kind of parting company with a lot of things that we typically did on these movies, and the animal side-kick was one of them. And we just decided, why not let Milo tell his own story, rather than always having to cut back to a little animal, always having to make a sad or happy face to let the audience know how to feel toward Milo."
See Disc 1, Bonus Features, "Visual Commentary", on *Atlantis: The Lost Empire*.

Kida's relationship is portrayed as it is. The fact is, however, that this story could have been written without including a female character – let alone a princess – at all, but one was included nonetheless. Also, rather than portraying her as simply a token woman or an object, she is a highly active, central character. And unlike Jasmine, who despite her strength and individuality is portrayed nonetheless as a reward of sorts for Aladdin, Kida and Milo are shown to have what may be the closest thing to a partnership of equals as can be found in a Disney film. It is not a relationship which is portrayed as either character's destiny. Instead, it seems to have been a "happy accident" in these characters' lives, and will bring benefits to them both.

These ideas – that finding true love may or may not be part of a woman's destiny and that respect cannot be separated from love – are fairly new themes in Disney films. The beginnings are to be seen in *Beauty and the Beast*, when Belle and Beast learn to respect and like one another first and love one another second, but their love for one another is not fully formed or romantically acted upon until fairly close to the film's end, when they have managed to overcome all of the emotional, psychological, and physical barriers which have kept them apart. With Belle, and with Jasmine and Pocahontas (and, to a lesser degree, with Kida, though she does not seek self-knowledge so much as an understanding of what happened to her society) – the other heroines with whom she shares the most in common – the paths to self-fulfilment, self-confidence, and self-understanding may include finding love to some degree. But, in fact, it is finding out about themselves – and their own personal strengths and weaknesses – which are far more important in resolving the questions posed by the stories in which they find themselves. What starts them onto their paths of self-discovery and potential romance, however, is not their own desire for adventure or their quests to find true love, but is instead their devotion to their fathers and their initial over-identification with themselves as being good daughters.

The good daughters – Belle, Mulan and Jane

The good daughter is, quite simply, a good daughter. A traditional motif and archetype within fairy tales the world over, the good daughter is (usually) a young woman who, out of loyalty to her good but naïve father, finds herself in a potentially threatening situation and must use all her personal resources to survive, an exercise which usually ends in personal triumph for the heroine. For Clarissa Pinkola Estés, tales of this nature hold a powerful archetypal significance as teaching tales for women: "So many tales – 'Beauty and the Beast', 'Bluebeard', 'Reynard the Fox' – begin with the father endangering the daughter. But in a woman's psyche, even though the father bumbles into a lethal deal because he knows nothing of the dark side of the world or the unconscious, the horrible moment marks a dramatic beginning for her; a forthcoming consciousness and shrewdness."[312] Estés, a psychologist and folklorist, uses the themes and symbolism in fairy tales and folk tales as healing tools for her patients. As she describes the implementation of story-telling as a tool for use in psychological healing, "What can be derived from those deep templates echoes the innate patterns of women's most integral psychological processes. In this sense, fairy tales and mythos are initiators; they are the wise ones who teach those who come after".[313] In other words, stories which contain the archetype of the good daughter are a very old and traditional element in fairy tales which continue to resonate in Western culture as important tales with which audiences can easily identify and from which they can benefit.

There are three Disney animated films of this period which portray the theme of the good daughter – *Beauty and the Beast* (one which Estés cites as a typical example of this type of tale), *Mulan*, and *Tarzan*. All three films feature heroines who, out of love and loyalty to their fathers, willingly put themselves in harm's way. In *Beauty and the Beast* and *Mulan* this is particularly true: Belle knowingly trades her own freedom to the Beast for her father's freedom, and Mulan disguises herself as a boy and runs away in the night in order to stop her elderly father from having to fight in a war by taking his place as a soldier. Although Jane (in *Tarzan*) does not follow quite this same pattern, she is nonetheless an unusually devoted daughter, following her father into the jungles to serve as his research assistant and clearly demonstrating that she is very much her father's care-taker and the practical member of the group.

Where there are differences in the characters of these three young women, they are usually more to do with the set of

312 Clarissa Pinkola Estés, *Women Who Run With the Wolves: Myths and Stories of the Wild Woman Archetype* (London: Rider, 1998), p. 396.

313 Estés, *Women Who Run With the Wolves*, p. 263.

circumstances in which each must function, and particular aspects of their personalities are brought to the fore as befits their stories. They all have in common certain traits: none fits in with the society surrounding her; none is initially interested in finding romantic love; none is initially interested in pursuing any particular goal; all, in some way, take care of their fathers and support their fathers' goals rather than having goals of their own; each, in her quest to serve her father's best interests, ends up both saving her father's life and finding a life of her own.

The first example of a good daughter is Belle, the heroine of *Beauty and the Beast*. From the start, Belle is described as a scholar and a bookworm, and is described by the people of her village as being strange and not fitting in because she is more inclined toward intellectual pursuits. In fact, as the townspeople describe it in the song which opens the film, Belle's looks are more valued by them than her intellect, and it is because of her intelligence that she does not fit in with the others in the town. The townspeople first sing in description of her that:

> Now it's no wonder that her name means beauty
> Her looks have got no parallel
> But behind that fair façade,
> I'm afraid she's rather odd
> Very different from the rest of us is Belle.

Later in the song, they lament that such a beautiful girl does not mix well with them:

> Look there she goes that girl is strange but special
> A most peculiar mademoiselle
> It's a pity and a sin
> She doesn't quite fit in
> For she really is a bonny girl
> A Beauty but a funny girl
> She really is a funny girl, that Belle!

The only person in the village who does not consider her strange is her father, Maurice, an eccentric inventor who is himself thought of by the townspeople as being slightly insane. Although they are quickly shown to be close and loving, her father, however, shows that he, too, shares the misconception of the others that it is upon someone's looks that they can be judged, replying to Belle's comment that she has no one in the village with whom she can talk, "What about that Gaston? He's a handsome fellow", even though Gaston is boorish, self-centred, sexist, and egotistical, as

Belle is obviously well aware. Indeed, throughout the film, the personality traits which are emphasised most about Belle are her intelligence, her ability to judge character, and her curiosity and intellectualism. Indeed, of all the characters in the film, it would seem that Belle is the only one whose beautiful looks reflect a beautiful soul. Yet even Belle changes over the course of the film, and grows from being an extension of her father to being a fully-formed individual in her own right.

From the start of the film, Belle is characterised as being of an intellectual bent, yet this portrayal is not wholly born out by the film. First of all, the main proof that is given as to Belle's identification with intellectualism is that she is an avid reader. She always has a book in her hand, is often shown reading while she walks, and is shown in the book shop (where the owner is kind enough to let her borrow rather than buy books), looking for something new to read although she has read every book in the shop, some more than once. What seems to be overlooked, however, is that the only book Belle is ever shown reading – the book which she herself describes as being her favourite – is what seems to be a romantic fairy story. Otherwise, her portrayal as an intellectual is supported by the fact that she feels stifled in her life, describing her home as being "this poor provincial town" and her experience of life there as always being the same. Furthermore, the provincial nature of the town is emphasised when its "leading citizen", Gaston, says to Belle that "It's not right for a woman to read! Soon she starts getting ideas, and thinking … ". The provincialism of the inhabitants is also emphasised by the fact that other young women of the town are totally in love with Gaston and chorus, "What's wrong with her!" "She's crazy!" "He's gorgeous!" when they see Belle reject Gaston's insulting, patronising, egotistical advances. Just before Belle embarks on her adventure, which begins with her attempt to rescue her father, she describes her boredom with her current situation in these terms:

> I want adventure in the great wide somewhere
> I want it more than I can tell
> And for once it might be grand
> To have someone understand
> I want so much more than they've got planned!

It is at this point in the film that Belle's horse, which her father had been riding on business, arrives back at their home, riderless. Belle quickly prepares herself to leave, and the horse takes her to the Beast's castle, where her father is being held prisoner. When she first meets the Beast, she is horrified both by his hideous appearance and by the fact that he is refusing to free her father. It is at this point that Belle earns her title of "good daughter": when the Beast will not free her father, Belle asks that she be allowed to take her father's place as the Beast's prisoner. Of course, as soon as he is freed, Belle's father works non-stop to free Belle, but never succeeds in doing this. Instead, the Beast eventually frees Belle because they learn that her father is lost and sick, and the first thing Belle does with her freedom is to immediately find and rescue her father once more. Her loyalty to her father is even turned against her by Gaston, who creates a plan to force Belle to marry him in order to save her father from being committed to an asylum. Ironically, it is thanks to her first sacrifice for her father – allowing herself to be held prisoner by the Beast – that Belle is able to save her father a second time, by proving that Maurice's story about a beast in a castle is true. It is also by the chain of events she inadvertently sets in motion by revealing the Beast's existence that her story is brought full-circle: when she saves the Beast from Gaston's attack on him, she realises that she is in love with the Beast and says so, thus freeing the Beast and his household from the spell and returning them all to human form. In each and every instance in the film, Belle is trying to help or take care of someone, considering her own needs to be secondary to those of her father and the Beast.

It is at the end, when she thinks first of herself – praying for the Beast not to die because she loves him – that Belle's good works are able to set the world to rights. This idea, however, is somewhat underplayed in the film. Her one "selfish" act – to think of her own sorrow if the Beast died rather than thinking about the impact of his death on his servants and the tragedy of his losing his life – is rewarded by the Beast's transformation from beast to human and his being returned to life. However, when she utters her prayer, "Please don't leave me! I love you!" she does so in a whisper, and is only heard by the audience (and the force which can break the spell). The transformation of the Beast, which immediately follows her prayer, is done so dramatically as to overshadow the event which caused it, and the fact that Belle said what

193

she said is not referred to again. The Beast/prince does not explain to Belle what transformed him back into a human (this is explained, as voice-over narration, at the start of the film), and so (presumably) not only does she not learn that it was she who brought about the Beast's transformation, it is also not even emphasised for the audience.

This film's portrayal of Belle effectively shows that the woman who is selfless, giving, and uses her wisdom only to support others is the good woman deserving a reward, rather than showing that it is okay for women to think first of themselves and secondly of others, at least sometimes. Of the characters in the film, Belle, in her constant selflessness and care-taking, has more in common with the Beast's servants than she does with the other major characters of the film. Belle's father, an inventor, puts his work first and allows Belle to take care of him and assist him rather than recognising that, as her father, it is his duty to put her first. Gaston, the town "macho man" who seeks to marry Belle because "No one else in town but she/is as beautiful as me", always acts in his own interest, and it is not his selfishness, but his vanity, which is ridiculed by the film and which brings about his downfall. Even the Beast thinks of his own wants and needs first and thinks of others last: it was this attitude which caused him to be cursed in the first place. Although, in the end, he does learn to love Belle and place her needs ahead of his own (which he shows when he releases Belle so that she can rescue her father), however, it is not this which transforms him. Rather, it is Belle's learning to love him, in spite of his appearance and her initial impressions of him, which finally returns him to human form. In other words, the film's final message seems to be that an unselfish act by a man improves nothing, but an unselfish act by a woman can transform the world. As the film closes, with Belle dancing in the arms of the prince, the film tries hard to make sure that we are left in no doubt that Belle's selflessness is what brought about this happy ending.

However, by the time *Mulan* was released in 1998, seven years after *Beauty and the Beast*, a number of changes had occurred in the studio's characterisations of women. Stronger, tougher women had begun to appear, both within Disney films and in the larger arena of Hollywood cinema, as more women began to move into such key movie-making roles as producer and director. Certainly, at Disney, women's names have begun to appear next to various production credits, although thus far no women have directed one of Disney's animated films. Elsewhere in Hollywood, however, the influence of women writers, directors, producers, and actors, amongst others, over the kinds of female characters being portrayed on-screen, had begun to make some definite changes in the over-all image of women as depicted by Hollywood. It is interesting to note that *Beauty and the Beast* was released in the same year as *Thelma and Louise* (1991), and that the two films were both nominees for Academy Awards during the same year.

While there are those commentators, feminist film historians, and members of the industry itself who have (rightly) pointed out that Hollywood cinema has a long way to go in terms of the types/roles of women it portrays,[314] nonetheless there are numerous examples of positive portrayals not only of female strength and independence, but also of female friendships, relationships, and opportunities. Films such as *Fried Green Tomatoes* (1991), *What's Love Got to Do With It* (1993), *The First Wives Club* (1996), *Practical Magic* (1998), and *There's Something About Mary* (1998) are all examples of films made during the 1990s which contain characters who are trying to carve out lives for themselves in which, although may not live (either through choice or through circumstances) "normal" lives, nonetheless they have found ways in which they can be themselves.

Enter *Mulan*, which was released in 1998. *Mulan* is about a young girl in (what appears to be) medieval China who, from her first scene until well into the second half of the film, is shown studying and memorising the rules by which she is expected to live. The only child of her parents (at least in the film version), she is shown in her first few scenes preparing to meet the local match-maker, and is worried that she will not be able to fulfil her role as a bride properly. The girl we are shown initially is a good, honest, forthright, intelligent, lively person with a kind heart and a strong sense of justice. Yet, in Mulan's world, none of these qualities are shown as having much value, especially in a woman. "Quiet, and demure, graceful, and polite, delicate, refined, poised – punctual!" These are (supposedly) the qualities which a "proper" young woman should possess and which Mulan is trying to memorise, writing them on her arm so that she will remember. Her very writing down of these qualities, not to

314 Yvonne Tasker discusses these issues at length in her book *Working Girls: Gender and Sexuality in Popular Cinema* (London: Routledge, 1998). Tasker, in her introduction, quotes Whoopi Goldberg's comments on the roles on offer to women, made while hosting the 1996 Academy Award ceremony. Karen Hollinger, in *In The Company of Women: Contemporary Female Friendship Films* (Minneapolis: University of Minnesota Press, 1998), also looks at the anti-feminist themes found in many films of the 1990s.

mention her behaviour in the rest of the scene, show that she has none of them, and yet the girl we are presented with is an entirely likeable one.

The day we first see Mulan is the day she is to be presented to the match-maker, and a great deal of time and attention in the first phase of the film is devoted to her experience of preparing for, going to, and returning from her interview with the match-maker, all of which is an unqualified disaster. Try though she might, everything that is expected of Mulan as a good daughter and potential bride is at odds with who Mulan is. Much emphasis is placed on just how much artifice is involved in being the "perfect bride", and the scene in which Mulan is dressed, made-up, and sent off to join the other future brides is an interesting one. She is shown working hard to copy the behaviour the other four brides are exhibiting, but she is slightly behind, out of step, and not nearly as good at being a "proper woman" as they. She is enthusiastic and tries hard, yet it is these very qualities which, ironically, make her fulfilment of this role so impossible. During her interview with the match-maker, she is told to recite "The final admonition", which she does by sneaking quick looks at the notes she has written on her arm. This "final admonition", which Mulan finds so difficult to live by as well as to recite, is "Fulfil your duties calmly and respectfully. Reflect before you act. This shall bring you honour and glory." Yet, as her interview goes completely haywire (ending with her accidentally setting fire to the match-maker's backside and being screamed at by the match-maker that "You may look like a bride, but you will never bring your family honour!"), Mulan goes home with her mother and grandmother, feeling disgraced. It is at this point that Mulan sings a song which tells the audience the film's theme:

> Look at me
> I will never pass for a perfect bride or a perfect daughter.
> Can it be I'm not meant to play this part?
> Now I see that if I were truly to be myself,
> I would break my family's heart.
> Who is that girl I see staring straight back at me?
> Why is my reflection someone I don't know?
> Somehow I cannot hide who I am though I've tried.
> When will my reflection show who I am inside?

As it turns out, the moment which Mulan wishes for in the

song – that her reflection be an accurate one – will not come until the final fifteen minutes of the film. It is as this earlier scene is ending, however, that news reaches Mulan's village that the Hun have invaded China and that her father has been called up to fight. Because her father is elderly and crippled – and because there is no one else to go to fight in his place – Mulan decides, rather than see her father go to what will certainly be his death, that she will disguise herself as a boy and take his place in the army.

The majority of the film is concerned with Mulan's experiences in the army (where she claims to be her father's son and calls herself Ping), during which she has to learn not only how to act like a man, but how to fight like a soldier (assisted, as part of the film's comic relief, by a dragon spirit voiced by Eddie Murphy). Her initial attempts at both these roles are so poor as to be comical, but eventually, having been told she can go home, Mulan becomes so determined to succeed that she very quickly begins to prove herself, both as a man and as a soldier. In particular during the scene in which her regiment fights the Hun, Mulan/Ping fights so bravely – and so intelligently – that she single-handedly wins the battle and saves her regiment from almost certain annihilation. In the process, however, she is badly wounded, and it is when the doctor is tending to her wound that her true sex is discovered. The penalty for a woman impersonating a man, as we learned early on in the film, is death, but because Mulan saved the life of Shang, her commanding officer, he decides not to execute her for impersonating a man, and instead leaves her behind, expecting her to return home once the army has moved on.

It is at this point in the film that Mulan is finally able to be successful as herself, and not as Ping. She is sitting alone and dejected when she sees that the Hun army, which had been assumed to be dead, has in fact survived the battle and are about to reach the Imperial city and attack the Emperor. Realising that her regiment is unaware of the danger, Mulan quickly rides to the Imperial city to catch up with them and warn them. However, now that she is a woman again, and furthermore because she had lied to them about who she was, no one will believe her warnings until it is too late and the Hun have managed to capture the Emperor. Mulan, however, leads several of her regiment, including Shang, in a daring and successful rescue, only this time she is dressed

197

as herself, and all those with her but Shang are dressed as women. In the end, the Emperor rewards Mulan with a sword, a crest, and an offer of a position in his cabinet, but Mulan refuses, saying that it is time for her to go home. In a dramatic moment, the Emperor, as part of his thanks to her, bows, and all of the thousands around the palace kow-tow to her. Mulan returns home to give her father the sword and the crest that the Emperor gave her, but he drops them on the ground, hugging Mulan tightly and telling her that "The greatest gift and honour is having you for a daughter". According to the film, it was Mulan's allowing her true character to shine through – once she had the courage to be herself – which made it possible for her to be truly happy. Though, unusually for a Disney film, *Mulan* is largely with-out romance, it becomes clear that Mulan is attracted to Shang but, as Ping, of course, cannot tell him this. As Mulan, however, is fighting (as a woman) alongside Shang to protect the Emperor, the idea that Shang is both impressed with – and attracted to – Mulan begins to become apparent. In the final scene of the film, back at Mulan's home, Shang comes to find her, on the pretext of returning her helmet, and the implication is that Mulan and Shang will be married at some point in the future. The implication is also that their rela-tionship will be very untraditional, but will also be a very happy one possessing mutual respect and understanding.

Ironically, this probable marriage to Shang, a celebrated war hero from a powerful and influential family, will also mean that Mulan will "strike a catch" which will be guaranteed to bring her family honour, and which will bring Mulan hon-our through her fulfilment as "a perfect bride" and "a perfect daughter", at least in the eyes of her society. The fact that this marriage will be of Mulan's choice and on her own terms, however, is important to the theme of the film. Mulan was not happy as "just" Mulan, the tomboy who could not act like a woman, nor was she happy as Ping, the soldier living in constant fear of discovery by his/her fellow soldiers. As Mulan the soldier, however, the combination of both roles in which Mulan could act out both sides of herself, Mulan finally achieves true success. Although in her song Mulan sang that "Now I see that if I were truly to be myself/I would break my family's heart" and "Somehow I cannot hide who I am though I've tried", the film's end shows that such sentiments are completely incorrect, and that it is by truly being herself that Mulan is able to win both honour and love.

Mulan is a special case as a Disney film for the issues it considers and, more importantly, the way, it chooses to examine these issues. Yet its predominant issues – self-identity and the notion of gender as performance – are a part of a small but significant Hollywood cinematic tradition in which women who dress as men find for themselves advancement, success, and the fulfilment of their dreams. Yvonne Tasker, in her book *Working Girls: Gender and Sexuality in Popular Cinema*, discusses the theme of female transvestism at some length, citing such films as *Victor/Victoria* (1982), *Yentl* (1983), and *The Ballad of Little Jo* (1993) as leading films in this off-beat sub-genre of the "coming of age" film. According to Tasker, there are two basic kinds of female cross-dressers: cross-gender and cross-class. As an example of class cross-dressing, Tasker points to *Working Girl* (1988), which stars Melanie Griffith as a lower-class secretary who, during her boss' absence, masquerades as a middle-class, middle-management yuppie, and is able to transform herself from lower- to middle-class by dressing in middle-class fashion. Cross-class dressing is similar in intention to cross-gender dressing, according to Tasker, because both are about social advancement: men have more power than women, and middle/upper-class women have more power than lower-class women. As Lauren Bacall, Marilyn Monroe, and Betty Grable attempted to show in *How to Marry a Millionaire* (1953), the idea seems to be that in order to become a member of a higher class, you have to at least look, if not live, the part.

In cross-gender dressing, however, the issues involved tend to be different. In films in which women dress and live as men, there is almost always a sense of desperation behind their transformation: their existence is threatened (as in *Victor/Victoria* and *The Ballad of Little Jo*), or their personalities do not allow them to function successfully as women within the strictures of their society (as in *Yentl* and *Mulan*). As men, such women are able to obtain a success and freedom which eluded them as young women within the societies in which they function. As Tasker writes, "If anarchic men dress as women to learn about self-control whilst enjoying the evident pleasures of transformation, narratives and images of women cross-dressing relate to opportunity and

199

achievement in different, though related ways. Both gendered and class cross-dressing is explicitly presented as allowing female protagonists an opportunity and a *freedom* (of
both physical movement and behaviour) that they would
not otherwise achieve."[315] Mulan's success – defeating the
Hun army and saving China from invasion, would seem to
support Tasker's later statement that "in the cinema, viewers
are offered an explanation of female-to-male cross-dressing
that can be understood as seeking to naturalise the transition, cast in terms of the desire for the privileges and freedom available to men. At the basic level of plot, the cinema
offers us women who achieve freedom and/or success as
male or masculine personas, their achievements typically
presented as unique."[316] After all, a single-handed defeat of
an entire army is a fairly rare achievement for anyone – male,
female, or transvestite. Yet *Mulan* goes beyond this basic
assumption – which is a more hardened twist on the idea of
"if you can't beat 'em, join 'em" – by having Mulan achieve
her greatest success not as Ping, but as a Mulan who has been
transformed by her experiences as Ping. When, as Ping, she
achieves the defeat of the Hun army by causing an avalanche
to fall on them and bury them, it would seem that she has
achieved an ultimate victory. This is short-lived, however,
when the key members of the Hun army manage to claw
their way out of the snow and launch a briefly successful
attempt to capture the Chinese emperor. Her final defeat of
the Hun comes only when Mulan is truly herself and relies
upon her own ways to defeat them.

In the first scene Mulan is in, she demonstrates her natural
– albeit unorthodox – talent for problem-solving, such as
tricking her rather unintelligent dog into chasing a bone tied
to a rod on his collar, tying a sack of seed to his tale, and then
sending him running all over the farm, thereby scattering
the seed for the chickens and giving Mulan extra free time
to memorise what she needs to say to the match-maker. Her
problem-solving is funny and successful, but simultaneously chaotic, causing momentary havoc on the farm. But,
while living as Ping, Mulan acquires the discipline and
tactical training necessary in a soldier, and is able, by aiming
a single rocket at a huge snowdrift just behind and above the
attacking Hun army, to set off the avalanche which seems
to defeat them. Mulan's success, though more substantial
this time, falls apart when the wound she suffers during the

315 Tasker, *Working
Girls*, p. 35.

316 Tasker, *Working
Girls*, p. 37.

battle brings about her discovery. It is when she is once more Mulan, but is openly using the training she received as Ping and combining the "masculine" traits of a soldier with female postures, dress, and accessories, that Mulan achieves her greatest and most lasting success. In a comical but still telling part of this final battle scene, Mulan persuades her fellow soldiers to dress as women so that all of them can – and do – walk right into the palace (under the gaze of the Hun guards) because, as women, they are not assumed to be a threat. They then pull out the fruits they are using as false breasts and use them to stun the guards before defeating them in hand-to-hand combat. Later, when the Hun leader is about to kill Shang in revenge, saying "You took away my victory", Mulan, standing nearby, says "No, I did", and pulls back her hair into the way she wore it as Ping. In that instant, she has the body and dress of a woman but the head of a man, and it is in this instant that the tide turns for her, allowing her to achieve her victory moments later when, in a wonderful combination of her masculine and feminine skills, Mulan uses a folding paper fan to grab – and take – a sword away from the Hun leader, using the sword to pin him to the roof of the palace in time for him to be hit and blown up by a rocket.

In the end, however, Mulan willingly gives up all the power she has gained, rejecting the offer of a seat on the Emperor's council, and returns home, where her first act is to bow to her father and present him with the sword and crest, saying that they are "gifts to honour the Fa family". It is also implied, shortly thereafter, that Mulan and Shang will be married, which means that Mulan will, in the end, follow the traditionally prescribed right of passage for a woman of her society, moving from her father's house to her husband's. The assumption is that, now that she is able to be herself, at least within the private sphere, she will be happier. Yet, as was shown in the initial scenes where Mulan was shown as a likeable but unruly tomboy, she was always able to be herself within her parents' house, and that, although they worried about her ability to fit in with society, they nonetheless loved her and put up no barriers to her freedom. Nothing has changed about Mulan – or her parents' views of her – during her absence or as a result of her achievements, mainly thanks to the fact that they always allowed her to be herself. The only change is her having (probably) found a man to be her husband who would be equally tolerant of her ways. In other words, the successful blending of her masculine and feminine sides, while a personal achievement for Mulan, has not necessarily changed anything for her in the world in which she lives.

Nonetheless, this idea of finding oneself – and of combining both sides of oneself (at least within the limited sphere of the family) – is to be found in the studio's (and this book's) next feature, *Tarzan*. While the main emphasis of the film is on Tarzan and his eventually successful combination of both the human/tame and the ape/wild sides of his nature, an element of this is also to be found in the characterisation of Jane. When we first meet Jane, which happens a little over thirty minutes into the film, she comes confidently onto the scene, and seems to be the sensible member of her family. Her father, Professor Porter, is portrayed as good, loving, and kindly, but also as a little silly and not terribly in touch with the world (he is immediately characterised as a rather eccentric academic). Jane, his only child, has apparently spent her life devoted to her father's work, and not only looks after him as a devoted daughter but also as his research assistant. Once introduced into the film, Jane is shown to have a bright, agile, and curious mind, but is also very much a prim and proper Edwardian[317] lady, striding through the jungle in a yellow bustled dress, with a corseted waist, safari hat, parasol and white gloves, carrying a sketch book. Her mannerisms, speech patterns, and demeanour are a stark contrast to Tarzan, whom she meets when he saves her from a group of angry baboons. Tarzan is fascinated by her since she is not only the first woman, but also the first human, he remembers seeing. Jane, too, is fascinated by Tarzan, owing to his wild appearance, his ability to communicate with animals, and his fascination with her (which, she rightly assumes, is because he has never seen other humans before). She is also rather frightened of him, however, because he is so strange and wild; her first (nervous) words, once she is safe from the baboons, are "I'm in a tree with a man who talks to monkeys!" As she tries, rather ungracefully, to edge out of the tree and away from him, and throughout the initial moments of her first encounter with him, she is plainly terrified. Once she sees that he will not harm her, and that he is not mute (even though he does not understand her language), her timidity is slowly overcome by her

317 Apart from her style of dress, we can deduce that the film is set around 1910 because, while looking through a telescope, Jane, Professor Porter, and Tarzan see what is most likely Haley's comet.

fascination for this "big, wild, quiet, silent, person-thing". In her description of their meeting to her father, she excitedly tells him of her encounter with Tarzan, and later, while drawing a picture of him for her father, begins to display an obvious attraction for Tarzan (albeit one which she herself cannot see), as she says, "He seemed confused at first, as if he's never seen another human being before. His eyes were intense, focused – I've never seen such eyes."

As the story progresses, and as Tarzan and Jane get to know each other better, a simultaneous change occurs in them: as he becomes more "civilised", she becomes less so. A major clue to this comes from Jane's dress, as dress in general is used in the film as a symbol of civilisation. As already noted, our first glimpse of Jane is as a very properly-dressed lady. When the baboons attack her, and as she is rescued by Tarzan, Jane loses one of her boots, her hat, her parasol, and one of her gloves, as well as having her hair loosened. Tarzan, as he is in the process of realising that Jane is the same kind of animal he is, examines her hand, before removing her remaining glove and holding his palm to hers, comparing their hands. In the next scene with Jane, she is dressed much more simply than previously, her hair only pulled back at the sides, her clothes only a simple skirt and blouse. Eventually, she wears only a skirt and camisole. When Jane is in the jungle with Tarzan, her hair is completely loose. When she is in the camp, her hair is pulled back at the sides. When she is preparing to leave for England, she returns to the yellow dress we saw her in initially, but when she decides to stay, and in the final shots of the film we see her, her father, and Tarzan swinging through the trees, she is dressed only in what could best be described as a leather mini-skirt and bra combo, reminiscent of Maureen O'Sullivan's famous costume (when she was wearing one) in *Tarzan and His Mate* (1934). Likewise, when Tarzan decides to go to England with them, he is seen wearing a suit of his father's which he has found in what remains of the hut his parents built when they became stranded. On the ship, realising that they have been tricked by their guide, Clayton, and imprisoned, Tarzan, now only partially dressed in the suit, hurls himself about frantically trying to escape. Once the group has been freed (by Tarzan's best friends, Tantor the elephant and Terk the gorilla) and Tarzan races through the jungle to stop the hunters from attacking his gorilla family, he sheds the rest of his human clothes en route. Once he is back with his family, he is again wearing only the loin cloth he has worn throughout the film.

Of course, there is one other human woman shown in *Tarzan* – Tarzan's mother. She and his father are in the opening shots of the film, along with the infant Tarzan. He is cradled in her arms as she and Tarzan's father escape in a lifeboat from their burning, sinking ship, land upon a strange shore, and build themselves a home in a giant tree in the jungle. She is portrayed as a delicate, beautiful young woman, but a strong, determined one as well, who works alongside her husband in the difficult work of saving their lives from the shipwreck and building a home. The shots that follow are of Tarzan's future ape-mother, Kala, who loses her baby to an attacking leopard. The film then follows her as she hears a baby's cries and follows the sound to the house Tarzan's parents have built, where we get our next shots of Tarzan's mother: one, in a framed photograph of the young family, and the other, lying dead with her husband in a corner of the hut, obviously the victims of the same leopard that killed Kala's baby. Yet, unlike Kala, Tarzan's mother has managed to save her baby, at the cost of her own life, having buried him in his cot under a pile of curtains, suitcases, and other things to keep him safe from the leopard. Kala adopts the infant, first having to fight off the leopard, this time successfully, and then rejoins her troupe.

As for Jane, her transformation in the film is subtle but significant. She starts out as an over-dressed, rather nervous young woman who runs after her father, taking care of him and helping him in his work while, most of the time, her father is so oblivious to the world around him, he is not even aware that they have been in danger until she tells him what has happened later on. Tarzan's influence on her, however, awakens her to the world outside of the proper, civilised existence she has known up to that point, awakening her to sights, sounds, and experiences she never dreamed possible and which she thoroughly loves. In the end, as she and her father are about to set sail for England and leave Tarzan behind, at the last minute, she changes her mind, swims back to shore, and throws herself into Tarzan's arms, shortly before announcing – in the few words of gorilla language which Tarzan taught her earlier – that she is staying with Tarzan. Although she remains largely herself, she has become freer to express and be herself than she was at the beginning of the film. Furthermore, she is noticeably calmer, as is demonstrated by her speech. At the start of the film, she talks a great deal and at a very fast pace. By the end of the film, she speaks in a much slower, more relaxed style, and has even begun learning to communicate without speaking. But, although at the film's end she is shown living a happy, care-free existence with Tarzan, his ape family, and her father, she is nonetheless, as we are reminded in the final fifteen seconds of the film, there as Tarzan's mate, and is living in a world which, no matter how much she loves it, is still largely alien to her, making her dependent on Tarzan's protection and guidance.

Tarzan is, of course, more about Tarzan than it is about Jane, but the film's moral "message", at least as implied by Disney's own description of the film, is that *Tarzan* is not just an adventure story. It also gives its audience "important reminders about acceptance and family!"[318] However, Jane, as a character in the film, is given a great deal of emphasis by the story, and portrayed in such a way that she can be identified with easily. So it is interesting that, at the end of the 1990s, a film is made in which a major female character gives up her home, the life she has known before, and even all but two other members of her own species in order to be with a man. Though it fits in with much of the cinematic traditions surrounding the Tarzan story, this does differ widely both from the book and the 1984 film *Greystoke: The Legend of Tarzan, Lord of the Apes*, which has Glenn Close's voice in common with the Disney version.[319] In both of these, Jane does not go to stay with Tarzan, but remains in England. Although it would not have been a happy ending for the film, it would not have been without precedent at the Disney Studio. After all, Pocahontas stayed behind while John Smith returned to England, thus ending their romance. So, Jane's rejection of her old life as the only way to be with her man provides something of an old-fashioned element for the film's end. However, at the same time, when Jane decides to stay with Tarzan, although she does so with her father's blessing, she is initially rejecting her father, and for the first time in the film stepping out of her role of the dutiful daughter. It is only after she swims ashore and announces to Tarzan and the gorillas that she is staying that her father decides to stay too.

318 From the description of the film on the cover of the February 2000 edition of the US video release. ©Buena Vista Home Entertainment.

319 Close provides the voice for Kala in the Disney version. In 1984, her voice was dubbed over Andie MacDowell's since MacDowell's Southern accent was deemed inappropriate, a fact with which many fans of *Greystoke* would be acquainted. *Leonard Maltin's 2000 Movie and Video Guide* (New York: Signet, 1999), p. 556.

Although the "good daughter" is a traditional folk/fairy tale theme, its appearance in the Disney cannon is fairly recent. As ideas such as political correctness and the mainstreaming of feminism have made it increasingly difficult for film studios (amongst other purveyors of mass culture) to show women giving up anything for marriage, old elements of male authority have been resurrected as a way around this recent taboo. While it may no longer be acceptable to a large segment of the American public to feature stories of women putting their needs as secondary to the needs of their husbands, the notion that a woman is willingly sublimating her needs to those of a kindly, loving father is slightly more acceptable. When, like Belle, Mulan, and Jane, she finally trades in the role of the good daughter for that of the good wife, the move is not portrayed as the lateral move which it in fact is (since the character is only trading one male authority figure for another), but as a liberation for the young woman, and a chance to finally "be herself". Belle has moved from life on the edge of her boring, provincial village to a castle where she has a library filled with books and a charming, intelligent, loving man to talk with and read to. Mulan has given up the life of a soldier, it is implied, to become the wife of a soldier whose skills are similar to her own, and who both understands and respects her. Jane, no longer burdened with stiff collars and uncomfortable clothes and living as her father's care-taker and research assistant, is shown as free to live life swinging from the trees wearing next to nothing and being adored by a wild man. Yet the fact remains that, in all three cases, the woman has moved (or will do someday, as is implied with Mulan) from life in her father's care to life in the care of her husband. However, each one's overall quality of life has improved, and through the more equal partnership they have established with a man, the situations they are moving into will be an improvement over the more subordinate one they had with their fathers.

The 'tough gals' – Esmeralda, Meg, Audrey and Captain Amelia

Of all of the Disney women and girls, there are four whose portrayals are starkly different from those of their "sister" characters at Disney. They are Esmeralda from *The Hunchback of Notre Dame,* Megara (Meg) from *Hercules,* Audrey from *Atlantis*, and Captain Amelia from *Treasure Planet*. From their first moments on screen until the very end of each's film, these characters exhibit a kind of strength, brashness, and confidence not to be found elsewhere amongst most of Disney's animated heroines. Although their portrayals have strong links with the character of Slue-foot Sue from "The Legend of Pecos Bill" segment of *Melody Time* (1948), these more modern characters surpass Slue-foot Sue in that they each have a voice and can match their gutsy personas with strong words. Although each has to overcome a number of disadvantages, and though three of the four have found true love at the ends of their films, nonetheless these characters are feisty, no-nonsense women who leave audiences in no doubt that, far from needing (or even wanting) a man, these are women who can – and do – take care of themselves.

The first shots we see of Esmeralda are of her pan-handling, dancing on the street for money. Esmeralda is a gypsy living in medieval Paris, and, though the laws of Paris make it difficult for the gypsies to survive, Esmeralda is nonetheless making a living for herself and her goat, and although her life is hard, she is happy, finding sources of freedom despite the oppression surrounding her. She makes this sense of independence and self-reliance clear when, having claimed sanctuary in Notre Dame cathedral from Frollo, the evil Minister of Justice, she sings a song of prayer to God, asking not for help for herself but to help those who are worse off than she. As the song puts it:

> I ask for nothing – I can get by,
> But I know so many less lucky than I.
> Please help my people   the poor and down-trod,
> I thought we all were the children of God.

Throughout the film, Esmeralda is notable for the strong sense of justice and highly moral stance she takes, and is frequently contrasted with Frollo, a sanctimonious, self-righteous man full of corruption who sees evil everywhere he looks. In an interesting twist for a Disney film, the evil villain who seeks to destroy the heroine is a man, and, also interestingly, he expresses the attitude that a strong sexuality such as Esmeralda possesses is a sign of her evil nature as well as proof (in his eyes) of her being a witch. This attitude towards sexuality is easily detected in early Disney films which show the villainesses as sexually mature, self-

207

possessed, and malevolent, while the heroine is young, naïve, and innocent. In *The Hunchback of Notre Dame*, however, Esmeralda's self-confidence – which includes confidence in her beauty and sex-appeal – are also proof of her goodness and strength, whereas Frollo's characterisation of her and her sexual confidence as evil is proof that he projects this evil onto her from his own twisted desires.

Eventually, Esmeralda finds an ally in Febus, the captain of the guard who is supposed to be in charge of Frollo's men but eventually rebels against him because of his cruelty. Together, as Esmeralda and Febus move from fighting against one another to fighting on the same side, they also realise that the attraction they feel for one another – present from their first encounter – is, in fact, love. In the book, Esmeralda dies at Frollo's hands, but in the film it is she who helps to defeat him. At the film's end, she emerges from the cathedral, hand-in-hand with Febus, to the triumphant cheers of the people of Paris. She and Febus are portrayed as being very much in love with each other and having a great deal of respect and admiration for one another. They are shown throughout the film as being equals in strength, sense of humour, and sense of justice and Right, yet it is Esmeralda who – repeatedly – saves Febus' life, and it is she who helps him to see that Frollo is not just corrupt, but evil. Far from being her protector or her mentor, Febus is shown as owing Esmeralda both his life and his having found his true path.

Likewise, it is Meg – the heroine of *Hercules* – who helps the hero find out who he is meant to be and where he most belongs. As the film is largely Hercules' story, Meg does not appear until a third of the way into the film. Yet her role from that point on is a pivotal one for Hercules, who quickly falls in love with her and spends much of the film winning her heart through his wholesomeness, honour, and honesty, qualities which – as we learn shortly after she is introduced – life has taught Meg not to look for in men. Meg states her ideas about men early on: "You know how men are – they think 'no' means 'yes' and 'get lost' means 'take me, I'm yours!'" Meg is portrayed as a wounded, cynical young woman who was hurt when she traded her soul to Hades to save her lover's life only to be abandoned by her lover for another woman. Her hurt and anger towards men runs so deeply that, in a quip to Hades (who now controls her and forces her to do his bidding) she responds to his order that she "handle" ("take care of") Hercules, "Hey, I've sworn off man-handling".[320] When we first see Meg, she is in the clutches of a menacing river guardian. Hercules, on his way to Thebes to try and become a hero, thinks that Meg is in danger and insists on trying to save her, despite her order to "Keep movin', Junior". When he asks her "Aren't you a damsel in distress?" her reply, said with a combination of authority and sarcasm, is typical of Meg: "I'm a damsel. I'm in distress. I can handle this. Have a nice day!" Hercules, however, insists that Meg has to be saved and, with some trouble (mainly owing to his lack of practical experience) defeats the river guardian, much to Meg's annoyance. As we learn later, Meg has been ordered by Hades to get the river guardian to assist him in his plans to conquer the universe, and Hercules' "rescue" has interfered with her assignment.

Like Esmeralda, Meg is street-wise and tough. Unlike Esmeralda, Meg is bitter and hurt. Over the course of the film, while under orders to stop him, Meg finds herself first liking Hercules (once she sees that his manner is not some "innocent farm-boy routine" but is in fact his true personality), then – much against her will – falling in love with him. Eventually, she refuses to help Hades in his attempts to defeat Hercules, and saves Hercules' life at the cost of her own, thus inadvertently freeing herself from Hades' service. Hercules, in turn, rescues Meg from the River Styx and brings her back to life, an act so brave and selfless that it restores Hercules to the status of god (which, in the film, is what he was when he was born). Because of his love for Meg, however, and her love for him, Hercules is allowed by Zeus to remain a mortal so that he can marry Meg and stay with her, since he has come to realise that it is at her side that he belongs. Meg, in turn, has lost her bitterness and been restored to the kind, selfless, trusting nature which led her to give herself up for a lover's life in the first place, and she becomes a happier, more trusting person, perhaps not so naïve as Hercules, but nonetheless just as honest and selfless. Having found and saved each other, Meg and Hercules are able to live happily ever after, each one (no doubt) keeping the other's weaknesses in check. Or, as Vivian/Julia Roberts says at the end of *Pretty Woman* when asked what the princess does when saved by the handsome prince, "She saves him right back!"

What both Esmeralda and Meg have in common is their

320 This remark is in response to Hades' directive that she needs to stop Hercules from attaining the status of hero, saying that his other "assistants" were not able to handle Hercules as a boy, and that he needs someone who can handle him as a man.

street-wise personas and sexual confidence, coupled with their innate goodness and personal senses of justice. Furthermore, as Disney heroines who are not only saved but do an equal share of the saving themselves, they are an unusual pair amongst the other women portrayed in Disney animation. They are both possessed of many flaws (Esmeralda is distrustful and confrontational, Meg is bitter and unfeeling), yet the flaws which hamper them most – and which they have acquired because of their difficult lives – are the ones which they also learn to overcome during the course of each's film.

A slight departure from these tough girl characters – at least in terms of the total lack of romance in the character's life – is Audrey from *Atlantis*. Audrey's youth is emphasised several times in the film, but she is still old enough to have not only become an extremely capable mechanic, but also to have accompanied the explorers on a previous expedition as well as this one to Atlantis. She is a total tomboy, wearing overalls for all but the final scene of the film, and teases Milo's timidity several times. She's shown as brave, cocky, confident, no nonsense, and – it is hinted – is even less squeamish than the doctor of the group. This is shown when Dr. Sweet tells Milo that he should not ask what Molière's story is, saying, "Believe me, you don't wanna know. Audrey, don't tell him. You told me, and I didn't want to know, and believe me, you don't wanna know!" She explains herself by saying that her father had wanted sons (to be a mechanic and a prize fighter), but had ended up with her and her sister. When Milo asks what happened with her sister, Audrey replies (as if it were a mundane piece of information): "She's two and 'O' with a shot at the title next month". When, as the expedition is about to leave Milo behind and take Kida, Milo makes a point of questioning their values; it is Audrey who is the first to take a stand against Rourke, the mercenary expedition leader, and stand with Milo against the destruction of Atlantis. It is her example, in fact, which persuades the other characters (except Rourke and Helga) to help Milo, and she is one of the principle fighters in the climactic battle scene to rescue Kida.

Although Audrey is not portrayed as "the" heroine of her film, she is nonetheless an important supporting character. She is unusual for a Disney character of her sex and age in that, instead of displaying any traces of sexuality or romantic longing at any point, she shows a complete lack of interest in such matters. Yet despite her overalls, she is portrayed as a pretty, voluptuous young woman who is definitely old enough (according to standards set for other Disney women) for romance. What is emphasised about Audrey, however, are her capableness, her intelligence, and her strength of character. Like Mulan, she has combined masculine and feminine roles in such a way as suits her character. Unlike Mulan, she has (apparently) never had to struggle to achieve this identity. Whether, however, this type of young female character is pointing the way toward a new trend in Disney women, remains to be seen. It could be argued however, that, in terms of this confidence in herself, Audrey is one of the most pro-feminist of Disney's characters, as well as being one of the most balanced, "ordinary" portrayals of a human woman to be found in any Disney film.

This brings us to Captain Amelia, the ship's captain in *Treasure Planet*. When Dr. Doppler and Jim Hawkins arrive on the ship they have hired to seek out Treasure Planet, they see a "man" (many of the main characters are humanoid "alien" creatures, as opposed to being homo sapiens) standing on the deck, wearing a uniform and surveying the activity around him with confidence. They address him as captain, and he corrects them, pointing up to the sails and saying, "There's the captain!" The camera pans up, and we see a lean, lithe creature moving amongst the sails like a gymnast. She lands on the deck, and introduces herself as Captain Amelia. From the moment she opens her mouth, speaking in a crisp, aristocratic English accent (her voice is provided by Emma Thompson), she demonstrates immediately that *she* is in charge, and that she will take no interference from anyone. Nonetheless, she is a good-humoured, no-nonsense, honest individual who gives credit where it is due, commending Mr. Arrow (her first-mate) on his overseeing the ship's preparations for launch. She also, in this first scene with her, proves that she is highly intelligent, an astute judge of character (she quickly sums up the doctor, Jim, and the crew that the doctor has hired), and a wise, shrewd woman. When, later in the film, the pirates mutiny and, outnumbered, the heroes of the film are forced to flee the ship, it is Amelia who leads them to safety, even managing to steer the "longboat" to the planet's surface despite its having been blown in half by the ship's cannon. She is injured in the landing, but those in her care are not, and it is Amelia who still serves as advisor – and as a guide for maintaining their honour – when the pirates find and capture them. When Silver demands that Jim give him the map or risk the captain and the doctor being killed, the doctor initially nods his head vigorously, encouraging Jim to hand over the map. Amelia, however, is just as vigorously shaking her head "no", reminding Jim that he should not bow to the pirate's demands. Realising that her position is the "right" one, the doctor quickly stops nodding his head and begins shaking his, mirroring the captain. Once they have all escaped and returned to their home port and to safety, Amelia, recognising that Jim has many excellent qualities (despite all the trouble he has caused and the poor choices he has made) and that he has within him the potential to be something better than he is, announces that she will recommend him to the Interstellar academy, saying, "they could use a man like you". Unlike the other heroines who have come before her in Disney animation, she never has an instant of self-doubt: she knows that her position is right, and she is willing to work hard to make sure that she achieves her goals. Once upon a time, these were traits which would have been seen amongst the villainesses, whose determination to defeat the heroines knew no bounds. In Amelia, who is *always* represented as good, this depiction comes full circle: strength of will, determination, and ingenuity have ceased to become flaws and signs of an evil nature in a woman's character, and have been transformed into proof positive that she is the best kind of ally, and the type of person who can save the day (or, at least, make saving the day possible).

Nonetheless, Amelia is still able to find time to fall in love – rather surprisingly – with Dr. Doppler. Since both these characters are supporting characters, their romance is not focused upon: there are a few looks (usually tinged with surprise, as well as growing attachment, on the parts of the doctor and the captain) and gestures, but no big romantic scene. At the end of the film, they are shown as having had a "litter" (she is feline in appearance, he has some rather canine characteristics) of babies and are dancing in a rather dashing, romantic way. But this has no role or function within the story's narrative, and almost seems to be the obligatory romantic undercurrent in the film. For this reason, it is an odd inclusion, and one wonders why the choice was made. Nonetheless, even this bit of romance never slows down Amelia: even in this final scene, dancing in the arms of her partner, she still wears her captain's uniform, implying that she is still a "spacer" (the film's term for sailor), still a leader, and still herself.

Sister act – Lilo and Nani

The final heroines to be discussed are unique in a number of ways: they are the only two "modern" female characters in a Disney animated feature, they are the only modern-day American women, they are the only two "ordinary" women (without special knowledge or abilities or status or magical powers), and they are the only two who are shown alongside their sister. They are Lilo and Nani from *Lilo and Stitch*. In the film, we learn that Lilo and Nani's parents were killed in a car accident, and Nani has been left as Lilo's guardian. Being a young woman herself, Nani is struggling to support them financially (and, in fact, spends a portion of the film unemployed and searching everywhere for a job), and is also struggling to look after and help her little sister, who is very loving and good-hearted, but full of hurt and anger over their parents' deaths. In some ways, Nani is portrayed as self-sacrificing, in that she has put her own life on hold (including her love-life; a friend of hers, David, wants her to go out with him, but she tells him no, saying that things for her are complicated, and glancing at Lilo when she says this). She also puts up with Lilo's choice of "dog", Stitch. Stitch is an incredibly bad-tempered, destructive alien, though none of the humans in the film are aware of this; in many ways, Stitch and Lilo are shown to have similar personality flaws, and it is their friendship, as well as Lilo's strong sense of "ohana" (the Hawaiian word for family) which will repair Lilo's and Stitch's damaged spirits and save their little family unit. However, above all else, Nani is shown to love and need Lilo, and knows that she is the only one (apart, perhaps, from Stitch) who understands and can help Lilo work through her grief.

Most interestingly about both Nani and Lilo, however, is how normally they are depicted. Nani works normal jobs: she is a waitress at what she describes as a "fake luau", and when she loses that job, looks for work within various other parts of Hawaii's tourist industry: as a hotel concierge, as a life guard, at a greengrocers, and in a coffee house. The clothes they wear are normal, too: Nani is often shown wearing shorts and t-shirts, jeans, or a bathing suit (when they are surfing and enjoying a day together as a family). Lilo wears mostly a little red muumuu, and plays with fairly normal toys. The two fight, like all sisters do, but they clearly love one another despite it. That they are just so ordinary (as compared to the Disney women who came before or have come since) is why they stand out amongst the women discussed in this study. They are so ordinary, in fact, that I hesitate to describe them as heroines. Instead – interestingly – their story is simply one about two sisters overcoming the grief of losing their parents, and about creating a new family which, as Stitch describes it, is "little, and broken, but still good". In many ways, Nani and Lilo function as a single-parent family for most of the film (in fact, after the initial test screening, the makers of the film went back and added numerous references to their being sisters because the test audience was shocked to see what they thought were a mother and daughter arguing as Lilo and Nani do earlier in the film[321]). As Dean DeBlois, one of the writers and directors of *Lilo and Stitch* has said, "I think a lot of people look at the film and they notice that there's something really different about it; it doesn't look traditional Disney, and yet there's something really nostalgic about it. And that kind of exemplifies what were trying to do with the film anyway."[322]

Wicked women – a dying breed

Whereas strong heroines are a growing trend in Disney animation of this later period, evil women are becoming an increasingly rare phenomenon. In this era of Disney animated features, there are only three evil women: Ursula (of *The Little Mermaid*), Yzma (of *The Emperor's New Groove*) and Helga St. Claire (of *Atlantis*). This ratio of three villainesses to thirteen heroines is much lower when compared to the "Classic" era, which had a ratio of five villainesses to eight heroines, and is lower even than the "Middle Period", which had one villainess to four heroines.

These modern villainesses cannot be discussed entirely as a group, however, because each stands out from the other in very definite ways. Granted, Ursula and Yzma are the most

321 From the *Lilo & Stitch* DVD extras: "Deleted Scenes: 'Bedtime Story'": UK DVD release of *Lilo and Stitch*, ©Disney.

322 From the *Lilo & Stitch* DVD extras: "The Look of *Lilo & Stitch*": UK DVD release of *Lilo and Stitch*, ©Disney.

traditional villainesses of the three, but Ursula is the only one who easily fits the traditional perimeters of "Disney Villainess": she is very much a "monstrous other" who opposes a young heroine. She possesses magical powers (and is referred to repeatedly as being a "sea-witch", and her attempts to thwart the heroine she opposes are based primarily upon jealousy of some physical attribute (in this case, Ursula wants Ariel's voice). There is also, in Ursula's case, an attempt to disguise herself when her previous efforts to harm the heroine have failed: in this case, Ursula disguises herself as Vanessa, a beautiful young woman with Ariel's voice, so that she may marry Prince Eric and capture Ariel's soul. When even this fails, she swells in size in an effort to crush her opponents, but Eric stabs her with the prow of a ship and kills her. Everything about her is a caricature of some earlier Disney heroine, to include her tactics. Even her look borrows elements from classic villainesses: she tries to appear glamorous and sophisticated, but her monstrous form (she has the body of a somewhat humanised octopus) undercuts this attempt. Like them, she also works in "black magic". Also like them, she is stopped from permanently injuring the villainess through the efforts of a male character who serves as the heroine's champion.

Yzma, at least physically, is similar to past villainesses: she tries to look glamorous, but is so ugly (in fact, she is repeatedly described in the film as being "scary beyond all reason") that she is anything but glamorous (despite her long black dress and pearls). What is more unusual – and therefore more interesting – about Yzma (voiced by Eartha Kitt), however is that she is the first female villain to oppose a main character who is male. In this case, Yzma is advisor to Emperor Kuzko (voiced by David Spade), but is fired early on in the film because of her constant attempts to take over his throne. Seeking revenge, she and her dim-witted assistant/sidekick Kronk (voiced by Patrick Warburton) attempt to poison Kuzko, but only succeed (thanks to Kronk's blunder) in transforming him into a llama. After Kronk again fails to kill Kuzko, the pair set off through the jungle to find Kuzko so that Yzma can retain her new role as ruler of the kingdom.

Yzma's motivation, in other words, comes not so much from jealousy as it does from an overwhelming desire for power. Her initial method – poisoning – is not derived from black magic, however. Instead, Yzma has a "secret" lab (which most of the characters seem to know about), and concocts the poison through her apparent knowledge of chemistry rather than a knowledge of witchcraft. In other words, Yzma may look like a witch, but she has no magical powers; in fact, she must rely heavily upon Kronk for help, but his ineptness and – surprisingly for an evil henchman – his generally good nature mean that Yzma's efforts are doomed before they begin, and even when she is defeated she is not destroyed, but instead transformed through her own poison into a kitten, in which form she remains at the film's conclusion. She may be physically described as "scary beyond all reason", but in fact she – along with all the other characters in this silliest and most slapstick of Disney's animated features – is very much a comic character, and is not menacing to anyone, to include the other characters in the film.

The final villainess of this period – and perhaps the most complex villainess of all of Disney's films – is Helga St. Claire, the lieutenant of the expedition which seeks to find Atlantis in the film of the same name. First and foremost of the most obvious qualities which set her apart from past villainesses, she is a beautiful young woman who possesses no magical abilities whatsoever. She wears ordinary cloth-ing, speaks in an ordinary voice, and works within – rather than trying to subvert – the rules of the group in which she operates (which, in this case, is a group of mercenaries). Most unusually – and it is this which makes her complex – she is the only villainess who seems, even fleetingly, to possess a conscience. When the expedition discovers that there are people living in Atlantis, she is the first one to comment that "This changes everything". The response she receives to this comes from the menacing Rourke, who tells her that "This changes nothing"; even though she goes along with the plans, there are moments when she seems to doubt that she is doing the right thing, and she is never the most extreme in terms of evil. In the end, when all of the others have sided with Milo and only she and Rourke are carrying out their plan to steal the Heart of Atlantis, she is betrayed by Rourke, who throws her out of the hot air balloon. She falls to the ground, but before she dies she fires up at the balloon, contributing greatly in stopping Rourke from suc-ceeding. Throughout, her motivation is shown to be her desire for money, not a desire for power or control. She also does not directly opposes Milo and Kida; they are merely on the "wrong" side, and therefore she is working against them. In the end, her revenge against Rourke's betrayal will be what saves Kida from being taken away, and ultimately what saves the existence of Atlantis.

These villainesses – but in particular Yzma and Helga – stand out from their predecessors. They have different motivations, and serve different purposes in their films. That – and the fact that villainesses are rare in later Disney films – are the features which most distinguish them from earlier eras of Disney villainesses. It should be noted, of course, that they are not the only evil characters in this era of the Disney studio's features: there are in fact fourteen major villains in this period (as well as numerous henchmen), more than in any other era of the studio's film history.[323] In the "politically correct" atmosphere of the 1990s in America, this focus on male villains may have been an attempt to steer away from sexist portrayals of evil, sexually frustrated women (except in the case of Yzma; she is portrayed in such comic terms, however, that she is at best a caricature of the early villainesses). Yzma's appearance, however, may demonstrate a "lightening" of this attitude. The characterisation of Helga, however, is complex enough – since she is more of a flawed, greedy woman rather than an evil witch – and is balanced enough in *Atlantis* by female characters with stronger morality that she could arguably be seen as not so much an anti-feminist figure as a misguided individual.

[323] There is only one pure villain in the "Middle Period", the Horned King in *The Black Cauldron* (though Amos in *The Fox and the Hound* and Mr. Snoops in *The Rescuers* come close). In the "Classic Era", there are the Headless Horseman (*The Adventures of Ichabod and Mr. Toad*) and Captain Hook (*Peter Pan*).

Conclusion

For all of the criticism directed at the Disney corporation, the 1990s witnessed a more dynamic period of changing patterns than has any other decade in the company's history (except – arguably – the 1930s). Certainly the overall size of the company expanded by leaps and bounds, not only saving it financially but also saving it literally from being broken up and sold off. Furthermore, the 1990s witnessed a rehabilitation in the Studio's reputation for film-making. As more money, time, and creativity were lavished on the animation studio, in particular, than was the case in the period immediately after Disney's death, Disney feature animation remained a leader in its industry despite more serious competition than had ever before been the case. The Disney Corporation expanded in every area in which it was involved, and on a financial level now looks safe for years to come.

In terms of its recognition of changes in American attitudes towards the portrayals of women – particularly those which are likely to be seen by younger audiences – there has been a noticeable shift in its characterisations of women. Certainly, the Studio recognises that its older portrayals – Snow White, Cinderella, and the rest – are being seen more often by young people now than at any other period in film history thanks to the rise in home entertainment technology. Interestingly, the studio makes no differentiation in its marketing of the older and newer films: they are all sold under the label "Walt Disney Masterpieces" and are all marketed as "classics". It has also recognised, however, that in its more recent offerings, it cannot rely upon the same formulae. Throughout the 1990s, the increasing normalisation of feminist values within American culture was reflected in the Studio's attempts to create more interesting, dynamic female characters who could serve as more positive role models.

Overall, these efforts have attained varying levels of success. Mothers have fared little better in the Disney films of the 1990s than ever. As with earlier heroines (and heroes), most characters have lost their mothers, though many have managed to hold onto their fathers. In terms of the overall portrayal of what it means to be feminine, and to be good, however, there have been significant changes. All of the heroines of the era covered by this chapter go on adventures, despite the fact that none of them are little girls. Age seems to have no effect either on the kinds of adventures they undergo or the degree of success they experience at their adventures' end. Although romance continued to be a major theme in Disney films, for almost all of the characters it ceased to be their major goal. Rather than sitting contentedly, waiting for their handsome princes to find them, the young women featured in the 1990s sought knowledge (Ariel, Belle, Jasmine, Jane, and Kida) or justice (Pocahontas, Esmeralda, Meg, Mulan, Audrey, Amelia, and Nani) in some form, and when romance came, it was less a goal and more a pleasant surprise – the icing on the cake. Darker themes also began to creep into these films – particularly in *The Hunchback of Notre Dame, Mulan, Tarzan,* and *Atlantis,* which seem to have been perceived by audiences as being less intended for younger children and more for adolescents and adults. Yet the heroines of 1990s Disney films, although more in keeping with feminist attitudes, are not by any stretch of the imagination heroines to feminists, with the possible exceptions of Audrey and Captain Amelia (though it must be remembered, however, that both are supporting characters in their films). They are often devout care-takers of those around them, require the protection – or at least the affirmation – of a male authority figure (usually in the form of a father, which, owing to the ages of many of the characters, is perhaps more acceptable to modern audiences), and live out adventures which are at least sanctioned, if not rewarded, by the patriarchies in which all of the characters live.

Conclusion

In the London edition of *Time Out* for the week of 28 June to 5 July 2000, there were a number of articles relating to the film *Chicken Run*, released in Britain that week.[324] Made by Nick Park and Peter Lord, the creators of "Wallace and Gromit", *Chicken Run* was the first feature-length film made by Aardman Studio, for some years a maker of very popular, successful, and Academy Award-winning shorts. At the beginning of the television listings section, as part of the promotion for a BBC documentary on *Chicken Run* and its creators at Aardman Studios, was a large picture of the various characters whom Aardman shorts have featured as well as some of *Chicken Run*'s characters. And, superimposed over the heads of four of the characters were four human faces: Nick Park, Steven Spielberg, Peter Lord, and Walt Disney. Though Disney's name and studio were not once mentioned in the article about the documentary, his image was nonetheless in the photo. In fact, because the maker of this picture chose to use a sepia-toned picture of a young Walt Disney's face, he stood out from the picture in a way which the other figures – people all mentioned in the article and involved in bringing *Chicken Run* to the screen – did not.

Clearly, thirty-four years after his death and (literally) an ocean away from where he produced his animation, Walt Disney's influence continued to be felt and his position within the history of animation remained high. Books on the history of animation almost always feature Disney in some way or another, even when the book is on an animation studio other than Disney, since much animation – particularly in America – is produced in reaction to Disney,

324 Dominic Maxwell, "Pecking Orders", *Time Out*, No. 1558 (28 June – 5 July 2000), p. 173.

221

with full homage to Disney, or – what seems to be more often the case – as a mixture of both.

Disney discourse

Disney's impact on American twentieth century popular culture is not limited to an influence on animation, however. In taking on the role of America's predominant story-teller for most of the twentieth century, Disney became an inseparable aspect of American popular culture, as well as an integral part of the American social fabric. Because of – or, perhaps, in reaction to – Disney's status in twentieth century America, critiques about the Disney studio – and the way it has represented certain ideas, themes, morals, and attitudes in its films – have become increasingly prevalent. Sometimes laudatory, more often angry – even hysterical – in tone, these polemics have attempted to portray the studio as not just a reflection of American society's overriding values, but also – even – as the cause of America's social ills. One aspect of Disney's films of which this is especially true is in their depictions of femininity through their human female characters. Snow White, Cinderella, Sleeping Beauty – these names are now as much wrapped up in the discourse surrounding the Disney studio as the name Walt Disney itself, and are just as often held up by critics of the studio's output as symptoms of what is wrong with Disney as are its corporate habits and merchandising powers.

By analysing the Disney studio's depictions of femininity over the course of the twentieth century, this book's intention has been to contribute to the small but growing body of academic work focused on understanding the cultural salience of the "world of Disney". Furthermore, by looking at the Disney studio's depictions of femininity, the study will hopefully contribute to a growing understanding of portrayals of women, femininity, and gender in Hollywood cinema. In *From Reverence to Rape*, Molly Haskell asserted that "Like two-way mirrors linking the immediate past with the immediate future, women in the movies reflected, perpetuated, and in some respects offered innovations on the roles of women in society".[325] Although most of the heroines of the Disney studio's films offer, at best, imperfect mirrors of what was expected of women by American society at various moments of the twentieth century,

325 Molly Haskell, *From Reverence to Rape: The Treatment of Women in the Movies* (Chicago: University of Chicago Press, 2nd edn, 1987).

nonetheless, in its effort to appeal to the sensibilities of its audience, Disney helped to create an important reflection of American society's rapidly changing attitudes and beliefs about women, gender, and femininity.

One aspect of Disney's films which is important to understanding twentieth-century American perceptions of women has been the fact that so many of Disney's films have focused on female characters. This focusing on women is something many of Disney's films share with the Woman's Film genre. In *A Woman's View*, Jeanine Basinger wrote of women's films that "The primary thing about the woman herself in the woman's film is that she be strong, interesting, beautiful, or glamorous enough to be able to command center stage. These are films that glorify women, that say that women's problems matter. They exist to give substance to women's feelings."[326] This is as true a statement about the Disney films examined here as it is about the women's films Basinger examines in her book. Many of the Disney heroines may be weak, or simple, or incredibly passive, leaving them vulnerable to shaming and criticism by scholars and the media. Many of them may be "too" good, or "too" beautiful, or "too" willing to let others run their lives for them. But have they ever problems! Threatened by evil witches and fairies, betrayed by their stepmothers, pursued by demonic individuals of all descriptions, when all they ever wanted to do was fall in love, get married, and maybe be useful to someone. But in almost all of these films, even when the focus has been a male character (such as in *Peter Pan* or the "Pecos Bill" segment of *Melody Time*), as soon as the woman or girl in these films was on the screen, she stole the show, making it, even if it started out being his, into *her* film. And one way or another, by the end of the film her problems are usually solved, those who sought to destroy her are dead or captured, and the heroine can go back to being the happy, beautiful young thing she had been before, albeit perhaps a little wiser. But, at least in the world of the film in which she is portrayed, the problems of Disney women *matter*. A boy may have been the ostensible focus of *Peter Pan*, but Wendy was the true lead of the film, and it was she who looked after everyone, solved as many problems as she could, and tried to keep things from going wrong. Peter Pan just flitted about, wanting to have adventures and be the centre of attention. Wendy was the glue that held both the

326 Jeanine Basinger, *A Woman's View: How Hollywood Spoke to Women, 1930–1960* (London: University Press of New England, 1993), p. 25.

characters' lives – and the film – together. Once Slue-foot Sue rode into the scene, everything Pecos Bill had done up until then was forgotten and Sue became the focus of the film until she was trapped forever on the moon. Only once she had been totally removed from the film could it turn its focus back to Bill, and even then the last few minutes of action were about Bill's mourning the loss of Sue, and it was out of Bill's love for Sue that he – and the coyotes – howled at the moon forever after. When there are no women to trouble them, the Disney men get along just fine. As soon as a woman shows up, the best he can do is react to her influence.

Yet most critics of the Disney studio's films overlook such points about Disney, finding it easier to deal in misinformation and half-truths than to engage in in-depth analysis. Disney – with its wide-spread influence, longish time-span, and later twentieth-century corporate power – was an easy target for 1990s critics of its role in popular culture. It was simple – and possibly true – to say that such films as *Snow White*, *Cinderella* and *Sleeping Beauty* might be giving young girls messages about love, self-motivation, and self-worth that were at odds with late-twentieth century feminist ideology. After all, Snow White, although in danger of being murdered by her evil, vengeful step-mother, is more concerned with cooking for, cleaning for, and mothering the dwarfs than she is about protecting herself, and certainly in the end can only be saved by the handsome prince who finds her and awakens her – with "love's first kiss" – from sleeping death. Furthermore, rather than doing something about taking back her kingdom from the evil queen, Snow White allows herself to be first degraded (by being turned into a scullery maid in what should have been her own castle), then persecuted and banished (when the queen orders Snow White's murder, but the huntsman allows her to flee). Finally, when Snow White falls in love, rather than doing anything to contact the prince herself or seek him out in any way, Snow White simply sits back in her chair and sings "Some day my prince will come", perfectly content to make do till he finds (and rescues) her.

But in pointing to such depictions, many critics have forgotten that, for the four inactive, passive Disney heroines of this study – Snow White, Cinderella, Aurora, and Anita – there are, at the time of this writing, twenty-one Disney heroines who are unquestionably active, self-motivated, strong-willed, intelligent, and independent – Slue-Foot Sue, Katrina van Tassel, Alice, Wendy, Miss Bianca, Penny, Widow Tweed, Eilonwy, Ariel, Belle, Jasmine, Pocahontas, Esmeralda, Meg, Mulan, Jane, Audrey, Kida, Nani, Lilo, and Captain Amelia. None of them are perfect. Some may even exhibit passive tendencies upon occasion. But when the chips are down, they go out and do what they must, and do not sit and wait to be rescued. Most of them even do some of the rescuing themselves. There are those critics who have found the flaws and damned the character, film, and studio for creating "negative" role models. But in doing so, they neglect the very positive aspects of many of these images, and the kind of women being presented by Disney as a whole. They also neglect to mention the very positive role models which Disney has consciously advanced over the course of the studio's history. In the 1950s incarnation of *The Mickey Mouse Club* television series (1955–1959), for example, Walt (who oversaw much of the show's development himself[327]) and the show's writers saw fit to include role models (namely, the girl Mouseketeers) who espoused such messages as:

> Beauty is as beauty does, that's what wise men say.
> So if you would be beautiful, do this every day:
> Listen to your teacher, because she is well trained
> This is what she has to say: "A beauty needs a brain!"

The Mickey Mouse Club, with an estimated audience of 12 million children and 7 million adults,[328] also depicted active role models for girls who were sometimes in direct competition with boys. Steven Watts points to one episode of the show, which featured a "1957 newsreel story on midget-car racing [which] focused on the girl among a group of boys who surprised everyone by winning the big race. Her father, the mechanic for her speedster, beamed proudly as the second-place finisher offered congratulations with an awkward kiss on the cheek."[329] As this example shows (particularly when examined alongside the headcount of active heroines in Disney films), even in the first period of Disney's feature animation, when all four of the films featuring inactive Disney heroines were first released (*Snow White and the Seven Dwarfs*, "The Legend of Sleepy Hollow" segment of *The Adventures of Ichabod and Mr. Toad*, *Cinderalla* and *Sleeping Beauty*), there is little evidence that the Disney

327 Steven Watts, *The Magic Kingdom: Walt Disney and the American Way of Life* (New York: Houghton Mifflin Company, 1997), pp. 335, 340.

328 Watts, *The Magic Kingdom*, p. 335.

329 Watts, *The Magic Kingdom*, pp. 341–342.

studio or Walt Disney were actively promoting (as has been suggested by some critics) passivity or stupidity in women as virtues to be emulated by girls and women; the evidence from those times when the studio was actually trying to educate children show, in fact, that they were promoting the opposite.

However, because Disney was not promoting passivity amongst women, it did not necessarily mean that the studio was attempting to promote sisterhood or depicting female friendship. Although Disney fare such as *The Mickey Mouse Club* may have portrayed the girls featured in the show as friends, this was not the case amongst its animated films. Women in Disney, if they have had other female characters to interact with in the first place, have been shown predominately as being in competition with one another or as outright enemies. Particularly in the films up to and including 1989's *The Little Mermaid*, Disney women did not get along well with one another. As the Women's Movement's emphasis on the idea of "Sisterhood" emerged, however, Disney seems to have acknowledged this – at least implicitly – by steering clear of portraying women as enemies. The relationship between Pocahontas and Nakoma in *Pocahontas* (1995) was one of the few female friendships found anywhere in Disney, and the only relationship between two women to be found in a Disney film after *The Little Mermaid* and until *Atlantis* (although in this case the relationships are not friendships, but simply people working together toward a common goal). However, with the exceptions of *Pocahontas*, *Atlantis*, and *Lilo and Stitch* (where the idea of sisterhood was made literal), Disney has refrained from featuring more than one major female character per film, and has tended to feature stories in its films in which the evil protagonist has been male. In this way, the studio has kept from portraying women in competition with one another. It has also, however, again until *Atlantis*, avoided showing women working together.

Yet, while Disney films rarely portray female friendships within individual films, there has been a growing tendency on Disney's part to portray its various female heroines as friends and peers in a marketing ploy for its film-related merchandise, particularly with the kinds of merchandise it sells at the Disney Store. At the turn of the twenty-first century, a highly successful and persuasive new marketing trend has been the grouping together of such characters as Snow White, Princess Aurora, Belle, Ariel, and Jasmine into what the Disney corporation calls "The Princess Collection". This "Princess Collection" places less emphasis upon the individual films from which each character originates and more emphasis on these characters as forming a kind of "Girls' Club". The marketing of "The Princess Collection" seems to be an attempt by Disney to reconstruct its image as a friend and supporter of women's solidarity, even going so far as to group the various villainesses together as a sort of "evil alternative" to the Princess Collection. Both groupings, however, seem to be an attempt by Disney to affiliate their films with a small but nonetheless strongly female-oriented film genre (a genre they themselves have not yet brought to the screen): the female buddy movie.

Female buddy films

In order to appreciate the extent to which Disney films do – or do not – participate in the discourse on women to be found throughout live-action Hollywood cinema, one must come to an understanding of how women fare within mainstream Hollywood films. Whilst the most obvious approach to this would have been to look at a selection of popular films from each decade in which one also finds Disney films (i.e. from the 1930s onward), it seemed best to combine this series of brief "case studies" with a look at popular film genres, so that Disney films as a group/genre would also be better understood in relation to other genres. But in showing women first as being enemies, and then showing female characters interacting either solely or predominately with men, Disney films have differed from other films produced in Hollywood, particularly within the genre of the Women's Film.

The idea of looking at women's films (particularly in the realm of the "female buddy movie") in order to come to a better understanding of the position of Disney films within American popular culture may initially seem contradictory. After all, particularly in Disney films prior to the 1980s, women who were major characters were represented as being anything from somewhat distrustful of other women (for example, Anita's polite but still apprehensive behaviour toward Cruella deVil in *One-Hundred-and-One Dalmatians*)

227

through largely antagonistic/competitive towards one another (as with Wendy and Tinkerbell in *Peter Pan*) to one character threatening the other's very existence (as in *Snow White* and *Sleeping Beauty*). The notion that even Disney films of the 1990s might be examined in relation to the female buddy genre seems problematic since, while Disney in the 1990s no longer seemed inclined to present women at odds with one another, there has likewise (except in *Pocahontas*, *Atlantis* and *Lilo and Stitch*) appeared to be no interest in portraying women as friends. The most recent trend in Disney films, in fact, is to present women as being largely in isolation from other women. They are surrounded by men, their friends and enemies are men, and they seem to function solely as women alone in a man's world. Again, one exception to this is *Pocahontas*, although it should be noted that Pocahontas is the only major female character and one of only two important living human characters in the film (Pocahontas' friend Nakoma being the only other actual woman in the film). The other women in the film are either dead or not human: Grandmother Willow, an important source of wisdom, friendship, and guidance for Pocahontas, is a magical willow tree; Pocahontas' mother (whose only identification is as such – her name is never mentioned), long dead by the beginning of the film, is represented as a spirit which manifests itself in the form of a blowing cloud of leaves, wind, and sparkles and which reveals herself at times of moral or ethical uncertainty, inspiring the living to do what is Right. Apart from these few exceptions, Disney women of the 1990s functioned in a vacuum, surrounded by, identifying with, and functioning in relation to men. It was not until 2001 that women began to function in the company of other women, and it is interesting to note that, in *Atlantis*, Kida, prior to the expedition's arrival, seems to be functioning as the token woman in a circle of male power and protection. Instead it is women from "the modern world" (the main action of *Atlantis* takes place in the year 1914) who bring with them a vision of independent women working together. Whether Kida will take this on board once they have gone, however, is left unknown at the end of the film.

In the chapter on "The Female Friendship Film and Women of Color" in her book *In the Company of Women*, Karen Hollinger points out that, in the field of scholarly examination of the viewing habits of African-American women, there is a strong trend, as described and documented by bell hooks and Jacqueline Bobo, for African-American women to read films in a highly selective way, accepting the elements of films which ring true for them and ignoring those aspects of films which do not. In other words, "African American women spectators learn from a lifetime of Hollywood film-going experiences either to turn completely away from the negative and distorted images they see of themselves on the screen or to recast these images in a more favorable light".[330] Similarly, Linda Williams argues in her chapter "When the Woman Looks" in *The Dread of Difference* that female audiences of horror films often refuse to watch the victimisation of the female characters on the screen because, rather than turning away in fear as has been traditionally assumed, they are in fact refusing to bear witness to the crimes against women which are being played out on the screen.[331] These interpretations of female spectatorship both argue that, in the majority of mainstream Hollywood films, stories are usually told, if not explicitly from a male point of view, then at least implicitly by making male characters the "boundaries" within which the films' central characters operate, thereby re-framing what are ostensibly women's stories into women's stories as seen through the eyes of the men in their lives. An example of this sort of re-framing is *Thelma and Louise* (1991). The story is technically about two women who are fleeing from the law (Louise shot and killed a man who was attempting to rape her friend Thelma, then panicked and fled the scene because she was afraid of being accused of murder), and many of the scenes are filmed from their point of view. But the majority of the scenes most critical to the development of the plot involve men: the rapist, the sheriff who is looking for them and pursues them across several states, the drifter Thelma has a one-night-stand with, and Louise's boyfriend, with whom she has several significant conversations. The scenes with the sheriff are given particular weight in the development of the plot, since he knows more about Louise's past (for instance, he knows that she was raped several years earlier), is the only really "benevolent" male character in the film, and has the weight of the law on his side. The two women's story is eventually viewed through the eyes of the male sheriff who is trying to save them, rather than being told

330 Karen Hollinger, *In the Company of Women: Contemporary Female Friendship Films* (Minneapolis: University of Minnesota Press, 1998), p. 187.

331 Linda Williams, "When the Woman Looks", in Grant, *The Dread of Difference*, pp. 15, 32.

through the eyes of Thelma and Louise, the only two major female characters in the film.

Other examples include *The Women* (1939), in which the life of the main character (played by Norma Shearer) is affected by the way she handles her husband's affair with Joan Crawford (the husband is the catalyst for most of the film's events, and in the end is the reward which Shearer's character receives for her patience); *Mildred Pierce* (1945), in which Mildred and her daughter's difficult relationship, as well as the growth of Mildred's business, is defined in the context of how her success as a businesswoman and lack of success as a mother affect her relationships with various men; and *The Color Purple* (1985), in which Celie's, Shug's, and Sophia's stories are framed by the actions of Celie's husband, Shug's father, and Sophia's husband (who is Celie's step-son). *The Women*, *Mildred Pierce*, *The Color Purple*, and *Thelma and Louise* are just four examples, spread across different eras of Hollywood cinema, of women's films in which the majority of the main characters' actions are defined in relation to the men in their worlds. But, stretching across the history of cinema as they do, they demonstrate the fact that Hollywood is entirely comfortable with making "women's films" which are less about the women themselves and more about women in relation to men.

Indeed, one of the rare examples of a popular and successful Hollywood film about women which is a women's film *and* allows women to interact with other women as their primary relationships (and which has no overt or covert lesbian/sexual themes) is *Steel Magnolias* (1989). There are, of course, men present in the film, but they are present merely to flesh out the lives and backgrounds of the story in a more plausible fashion. They fulfil at best only minor plot functions, do not serve as catalysts to the women's thoughts, dreams, or actions, and are without question secondary to the film's plot. Such films about groups of men, in which men are the only major characters (and sometimes are the only characters at all, major, minor, or otherwise) are commonplace.[332] Films in which women function in a female-centred or female-motivated universe (and which, again, are not about female/female sexual relationships but instead deal solely with women as mothers, daughters, friends, and – above all

[332] The various James Bond films, the majority of Hollywood Westerns, *The Ten Commandments* (1956), *Spartacus* (1960), *Patton* (1970), the *Lethal Weapon* films, the *Die Hard* films, *Con Air* (1997), *Pulp Fiction* (1994), *The Dirty Dozen* (1967), *Kelly's Heroes* (1970), *To Hell and Back* (1955), *The Guns of Navarone* (1961) (and its sequel *Force 10 from Navarone*, 1970), *Scent of a Woman* (1992), and *Saving Private Ryan* (1998) are just a few randomly chosen examples, but there are literally hundreds of other illustrations.

– autonomous individuals) are so rare as to excite comment from fans, critics, the media, and scholars alike.

In recent years, a new sub-genre of the buddy film has begun to emerge, that of the "witch" buddy film. The television series *Sabrina the Teenage Witch* (1996 to 2003) and *Charmed* (1998 to 2006), as well as the films *Hocus Pocus* (1993), *The Craft* (1996) and *Practical Magic* (1998), are a few examples of instances in which witches – both good and bad – have been given a friend or two and set off on an adventure. This portrayal of the witch is very much a recent phenomenon, reflecting to some extent the beginnings of a change towards the idea of the witch. Not only has the witch become increasingly a subject of cultural examination, but also the ways in which witches – and in particular the various witch-hunts and witch trials of the past – have been studied in recent times has been evidence of a change in the ways in which a feminist interpretation of this subject has taken hold in American culture. One example of this is the way that discourse surrounding the Salem witch trials have altered over the course of the twentieth century. By the time Arthur Miller's play *The Crucible* was produced in 1953, the idea that the witch trials might have been an example of mass hysteria and even vengefulness had begun to take hold. In the 1987 film *The Witches of Eastwick*, Darrell van Horn (played by Jack Nicholson) comments that the witch hunts and accusations of witchcraft had been a ploy of the medical profession for doing away with mid-wives. Scholarly examinations of the history of witches in America, such as Elizabeth Reis' *Spellbound: Women and Witchcraft in America*,[333] have looked at the history of witches from a feminist perspective, and have included writings on those modern-day women who call themselves witches but who are, in fact, devotees of various goddess-based pagan religions which have undergone small-scale revivals in recent times.

Although the older image of the witch continues to resonate within American cultural representations, it is increasingly blended with the feminist reinterpretations of the witch as both a phenomenon of history and an archetypal image of an aspect of Womanhood. Particularly in the first period of Disney films examined in this book, the role of the witch/evil woman is vital, since it is on her actions that the films' plots turn. Over the course of the century, however, as feminist interpretations of witches evolved, this change

333 Elizabeth Reis (ed.), *Spellbound: Women and Witchcraft in America* (Wilmington, DE: Scholarly Resources, 1998).

in conceptions of the witch has been reflected in the Disney animated films. While, in films up to *The Little Mermaid* (1989), the witch often appears, after 1989 the witch as a character has all but disappeared from Disney animation. Yet there is still an acknowledgement of recent interpretations of the reasons for witchcraft accusations to be found in recent Disney animated films. Esmeralda, in *The Hunchback of Notre Dame* (1996), is a perfect example of a portrayal of a woman as being young, beautiful, good (and yet also sexually aware and powerful) who is repeatedly referred to as a witch by the evil, twisted Judge Frollo. By and large, however, Disney films portray witches in more traditional – i.e. evil – roles.

For much of the Disney studio's film history, the witch has been shown as – ultimately (as is the case with the evil queen in *Snow White*, who starts out as a beauty but ends up ugly) – being ugly, old, and repulsive, and she has always been punished in the end. In this way, she has been contrasted with the beautiful, young, and attractive heroines. The only young, attractive villain has been Helga St. Claire of *Atlantis*, and her portrayal was more complex on a number of levels. She is very much an exception to the rule, however. In general, prior to 2001, a Disney woman's beauty has been portrayed as being a reflection of her goodness, and a woman's physical ugliness has likewise served as proof of her evil. The beautiful woman was the woman who deserves – and in the natural order of things obtained – all of the best things in life: love, security, justice. In fairy tales, the heroine is almost always depicted as beautiful, and in only the rarest of circumstances is beauty granted to the wicked or impure at heart. In those instances where it is, however, something in the story usually causes the true ugliness of the wicked woman to be revealed, such as in Snow White's stepmother's transformation of herself into a hag. This message that good equals beauty is very much alive, and is continuously conveyed through the media to remind women that, if they want to be beloved, they must also be beautiful. The irony present in advertisements with this message, i.e. that all women, just like the evil women in stories, must use artifice if they want to preserve their beauty, seems lost upon those who use this message.

Within the Disney films, in particular in the films of the 1930s, 1940s, and 1950s, evil women – women who display anger, jealousy, frustration, desire, and cunning – are often portrayed as not only evil, but also as being capable of black magic. They are portrayed as women in their 30s, 40s, or 50s, single or widowed, and very angry with the world around them. They may or may not be mothers, but they are never maternal. What is more, they are aware of the importance of artifice in maintaining their feminine status. They keep the young heroines in rags in order to prevent the beauty that comes from the heroine's goodness from overshadowing the beauty they have achieved through artifice. They are always shown to be aware of how much work it takes to achieve the currently standard form of femininity, and are vain, obsessive creatures. When they have magical powers (as most of them do) they use their speech – their words – to cast spells. When they cannot work magic, they nonetheless have the power to use their voices – by giving commands and telling lies – to work against their young, less verbally-gifted victims. The male villains in Disney films – Captain Hook, Gaston, Jafar, Ratcliffe, Frollo, Hades, The Hun, Clayton, and Rourke are the only human male antagonists – are evil, but they also have, for the most part, a comical element to them which will eventually contribute to their downfalls. They are, in other words, characters we love to hate, but they are not necessarily frightening. It is the traditional evil women in Disney – the Evil Queen/Hag, the Evil Step-mother, the Queen of Hearts, Maleficent, Madame Medusa, and Ursula the Sea Witch – who are portrayed in nightmare-ish seriousness, and as not being simply bad, mean, or evil, but also insane. The villains have goals to achieve in the world which the hero/ine stands in the way of; the evil woman has goals, but they are usually more personal, and are portrayed as sinister in comparison: they seek to be the fairest, to marry off their daughters, to rule with absolute authority. It is with such images that children are bombarded when watching these films. How much – or how little – children (and adults) are effected by such portrayals is something which is not yet fully understood.

Conclusion

At the moment, the best course of action in forming theories about how children are affected by the images of gender roles they see in films has to be inferred from the larger culture surrounding them, the accompanying media images which make reference to gender roles, and the films/television series which achieve success/popularity within American culture. After all, as has been noted earlier, if a film achieves popular success, it is because normally it has something about it which echoes ideas/cultural norms/accepted standards which can be found throughout society. It "strikes a chord", in other words, with some larger social trend. People respond to a film because it has something to offer them – something with which they can relate. It addresses a need they have for information on a subject, or even addresses a topic which they feel needs discussion within the larger society. Films which achieve these last two goals are usually films which have some sort of controversy connected to them, but which are still nonetheless highly popular and successful. The 1993 film *Philadelphia*, starring Tom Hanks as a gay man who is dying of AIDS, for example, was a film which aroused some protest from various religious groups for its sympathetic portrayal of homosexuality and its defence of the rights of those suffering from AIDS and HIV, but which achieved significant popular and critical success, winning the Academy Awards for Best Actor and Best Song (Bruce Springsteen's theme song for the film). Coming as it did at a time when the issues of AIDS/HIV and homophobia were just beginning to be considered acceptable topics for public discourse in America, *Philadelphia* was an example of the sort of film which can both cause controversy and touch a nerve within society as a whole.[334]

The fact is, however, that Disney films rarely cause controversy, and what little there is usually has no affect upon the general public's decision to see (or allow their children to see) a particular Disney film. What is it about Disney films which gives them this sort of immunity from parental scrutiny? Is it simply the Disney name? Is it the reputation which Disney has for providing safe, moralistic "family-appropriate" entertainment? These are issues which need to be addressed within the broader framework of an examination of the films made by the Disney studio at various points in the years since 1937 (in which it has been releasing feature films), as well as the reputation which it has built up over the near century-length span of time in which it has existed as a critically and commercially successful animation studio. In doing this, the intention has been to address the issues which have been raised in this chapter and to put them

334 For more on this subject, see Kyle William Mechar, "Every Problem has a Solution: AIDS and the Cultural Recuperation of the American Nuclear Family in Jonathan Demme's *Philadelphia*", *Spectator*, vol. 15, no. 1 (Autumn 1994), pp. 78–93.

within the context of the decades in which various films were made and released, as well as in the context of the paths, towards various levels of success, faced by individual Disney films.

This study has attempted to show that the Disney studio's depictions of femininity, which, as the ability of the studio to animate more complicated, realistic figures increased, grew increasingly complex over the course of the twentieth century, did in fact resemble depictions of women in other areas of mainstream Hollywood cinema. It has also, through in-depth analysis of the films, the types of characters being depicted within each major time period of the Disney studio, and the ways these depictions changed between 1937 and 2005, sought to demonstrate that, far from portraying weak, passive female human characters, the Disney studio has presented an image of women – and femininity – which, although not perfect, is largely positive in its overall make-up.

By writing this book, it has been my intention to, firstly, correct the perception of how women are represented in Disney's animated features, and secondly, to begin a dialogue – based on this analysis – about how these representations function within American society and popular culture. Because this analysis of Disney's animated feature films contradicts to some degree many popular conceptions of Disney films as a group, the findings it presents in its analysis will hopefully counteract the impression that these films are so thoroughly sexist by offering a more balanced look at depictions of femininity in Disney films. As scholars have begun examining cinema's complex and multifaceted place within society, it has become evident that a greater focus must be placed on the dialogue between Hollywood film-makers and Hollywood film audiences. The role of this work – hopefully – is that it will contribute to this larger dialogue by correcting many wide-spread misconceptions about one of the most influential studios – and film genres – of the twentieth century.

Appendix 1

Disney's full-length animated feature films

The complete list

1. *Snow White and the Seven Dwarfs* (1937)
2. *Pinocchio* (1940)
3. *Fantasia* (1940)
4. *Dumbo* (1941)
5. *Bambi* (1942)
6. *Victory Through Airpower* (1943)
7. *Saludos Amigos* (1943)
8. *The Three Caballeros* (1945)
9. *Make Mine Music* (1946)
10. *Fun and Fancy Free* (1947)
11. *Melody Time* (1948)
12. *The Adventures of Ichabod and Mr. Toad* (1949)
13. *Cinderella* (1950)
14. *Alice in Wonderland* (1951)
15. *Peter Pan* (1953)
16. *Lady and the Tramp* (1955)
17. *Sleeping Beauty* (1959)
18. *101 Dalmatians* (1961)
19. *The Sword in the Stone* (1963)
20. *The Jungle Book* (1967)
21. *The Aristocats* (1970)
22. *Robin Hood* (1973)
23. *The Many Adventures of Winnie the Pooh* (1977)
24. *The Rescuers* (1977)
25. *The Fox and the Hound* (1981)
26. *The Black Cauldron* (1985)
27. *Basil, the Great Mouse Detective* (1986)
28. *Oliver and Company* (1988)
29. *The Little Mermaid* (1989)

30. *The Rescuers Down Under* (1990)
31. *Beauty and the Beast* (1991)
32. *Aladdin* (1992)
33. *The Lion King* (1994)
34. *Pocahontas* (1995)
35. *The Hunchback of Notre Dame* (1996)
36. *Hercules* (1997)
37. *Mulan* (1998)
38. *Tarzan* (1999)
39. *Fantasia 2000* (2000)
40. *The Emperor's New Groove* (2000)
41. *Atlantis* (2001)
42. *Lilo and Stitch* (2002)
43. *Treasure Planet* (2003)
44. *Home on the Range* (2004)
45. *Brother Bear* (2004)
46. *Chicken Little* (2005)

My subject list
The Classic Period
1. *Snow White and the Seven Dwarfs* (1937)
2. *Melody Time* (1948)
3. *The Adventures of Ichabod and Mr. Toad* (1949)
4. *Cinderella* (1950)
5. *Alice in Wonderland* (1951)
6. *Peter Pan* (1953)
7. *Sleeping Beauty* (1959)
8. *101 Dalmatians* (1961)

The Middle Period
9. *The Rescuers* (1977)
10. *The Fox and the Hound* (1981)
11. *The Black Cauldron* (1985)

The Modern Period
12. *The Little Mermaid* (1989)
13. *Beauty and the Beast* (1991)
14. *Aladdin* (1992)
15. *Pocahontas* (1995)
16. *The Hunchback of Notre Dame* (1996)
17. *Hercules* (1997)
18. *Mulan* (1998)
19. *Tarzan* (1999)
20. *The Emperor's New Groove* (2000)
21. *Atlantis* (2001)
22. *Lilo and Stitch* (2002)
23. *Treasure Planet* (2003)

238

Appendix 2

Disney films analysed in this study, with plot summaries*

Snow White and the Seven Dwarfs (1937)

An evil queen asks the slave in her magic mirror 'who is the fairest one of all?' to which the slave replies that Snow White is. Made jealous by the subsequent sight of Snow White being wooed by the prince, she orders her huntsman to take Snow White into the woods and kill her. The huntsman, overcome by Snow White's goodness, tells her of the Queen's rage, bidding her to flee. Later, Snow White is led by the animals to the seven dwarfs' cottage. Snow White and the animals clean the house, hoping to persuade the dwarfs to let her stay. Snow White becomes tired and goes upstairs to sleep. The dwarfs return home, and a comic scene ensues as the dwarfs notice that everything is clean and assume 'there's dirty work afoot' and in which we learn each of the dwarfs' personalities. They then find Snow White, asleep, laying across several of their beds. Upon awakening, she tells them of the Queen's jealousy, asking if she can live with them. They agree. Leaving for work the next morning, they warn Snow White to be on guard. The Queen, meanwhile, has used her black magic to disguise herself and has learned Snow White's whereabouts. The Queen goes to the Seven Dwarfs' cottage, bringing Snow White a poisoned apple. Snow White takes a bite and falls unconscious. Meanwhile, the dwarfs, alerted by the animals that the Queen is with Snow White, hurry to the cottage to protect her, but succeed only in chasing the Queen to her death. We are then told (by means of an inter-title) that because she was so beautiful the dwarfs did not bury Snow White (whom they think is dead). The prince, having searched for Snow White all along, arrives and sees the dwarfs and the animals praying around Snow White's coffin. He lifts the cover, kisses her, and kneels down. Snow White awakens. After bidding good-bye to the dwarfs, she and the prince head into the sunset to live happily ever after.

*Listing in chronological order

239

Melody Time (1948)

In this package film, which is comprised of seven short segments, this study focuses on the last segment, 'Pecos Bill', as told and sung by Roy Rogers and the Sons of the Pioneers. The story is mainly a tall tale explanation of why coyotes howl at the moon, but also relates various incidents from the life of Pecos Bill (such as how he came to be raised by coyotes, how he got his horse, Widowmaker, how he created the Painted Desert, the Rio Grande, and the Gulf of Mexico, and how Bill made Texas the 'Lone Star State'. The explanation of why coyotes howl at the moon is centred around Bill's romance with Slue Foot Sue, the first woman Bill ever saw and whom he would have married. They court, fall in love, and decide to marry. For her wedding, Sue wants to wear a bustle and ride Widowmaker, to both of which Bill agrees. Widowmaker, however, is terribly jealous of Sue and fights hard to keep Sue from mounting him, but she does so anyway. Widowmaker's constant bucking, however, causes Sue's metal bustle to start bouncing uncontrollably, until she is finally thrown from Widowmaker's back. She hits the ground bustle-first and bounces higher and higher. Bill, however, as the greatest cowboy who ever lived, is naturally an expert with a lasso, and confidently attempts to lasso Sue and save her from her bouncing. Widowmaker, however, seeing his chance to be rid of Sue forever, secretly puts his hoof down on the end of the rope, causing it to fall just short of catching Sue. Apparently, Bill is so shocked at missing that he only tries once, and Sue, after bouncing for hours, eventually bounces so high that she lands on the moon, and stays there forever. Bill is so full of grief that he leaves behind human society and returns to life amongst the coyotes (who raised him from infancy), and in his grief looks at the moon (where he knows Sue is trapped forever) and howls. The coyotes, in sympathy, howl with him, and continue to do so until this day. The segment and the film as a whole both end with the singing of a mournful cowboy song.

The Adventures of Ichabod and Mr. Toad (1949)

In this film, which is also a package film, there are two segments: the story of Mr. Toad's mania with a motorcar, imprisonment, escape, and the eventual clearing of his name from Kenneth Grahame's *The Wind in the Willows*. The second segment is a re-telling of Washington Irving's *The Legend of Sleepy Hollow*, as sung and narrated by Bing Crosby. This study focuses solely on the second half of this film. The story is of Ichabod Crane, an eccentric schoolmaster in colonial times in the village of Terrytown, New York, and the nearby Sleepy Hollow. Ichabod is shown to be a sophisticated, educated man who is culturally superior to those around him in Terrytown, but he also has two weaknesses: his superstitions, and his interest in the wealthy, beautiful, manipulative Katrina van Tassel, the local belle. Katrina's father has an annual Halloween party, to which Ichabod is invited, at which it is traditional for the guests to share ghost stories. Brom Bones, the local strongman and Ichabod's rival for Katrina, decides to play upon Ichabod's superstitious streak and tells the local legend about a headless horseman, who rides every Halloween through Sleepy Hollow, searching for a head to replace the one he lost (though how he came to lose his own head we are never told). Ichabod is visibly terrified by this story, but nonetheless, at midnight, sets off through Sleepy Hollow on his way home. He gets about half way though the Hollow, nervous and paranoid the whole time, when he realises how silly he is being. It is then, however, that the headless horseman appears, and chases Ichabod around the Hollow with a sword trying to cut off his head. Eventually, Ichabod is shown to make it across the bridge which serves as a boundary to the headless horseman, but the story goes on to say that, the next morning, only Ichabod's hat and a shattered pumpkin were found, but that Ichabod was never seen again. It is rumoured that Ichabod married a wealthy widow in another county, but the local people stand by their belief that he had been 'spirited away' by the headless horseman.

Cinderella (1950)

This is a version of the classic fairy tale, albeit with a few Disney touches, such as the talking mice who are Cinderella's friends. The story starts with a narration telling us that Cinderella was the only child of a wealthy widower, who married a woman 'of good family' with two daughters about Cinderella's age, more for Cinderella's sake than his own. He dies, however, and Cinderella's step-mother reveals herself to be a malicious, vindictive woman who is jealous of Cinderella's beauty and goodness (because these traits make her superior to her own two ugly, awkward daughters). The step-mother, who also squanders Cinderella's family fortune, eventually forces Cinderella to work as a servant in her own home, and to wait hand and foot on her step-mother and step-sisters, all of whom treat her badly. Meanwhile, the king declares that he will hold a grand ball, which every eligible maiden in the kingdom must attend, so that his son the prince may (hopefully) find a wife amongst them. Cinderella reminds her step-mother that the invitation includes her too, and the step-mother reluctantly agrees. When Cinderella appears, dressed in her step-sisters' cast-offs and an old dress of her mother's (which the mice have kindly re-fashioned for her), however, her step-mother tricks the step-sisters into tearing the dress to bits. They then depart for the ball, leaving Cinderella behind. She runs into the garden, weeping. Her fairy godmother appears, however, gives her a beautiful gown and a magnificent coach, and tells her she may go to the ball but that the spell ends at midnight so she must leave before then. Cinderella agrees. At the ball, Cinderella meets the prince, and they fall in love. At midnight, Cinderella flees just as the spell is vanishing, and all that survived are her glass slippers, one of which she has left behind in her flight. A search of the kingdom ensues, and eventually the king's advisor finds Cinderella, sees that it is her glass slipper, and takes her off to the castle. The final scene is of Cinderella and the prince leaving the castle, having just been married, riding away to live happily ever after.

Alice in Wonderland (1951)

This film is a combination of Lewis Carrol's books *Through the Looking Glass* and *Alice in Wonderland*, and is comprised of random segments from each book. In the film, Alice follows the white rabbit down the rabbit hole, and then searches Wonderland for him, encountering a series of strange characters and circumstances, such as the mad tea party, an encounter with Tweedledee and Tweedledum, the garden of talking flowers, the Caterpillar, the Cheshire Cat, and the palace and gardens of the Queen of Hearts. Alice has nothing but trouble trying to find the rabbit, and it is his trail which leads her through these various situations. Eventually, Alice is put on trial by the Queen of Hearts, and escapes the courtroom, being chased by the Queen and various characters, through a tunnel, at the end of which she realises that she is dreaming, and manages to wake herself up. Upon awakening, she realises that the whole thing was simply a bizarre dream, and heads back to her house for tea.

Peter Pan (1953)

Based on J.M. Barrie's book, the film version focuses on Wendy, who accompanies Peter Pan (along with her two younger brothers, John and Michael) back to Neverland so that she does not have to grow up (we learn, early on, that her grumpy father, who bears a strong resemblance to Captain Hook, has declared it to be Wendy's last night in the nursery, and Wendy tells Peter Pan, who has come to her house looking for his shadow, that she has 'to grow up tomorrow'). Growing up is anathema to Peter Pan, and he sees taking Wendy to Neverland as rescuing her. He also, however, says she can be a mother to the lost boys. Peter sprinkles Wendy and her brothers with some fairy dust from Tinkerbell (much against Tinkerbell's will, as she is terribly jealous of Peter Pan's interest in Wendy and tries to get Wendy killed during the course of the film), they go on a series of adventures, such as the Lost Boys' games with the Indians, the rescue of Tiger Lily, the meeting with the mermaids, and the on-going war with Captain Hook and his pirates. At the end of the film, Peter Pan, Wendy, Tinkerbell, and the boys all manage to work together to defeat Hook and his pirates, capture the pirate ship, and fly it back to London to take Wendy, Michael, and John home.

Sleeping Beauty (1959)

The Disney version of this story is based (according to the title cards) on the Charles Perrault version of the fairy tale of Sleeping Beauty. The King and Queen of a happy kingdom spend many years unhappy because they have no children, but then, at the start of the film, they have a daughter, whom they name Aurora. They hold a celebration to honour her birth, to which all but the evil fairy, Maleficent, are invited. Three good fairies come to the celebration. Two of the fairies, named Flora and Fauna, bestow upon the infant princess the gifts of beauty and song, but then Maleficent arrives and, in revenge for being slighted, curses Aurora, saying that, on her sixteenth birthday, she will prick her finger on the spindle of a spinning wheel and die. The third good fairy, Merriweather, although not powerful enough to remove Maleficent's curse, nonetheless is able to change the curse from death to sleep, from which Aurora will be awakened by true love's first kiss. In order to protect her from the curse, however, the king and queen give their daughter to the three good fairies, who disguise themselves as peasant women and raise Aurora – whom they call Briar Rose – in a cottage in the forest. Briar Rose grows up knowing nothing about her true parentage. Meanwhile, Maleficent, furious at being thwarted in her curse against the princess, spends the next sixteen years searching for her. The day of Briar Rose's sixteenth birthday, she meets a handsome young man and falls in love with him (and he with her), but when she returns home the fairies tell her that she is a princess and that she must return to the castle to live with her parents, and that she is already betrothed to the prince of a neighbouring kingdom. Although heartsick, Briar Rose makes no protest, and obediently puts on the regal clothing the fairies give her and goes with them to the castle. The fairies give her some time on her own, and Maleficent uses this time to cast a spell on Aurora, leading her into a secret room and getting her to prick her finger on a spindle. Aurora falls into a death-like sleep. The fairies find her, and put an enchantment on the whole castle so that no one knows what has happened. Meanwhile, the young man, who turns out to be the prince to whom Aurora is betrothed, is captured by Maleficent and learns what has happened to Aurora. With the help of the three good fairies, he escapes his prison, kills Maleficent, and awakens Aurora with a kiss. They come down into the banquet hall, Aurora and her parents are reunited, and they all live happily ever after.

One-Hundred-and-One Dalmatians (1961)

Based on Dodie Smith's children's novel, this is the story, told from the point of view of Pongo, the adult male Dalmatian, starts with him and his 'pet' Roger's meeting and marrying their wives (Roger marries Anita, and Anita's dog, Perdita, marries Pongo). Early on in the film, Perdita and Pongo have a litter of fifteen puppies. But an old school mate of Anita, the evil, insane Cruella deVil, tries to buy the puppies, and then has them stolen, because she wishes to make a coat out of the fur of Dalmatian puppies. Pongo and Perdita run away from Roger and Anita in order to find and rescue their puppies, and eventually track down the puppies at Cruella's country mansion, Hell Hall. There, they discover that Cruella has collected eighty-four other Dalmatian puppies, also to be made into coats. With the help of some other animals, Pongo and Perdita rescue all of the puppies and get them safely back to London (to Roger and Anita's house), and Cruella deVil and her henchmen are left stranded, the cars wrecked, in the middle of the frozen countryside, defeated. Roger, a songwriter, has just had a great success with one of his songs, and he and Anita, now that they have one-hundred-and-one dogs, decide to buy a house in the country so that they have plenty of room for all the puppies.

The Rescuers (1977)

Based on Margery Sharpe's novels The Rescuers and Miss Bianca, this is the story of two mice, Bernard and Bianca, who, as representatives of the all-mouse Rescue Aid Society, go to save a little orphan girl, Penny, who has been kidnapped by a mad woman, Madame Medusa, who needs a child to fit into an old well which has a pirate treasure hidden in the bottom of it. Through a series of adventures, Bernard and Bianca find and rescue Penny, and take her – and the diamond which Medusa made Penny bring up from the well – back to New York. Penny gives the diamond to a museum, and she is adopted and goes to live in a happy home of her own for the first time. Bianca and Bernard report back to the Rescue Aid Society's headquarters (which are hidden in the United Nations building), and Bianca quickly volunteers them for another mission.

The Fox and the Hound (1981)

This is the story of a fox puppy, Tod, whose mother is shot by a hunter and who is taken in by an old woman, Widow Tweed, and raised as a pet. He becomes friends with a hound dog puppy, Copper, who belongs to a hunter. Unaware that they are supposed to be enemies, the two become best friends. As they grow up, however, Copper is taken off by the hunter and trained to be a hunting dog and to kill foxes, and when he returns he and Tod are no longer friends. Meanwhile, the hunter, who hates foxes, is always trying to shoot Tod. In fear for his safety, Widow Tweed takes Tod to an animal reserve and returns him to the wild. He wanders into the nearby woods, and there encounters Copper, who is being attacked by a bear. Tod is able to rescue Copper, but then the hunter shows up and tries to shoot Tod. Copper then saves Tod from the hunter, but the two part ways after that, and though they are shown to think of one another fondly and remember the joys of their youthful friendship, the film makes clear that, though they will never directly threaten each other, because they belong to two different worlds, Tod and Copper will never be able to be friends again.

The Black Cauldron (1985)

Loosely based on the Lloyd Alexander books *The Book of Three* and *The Black Cauldron*, this is the story of Taran, an assistant pig-keeper, who is charged with the care of Henwen, and oracular pig. Henwen is captured by the evil Horned King, and Taran sets out to rescue her. In the process, he is befriended by a creature called Gurgi. In the Horned King's castle, he also meets a young princess, Eilonwy, and an old musician, Fflewddur Fflam, who together with Gurgi accompany Taran on his quest to obtain and destroy the black cauldron and to rescue Henwen. By learning to work together, Taran, Eilonwy, Gurgi, and Fflewddur Fflam destroy the black cauldron's powers, defeat the Horned King, save Henwen, and become a band of loyal, heroic friends.

The Little Mermaid (1989)

Based on the Hans Christian Anderson version of the fairy tale, the film tells the story of Ariel, the mermaid daughter of King Triton (the Sea King). Young, adventurous, and curious, Ariel has a beautiful voice and an all-consuming fascination with the human world. She has never been on land before, but she scavenges shipwrecks on the ocean floor in search of human artefacts to feed her hunger for knowledge. Spotting a ship, Ariel secretly watches the humans on board, and falls in love with a young man, Prince Eric. A storm suddenly arises, and Eric is nearly drowned. Ariel rescues him, and takes him to shore. Eric is unconscious, however, and does not know who has rescued him, though he later has a fleeting memory of Ariel's beautiful voice, singing to him. Meanwhile, the Sea Witch, Ursula, who is looking for a way to capture the Sea King's powers and kingdom, discovers that Ariel has fallen in love with a human, and makes a deal with Ariel: if Ariel will give Ursula her voice, Ursula will give Ariel legs and make her able to live as a human for three days. If, by sunset of the third day, Ariel has made Eric fall in love with her and kiss her, she will remain human forever. If she has not, however, she will become a mermaid again and will become the property of Ursula forever. Ariel accepts these terms and is turned into a human. She is taken to land by her friends, and after quickly learning to walk, is found by Eric. He recognises her as the beautiful young woman who saved his life (and whom he has been searching for) until he realises that she is mute, and then decides it must not have been her. Nonetheless, he is drawn to her, and they spend the next two days together. Eric is on the verge of falling in love with Ariel until the Sea Witch, fearful that Ariel will succeed, comes on land disguised as a human and puts a spell on Eric, making him think that it was she who rescued him. He declares that they will be married. Ariel's animal friends discover the truth, however, and help Ariel stop the wedding and help Ariel retrieve her voice. Eric realises that it is Ariel he has been searching for, but too late, and she becomes a mermaid again and is taken away by the Sea Witch. Eric, the Sea King, and Ariel then all fight together to defeat Ursula. They succeed, peace and happiness are restored, and all is well. The Sea King, seeing how much in love his daughter and the human are, turns Ariel into a human again, and she and Eric are married and live happily ever after.

Beauty and the Beast (1991)

The film opens by establishing, though a lavish musical number, that Belle, the beautiful, intelligent daughter of the local, eccentric inventor, is out of place in the village where she lives and, though admired by the townsfolk for her beauty, think she is strange because of her intellect, and also because of her rejection of the advances made by the local 'stud', Gaston. Belle's father, Maurice, invents a machine to enter in the county fair and goes off to show the machine, but loses his way in the forest and comes upon the Beast's castle. He goes in to ask if he may rest there for the night, but is taken prisoner by the Beast. Belle learns of this and goes to rescue Maurice, and makes a bargain with the Beast to remain as his prisoner in exchange for her father's release. The Beast sends Maurice back to town, and Maurice then spends the next part of the film trying to rescue Belle from the Beast. Meanwhile, although Belle refuses to have anything to do with the Beast, she makes friends with his servants, who have been changed into enchanted objects at the same time that the Beast had been transformed from a handsome prince. Belle tries to escape but is attacked by wolves. The Beast saves her life, however, and she takes him back to his castle and tends to his wounds. The two become friends, after this, and Belle remains with him. They begin to fall in love with one another, but will not admit it to the other (or to themselves). Eventually, out of love for her, the Beast releases Belle, and she goes to save her father. Gaston, meanwhile, in an attempt to blackmail Belle into marrying him, has made an arrangement to have Maurice committed if Belle refuses to marry him. She proves that

Maurice's story of her imprisonment by the Beast is true, and Gaston immediately sets out to kill the Beast. Belle returns to the castle and saves the Beast's life, who then defeats Gaston but is gravely injured in the process. As he dies, Belle realises that she is in love with him, and at that moment he is transformed (by her love) back into a human, as are his servants. Belle and the Prince (which is what the Beast has become) are married and live happily ever after.

Aladdin (1992)

The film opens by giving the background of the story, explaining the nature of the Cave of Wonders (where Aladdin will discover the genie's lamp) and showing the character of Jafar, who will be Aladdin's enemy throughout the film. It then shows Aladdin, the plucky 'street rat', and his monkey friend, Abu, portraying Aladdin as a bright, spirited, pragmatic boy who is also very kind and generous (he steels a loaf of bread from the market for his breakfast, but then gives it to a pair of orphaned children). The film then shows Jasmine, the princess of Agraba, and her father the Sultan. Jasmine is shown to be similar to Aladdin in her intellect and spirit, and reveals that she feels stifled and cut-off by being confined to the castle (as is expected of all princesses). Her father is shown to be a good, kindly, but bumbling old man. His naïveté is also demonstrated by the fact that his advisor, Jafar, is the person in whom he has the most trust. Jasmine disguises herself as a commoner, sneaks out of the castle in search of adventure, and meets Aladdin. They recognise that they are kindred spirits and are shown to be attracted to each other. Aladdin is nearly arrested by the police, and Jasmine reveals her true identity in order to save him, but the police, who reveal that Aladdin's arrest was ordered by Jafar, take them back to the palace. Jafar then tells Jasmine that Aladdin was executed for kidnapping her. Meanwhile, Jafar disguises himself as an old man and persuades Aladdin to sneak out of prison, enter the Cave of Wonders, and bring him the lamp. Aladdin agrees, but Jafar betrays him and Aladdin is trapped in the cave. Abu, however, has stolen the lamp back from Jafar, and Aladdin, while cleaning it off, rubs it and releases the genie. Genie frees them from the Cave and grants Aladdin three wishes. Aladdin asks to become a prince so that he may court Jasmine. He returns to the castle and, after a series of events, wins Jasmine's heart, but is once more betrayed by Jafar. Eventually, Jafar manages to steal the lamp and forces Genie to do his bidding, but Aladdin manages to recapture the lamp and defeat Jafar for good. He then uses his third wish to free Genie from his lamp. Aladdin marries Jasmine, and they all live happily ever after.

Pocahontas (1995)

In a retelling of the American legend of Pocahontas the Algonquian princess and her rescue of English explorer Captain John Smith, Disney portrays Pocahontas as a wise, curious, spirited young woman in search of her destiny. Pocahontas meets John Smith in the forest as the other Algonquian are encountering the other British settlers. But whereas Pocahontas and John Smith learn to communicate with and understand one another (and even fall in love), the Algonquian and the British fear and distrust one another and, throughout the film, move closer towards war. Pocahontas and Smith work hard to keep their two peoples from fighting, but eventually, when the Algonquian believe that Smith has killed Kocoum, they capture him and take him back to their village, intending to execute him the next morning, as both the Algonquian and the British prepare to go to war against each other. Pocahontas, however, manages to arrive on the scene just in time to stop her father, Chief Powhatan, from executing Smith, and Powhatan realises that war would be wrong and that he should try to work with the British and learn to be friends with them instead of enemies. The British, too, see the error of their ways and resolve to be friends with the Algonquian. This turn of events is nearly thwarted by the evil Governor Ratcliffe, who tries to shoot Powhatan, but Smith throws himself in front of Powhatan and takes the bullet. Smith is then put on a ship to be taken back to England for medical treatment, and though he asks Pocahontas to come with him, she decides that her destiny is to stay with her people and to help the British and the Algonquian learn to live at peace with one another.

The Hunchback of Notre Dame (1996)

Loosely based on the Victor Hugo novel, the film begins with the story of how Quasimodo came to live in the bell tower of Notre Dame cathedral, and reveals the character of the sinister Judge Claude Frollo. The story then jumps forward in time to when Quasimodo is a young man who has never been outside of the cathedral and is a mysterious figure to the people of Paris. Desperate to be amongst people, Quasimodo covers himself in a cloak and goes to join the people in the Festival of Fools, which he has longingly watched from the bell tower every year. There, he meets Esmeralda, a beautiful young gypsy woman. Quasimodo is crowned the King of Fools and is full of joy for the first time in his life, when some soldiers start tormenting him by throwing vegetables at him, all under the eyes of Frollo, who does nothing to save him. Soon, Quasimodo is frightened and humiliated. Esmeralda, however, comes forward and rescues him, defying Frollo and accusing him of being cruel and unjust. She then manages to escape the soldiers and gain sanctuary in Notre Dame. Febus, the captain of the guard, follows her in to meet her (he is both captivated by her beauty and impressed by her bravery and character). Frollo then enters, and it is revealed that he too is attracted by Esmeralda, but in a more frightening, twisted way. The rest of the film covers Frollo's attempts to destroy the gypsies of Paris and possess Esmeralda (or else see her burned as a witch), and recounts Febus' and Esmeralda's growing attachment – then love – for one another. Frollo finally manages to capture the gypsies and tries to burn Esmeralda for witchcraft, but Quasimodo manages to rescue her from the fire and get her to the safety of the sanctuary offered by the cathedral. Frollo orders the army to surround and attack the cathedral, but Febus manages to free himself and the gypsies, and rouses the people to defend the cathedral and aid Quasimodo against Frollo. Esmeralda, who at first seems to be dead, regains consciousness, and together with Febus and Quasimodo, destroy Frollo and save the day. Quasimodo steps out of the cathedral into the light of day, and is accepted by the people, and all ends happily.

ineptitude, Kronk fails, and Kuzco ends up amongst the belongings of Pacha, a peasant who is faced with the prospect of Kuzco tearing down his house in order to build himself a summer house (Kuzco-topia). The two form an agreement whereby Kuzco will spare Pacha's home if Pacha will help him return to his palace. Through a series of misadventures and with much slapstick, Kuzco and Pacha learn to trust – and even like – each other, while Yzma and Kronk pursue them. Kronk is revealed to be not so much evil as too dumb to see how evil Yzma is, and by the end of the film, Kuzco, restored to human form, has become less self-centered and spoiled, he and Pacha form a life-long friendship. Pacha's home has been saved, and his family is protected forever. Yzma has been transformed into an irritated but otherwise harmless kitten, and Kronk has become a Junior Chipmunk leader for Pacha's children and their friends.

Atlantis (2001)

The film opens with the destruction of Atlantis. It then cuts to Washington, D.C. in 1914, where we meet Milo Thatch. Milo, works in the boiler room of a museum, longs to lead an expedition to Iceland in the hopes of finding the lost city of Atlantis. He quits his job at the museum, but is immediately hired by a millionaire, Mr. Whitmore, who was friends with Milo's grandfather, to serve as a linguist on an expedition to Atlantis. He joins a group of other explorers (Audrey, a mechanic; Vinny, a demolition expert; Sweet, the medical officer, Moliere, a geologist, Cookie, the cook; Rourke, the leader, Helga, his lieutenant, and Mrs. Packard, their radio operator), all of whom are described as being "the best of the best". On their way to Atlantis, their ship is attacked and most of the crew (except for a few soldiers and the above-named band) are lost, so the others journey onward. They eventually reach the edge of Atlantis, where they meet Princess Kida, the heir to Atlantis' throne, who is leading a small band of warriors. They welcome the explorers to Atlantis, and lead them to the city. The king, Nedakh, does not trust the outsiders, but Kida hopes that they bring knowledge which will help the Atlantians stop the slow decline of their civilisation. Kida and Milo begin working together to solve the mystery of the Heart of Atlantis. Soon, it is revealed that the real purpose of the expedition (unbeknownst to Milo) is to capture and bring back to the surface world the Heart of Atlantis. They realise that to do so would mean the complete death of Atlantis, but Helga and Rourke determine to press on with their plan, having been blinded by greed. The others initially continue to side with Helga and Rourke, but quickly have a change of heart, and work with Milo to stop Helga and Rourke, and to rescue Kida, who, in a trance, has become joined with the Heart of Atlantis and whom Helga and Rourke are kidnapping. Helga and Rourke are killed in a battle, Kida/the Heart of Atlantis is returned to its former glory over the city, and Kida returns to mortal form. The survivors of the expedition prepare to return home (and are given huge piles of gold by the Atlantians as thanks for saving their civilization), and Milo decides to stay with Kida, with whom he has fallen in love. The king has since died, so Kida is now queen of Atlantis, and it is implied that she and Milo will work together to rebuild Atlantis to its former glory. The survivors of the expedition return to Whitmore, tell him what has happened, and they agree not to reveal that they found anything, but instead concoct stories to explain why Rourke, Helga, and Milo are missing. All live happily ever after.

Lilo and Stitch (2002)

The film opens with a trial, held by the Galactic Federation, of Dr. Jumba Hookiba, a somewhat mad scientist (who prefers to be called an "evil genius"), and his creation, "Experiment 6-2-6". Both are imprisoned, but Experiment 6-2-6 escapes while being transported into exile. He steals a ship and ends up crash-landing on Earth, onto one of the Hawaiian islands. Meanwhile, a good-hearted but lonely, sad, angry, and troubled little orphaned girl, Lilo, and her older sister/guardian, Nani, are being watched by a "special" class of social worker, Cobra Bubbles, because Nani, a very young woman, is not coping well with her new role as her little sister's sole carer. Nani overhears Lilo's prayer for a friend. Deciding to answer this prayer (and hopefully help her sister deal with her grief over their parents' deaths), Nani decides to get Lilo a dog, they go to the animal shelter where Experiment 6-2-6 has been taken after being found when he arrived. Because he realises that he is being tailed by Jumba and an "expert" on the Earth, Pleakley, he goes along with Lilo's belief that he is a dog, and, now named "Stitch" by Lilo and adopted by her from the dog shelter, stays with Lilo, using her as a kind of human shield to avoid capture by Jumba and Pleakley. Lilo's attempts, based on Cobra Bubbles' orders, to turn Stitch into a "model citizen" based upon her idol, Elvis Presley, all fail miserably (and cause Nani to lose a series of jobs in the process), and, after Stitch, Jumba and Pleakley cause Lilo's and Nani's house to burn down, Cobra Bubbles arrives to take Lilo into foster care. Lilo runs away, however, and, along with Stitch, is captured by the unscrupulous Capt. Gantu (who is chasing both Stitch and the bumbling Jumba and Pleakley) and put on a ship to be taken away from the Earth. Stitch escapes, and, with the help of Nani, Jumba and Pleakley, chases down Gantu's ship and rescues Lilo. When the Galactic Federation arrives to take Stitch into custody, the official representative, the Grand Councilwoman, realises that there is good in Stitch, that he has become part of a family with Lilo and Nani, and that Lilo has legally adopted him (for a $2 adoption fee) from the dog shelter. She retires Capt. Gantu because of his incompetence and poor behaviour, sentences Stitch to exile on Earth, and puts the family under the protection of the United Galactic Federation (thereby preventing Lilo's being taken into foster care). She and Gantu leave the Earth, and a new, extended "family", comprised of Lilo, Stitch, Nani, Nani's boyfriend David, Cobra Bubbles, Jumba and Pleakley lives happily ever after.

Treasure Planet (2003)

Based loosely upon the novel *Treasure Island* by Robert Louis Stevenson, the film begins with the legend of Captain Flint, a notorious space pirate, being introduced, along with the young Jim Hawkins, who is fascinated with the story. His mother, Sarah, is introduced, and a happy, loving relationship is shown between them. The film fast-forwards to twelve years later, and we find Jim has grown into a

Wordcraft in Early New England', in Elizabeth Reis (editor), *Spellbound: Women and Witchcraft in America* (Wilmington, DE: Scholarly Resources, Inc., 1998), pp. 25–51.

Krämer, Peter. 'A Powerful Cinema-going Force? Hollywood and Female Audiences since the 1960s', in Melvyn Stokes and Richard Maltby, *Identifying Hollywood's Audiences: Cultural Identity and the Movies* (London: British Film Institute, 1999), pp. 93–108.

Lewis, Jon. 'Disney after Disney: Family Business and the Business of Family', in Eric Smoodin (editor), *Disney Discourse: Producing the Magic Kingdom* (London: Routledge, 1994), pp. 87–105.

Maltby, Richard. 'Sticks, Hicks and Flaps: Classical Hollywood's generic conception of its audiences', in Melvyn Stokes and Richard Maltby (eds) *Identifying Hollywood's Audiences: Cultural Identity and the Movies* (London: BFI Publishing, 1999), pp. 23–41.

Mandeville, A. Glenn. 'Once Upon a Dream: Behind the Scenes of the classic 1959 Disney film Sleeping Beauty'. From *Dolls: The Collector's Magazine* vol. 16, no. 5 (June/July 1997), pp. 97–101.

Merritt, Russell. 'Walt's Hollywood Beginnings'. Accessed via 'Library/Hollywood/ Hollywood (Walt's Hollywood Beginnings)' of the CD-ROM *Walt Disney: An Intimate History of the Man and his Magic*. CD-ROM. (Santa Monica, CA: Pantheon Productions Inc, 1998). ©1998 Walt Disney Family Educational Foundation, Inc. and its licensors. All rights reserved. ©1998 Disney Enterprises, Inc. All rights reserved.

Murphy, Patrick D. '"The Whole Wide World Was Scrubbed Clean": The Androcentric Animation of Denatured Disney', in Bell, Haas, and Sells, *From Mouse to Mermaid: The Politics of Film, Gender, and Culture* (Indianapolis: Indiana University Press, 1995), pp. 175–192.

Scott, Joan. 'Ordeal by Disney: Little Bit Goes a Long Way'. From *Film Comment*, vol. 23, no. 6 (November/December 1987), pp. 52–59.

Sells, Laura. '"Where Do the Mermaids Stand?": Voice and Body in *The Little Mermaid*, in Bell, Haas, and Sells, *From Mouse to Mermaid: : The Politics of Film, Gender, and Culture* (Indianapolis: Indiana University Press, 1995), pp. 175–192.

Serwer, Andrew E. 'Analyzing the Dream'. From *Fortune* vol. 131, no. 7 (17 April 1995), p. 71.

Sikov, Ed. 'Disney Complex: A Nightmare on Walt's Street'. From *Premiere (UK)*, vol. 2 no. 7 (August 1994), pp. 69–71.

Williams, Linda. 'When the Woman Looks', from Grant, Barry Keith (ed.). *The Dread of Difference: Gender and the Horror Film* (Austin: University of Texas Press, 1996), pp. 15–34.

Welter, Barbara. 'The Cult of True Womanhood,' *American Quarterly*, 18 (1966), pp. 151–174.

Wittner, Lawrence S. 'Gender Roles and Nuclear Disarmament Activism, 1954–1965', in *Gender & History*, vol. 12 no. 1 (April 2000), pp. 197–222.

Zicchi, Amy. '... And the Dream Continues: The storybook craze brings and entire cotillion of Sleeping Beauties'. From *Dolls: The Collector's Magazine* vol. 16, no. 5 (June/July 1997), pp. 102–103.

Appendix 4

Filmography*

The Adventures of Ichabod and Mr. Toad

Rel. 1949. Colour, 68 mins. Production Supervisor: Ben Sharpsteen. Directors: Jack Kinney, Clyde Geronimi, James Algar. Directing Animators: Franklin Thomas, Oliver Johnston, Jr., Wolfgang Reitherman, Milt Kahl, John Lounsberry, Ward Kimball. Story: Erdman Penner, Winston Hibler, Joe Rinaldi, Ted Sears, Homer Brightman, Harry Reeves. Character Animators: Fred Moore, John Sibley, Marc Davis, Hal Ambro, Harvey Toombs, Hal King, Hugh Fraser, Don Lusk. Music Director: Oliver Wallace. Based on "The Legend of Sleepy Hollow" by Washington Irving and *The Wind in the Willows* by Kenneth Grahame. Songs for "Ichabod" segment by Don Raye, Gene DePaul. "Ichabod" segment narrated (and songs performed) by Bing Crosby. Songs for "Willows" segment written by Frank Churchill and Charles Wolcott, with lyrics by Larry Morey and Ray Gilbert. Voices in "Willows" segment: Basil Rathbone, Pat O'Malley, Claud Allister, John Ployardt, Collin Campbell, Campbell Grant, Ollie Wallace.

Aladdin

Rel. 1992, colour, 90 mins. Released by Walt Disney Pictures. Directors: John Musker, Ron Clements. Producer: Donald W. Ernest. Script: John Musker, Ron Clements, Ted Elliott, Terry Rossio. Art Director: Bill Perkins. Music: Alan Menken, Howard Ashman, Tim Rice. Voices: Scott Weinger, Robin Williams, Linda Larkin, Jonathan Freeman, Gilbert Gottfried, Frank Welker, Douglas Seale; Singing Voices: Brad Kane, Lea Salonga.

Alice in Wonderland

Rel. 1951, colour, 72 mins. Released by Walt Disney Pictures. Production Supervisor: Ben Sharpsteen. Special Process: Ub Iwerks. Editor: Lloyd Richardson. Writers: Winston Hibler, Bill Peet, Joe Rinaldi, Bill Cottrell, Joe Grant, Del Cornell, Ted Sears, Erdman Penner, Milt Banta, Dick Kelsey, Dick Huemer, Tom Orb, John Walkridge. Directors: Clyde Geronimi, Wilfred Jackson, Hamliton Luske. Animation Directors: Milt Kahl, Ward Kimball, Frank Thomas, Eric Larson, John Lounsbery, Ollie Johnston, Wolfgang Reitherman, Marc Davis, Les Clark, Norman Ferguson. Music Supervision: Oliver Wallace. Songs: Gene Depaul, Mack Davis, Jerry Livingston, Al Hoffman, Bob Hilliard, Don Raye, Sammy Fain. Voices: Kathryn Beaumont, Ed Wynn, Richard Haydn, Sterling Holloway, Jerry Colonna, Verna Felton, Bill Thompson.

Atlantis

Rel. 2001, colour, 96 mins. Released by Walt Disney Pictures. Producer: Don Hahn. Directors: Kirk Wise, Gary Trousdale. Voices: Michael J. Fox, Cree Summer, James Garner, Claudia Christian, Florence Stanley, Leonard Nemoy, John Mahony, Jacqueline Obradors, Corey Burton, Don Novello, Phil Morris, Jim Varney, David Ogden Stiers.

Beauty and the Beast

Rel. 1991, colour, 81 mins. Released by Walt Disney Pictures and Silver Screen Partners IV. Executive Producer: Howard Ashman. Producer: Don Hahn. Associate Producer: Sarah McArthur. Directors: Kirk Wise, Gary Trousdale. Screenplay: Linda Woolverton. Camera

---

*Please note that the cast lists given are partial. For earlier films, the entire cast and crew were not named in the original credits. In the more recent films, the cast and crew lists are so extensive that for reasons of space, it was impossible to list them in full.

263

Manager: Joe Jiuliano. Editor: John Carnochan. Songs: Howard Ashman. Alan Menken. Original Score: Alan Menken. Voices: Paige O'Hara, Robby Benson, Richard White, Jerry Orbach, David Ogden Stiers, Angela Lansbury, Bradley Michael Pierce, Rex Everhart, Jesse Corti, Hal Smith, Jo Anne Worley.

The Black Cauldron

Rel. 1985, colour, 77 mins. Released by Walt Disney Pictures. Executive Producer: Ron Miller. Producer: Joe Hale. Production Executive: Edward Hansen. Production Co-ordinators: Joseph Morris, Dennis Edwards, Ronald Rocha. Production Manager: Don Hahn. Directors: Ted Berman, Richard Rich. Story: David Jonas, Vance Gerry, Ted Berman, Richard Rich, Al Wilson, Roy Morita, Peter Young, Art Stevens, Joe Hale, based on the books by Lloyd Alexander. Voices: Grant Bardsley, Susan Sheridan, Freddie Jones, John Byner, John Hurt.

Cinderella

Rel. 1950, colour, 74 mins. Released by Walt Disney Pictures. Production Supervisor: Ben Sharpsteen. Special Process: Ub Iwerks. Editor: Don Halliday. Directors: Clyde Geronimi, Wilfred Jackson, Hamilton S. Luske. Original Story: Charles Perrault. Animation Directors: Milt Kahl, Ward Kimball, Frank Thomas, Eric Larson, John Lounsbery, Ollie Johnston, Wolfgang Reitherman, Marc Davis, Les Clark, Norman Ferguson. Music Directors: Oliver Wallace, Paul Smith. Songs: Jerry Livingston, Al Hoffman, Mack David. Voices: Ilene Woods, William Phipps, Eleanor Audley, Rhoda Williams, Lucille Bliss, Verna Felton.

The Emperor's New Groove

Rel. 2000, colour, 79 mins. Released by Walt Disney Pictures. Director: Mark Dindal. Voices: David Spade, John Goodman, Eartha Kitt, Patrick Warburton, Wendie Malick, Tom Jones, Kellyann Kelso.

The Fox and the Hound

Rel. 1981, colour, 83 mins. Released by Walt Disney Productions. Directors: Art Stevens, Ted Berman, Richard Rich. Assistant Directors: Don Hand, Mark A. Hester, Terry L. Noss. Executive Producer: Ron Miller. Producers: Wolfgang Reitherman, Art Stevens. Production Managers: Edward Hansen, Don A. Duckwall. Script: Larry Clemmons, Ted Berman, Peter Young, Steve Hulett, Dave Michener, Burny Mattinson, Earl Kress, Vance Gerry. Based on the novel by Daniel P. Mannix. Supervising Animators: Randy Cartwright, Cliff Nordberg, Frank Thomas, Glen Keane, Ron Clements, Ollie Johnston. Voices: Mickey Rooney, Kurt Russell, Pearl Bailey, Jack Albertson, Sandy Duncan, Jeanette Nolan, Pat Buttram, John Fiedler, John McIntire, Richard Bakalyan, Paul Winchell, Keith Mitchell, Corey Feldman.

Hercules

Rel. 1997, colour, 93 mins. Released By Walt Disney Pictures. Executive Producer: Alice Dewy. Producers: John Musker, Ron Clements. Directors: John Musker, Ron Clements. Art Director: Andy Gaskill. Editor: Tom Finan. Story: Barry Johnson. Screenplay: John Musker, Ron Clements, Donald McEnery, Bob Shawn, Irene Mecchi. Music: Alan Menken. Lyrics: David Zippel. Score: Alan Menken. Voices: Tate Donovan, Joshua Keaton, Danny DeVito, James Woods, Susan Egan, Rip Torn, Samantha Eggar, Lillias White, Cheryl Freeman, LaChanze, Roz Ryan, Vaneese Thomas, Bobcat Goldthwait, Matt Frewer.

The Hunchback of Notre Dame

Rel. 1996, colour, 87 mins. Released by Walt Disney Pictures. Executive Producer: Howard Ashman. Producer: Don Hahn. Co-Producer: Roy Comli. Associate Producer: Phil Lofaro. Directors: Kirk Wise, Gary Trousdale. Art Director: David Goetz. Editor: Ellen Keneshea. Animation Story: Tab Murphy, based on Victor Hugo's novel Notre Dame de Paris. Animation Screenplay: Tab Murphy, Bob Tzudiker, Irene Mecchi, Noni White, Jonathan Roberts. Editor: John Carnochan. Songs: Music by Alan Menken, Lyrics by Stephen Schwartz. Original Score: Alan Menken. Voices: Tom Hulce, Demi Moore, Tony Jay, Kevin Kline, Paul Kandel, Jason Alexander, Charles Kimbrough, Mary Wickes, David Ogden Stiers.

The Little Mermaid

Rel. 1989. Colour, 83 mins. Released by Walt Disney Pictures. Directors: John Musker, Ron Clements. Assistant Director: Michael Serrian. Producers: Howard Ashman, John Musker. Script: John Musker, Ron Clements, based on the original story by Hans Christian Anderson. Music: Alan Menken. Voices: Jodi Benson, Pat Carroll, Samuel E. Wright, Kenneth Mars, Buddy Hackett, Christopher Daniel Barnes, Rene Auberjonois, Ben Wright.

Lilo and Stitch

Rel. 2002. Colour, 85 mins. Released by Walt Disney Pictures. Directors: Dean DeBlois, Chris Sanders. Script: Chris Sanders, Dean DeBlois. Producers: Lisa M. Poole, Clark Spencer. Music: Bernie Baum, Bill Giant, Jerry Leiber, Elvis Presley, Alan Silvestri, Mike Stoller, Francis Zambon. Editor: Darren T. Holmes. Voices: Daveigh Chase, Chris Sanders, Tia Carrere, David Ogden Stiers, Kevin McDonald, Ving Rhames, Zoe Caldwell, Jason Scott Lee, Kevin Michael Richardson, Susan Hegarty, Amy Hill.

Melody Time

Rel. 1948. Colour, 74 mins. Released by RKO. Production Supervisor: Ben Sharpsteen. Cartoon Directors: Clyde Geronimi, Wilfrid Jackson, Hamilton Luske, Jack Kinney. Story: Winston Hibler, Harry Reeves, Ken Anderson, Erdman Penner, Homer Brightman, Ted Sears, Joe Rinaldi, Art Scott, Bob Moore, Bill Cottrell, Jesse Marsh, John Walbridge. Directing Animators: Eric Larson, Ward Kimball, Milt Kahl, Oliver Johnston, Jr., John Lounsberry, Les Clark. Cast: Roy Rogers, Luana Patten, Bobby Driscoll, Ethel Smith and the Dinning Sisters, Bob Nolan, Sons of the Pioneers. Voices: Buddy Clark, The Andrews Sisters, Fred Waring and his Pennsylvanians, Frances Langford, Dennis Day, with Freddy Martin and his Orchestra, featuring Jack Fina

Mulan

Rel. 1998. Colour, 88 mins. Released by Walt Disney Pictures. Directors: Barry Cook, Tony Bancroft. Producer: Pam Coats. Associate Producers: Kendra Haaland, Robert S. Garber. Screenplay: Rita Hsiao, Christopher Sanders, Philip Lazebnik, Raymond Singer, Eugenia Bostwick Singer. Based on a story by Robert D. San Souci. Story: John Sanford, Chris Williams, Tim Hodge, Julius L. Aguimatang, Burny Mattinson, Lorna Cook, Barry Johnson, Thom Enriquez, Ed Gombert, Joe Grant, Floyd Norman. Music/Score Producer: Jerry Goldsmith. Songs: Matthew Wilder, David Zippel. Editor: Michael Kelly. Associate Editors: William J. Caparella, James Melton. Art Director: Ric Sluiter. Voices: Ming-Na Wen, Lea Salonga, Soon-Teck Oh, B.D. Wong, Donny Osmond, Freda Foh Shen, Eddie Murphy, Harvey Fierstein, George Takei, Jerry S. Tondo, Gedde Watanabe, Matthew Wilder, Miguel Ferrer, Frank Welker, James Shigeta, James Hong, June Foray, Pat Morita, Miriam Margolyes, Marni Nixon.

One Hundred and One Dalmatians

Rel. 1961, colour, 76 mins. Released by Walt Disney Pictures. Production Editors: Donald Halliday, Roy M. Brewer, Jr. Art Direction/Production Designer: Ken Anderson. Production Supervisor: Ken Peterson. Script: Bill Peet, based on the book by Dodie Smith. Directors: Clyde Geronimi, Wolfgang Reitherman, Hamliton S. Luske. Colour Styling: Walt Peregoy. Special Processes: Ub Iwerks, A.S.C., Eustace Lycett. Animation Directors: Milt Kahl, Frank Thomas, Ollie Johnston, Eric Larson, John Lounsbery, Marc Davis. Music: George Bruns. Songs: Mel Leven. Orchestrations: Franklyn Marks. Sound: Robert Cook. Voices: Rod Taylor, J. Pat O'Malley, Betty Lou Gerson, Martha Wentworth, Ben Wright, Cale Bauer, Dave Frankham, Fred Worlock, Lisa Davis, Tom Conway, Tudor Owen, George Pelling, Ramsay Hill, Sylvia Marriott, Queenie Leonard, Marjorie Bennett, Micky Maga, Barbara Beaird, Mimi Gibson, Sandra Abbott, Thurl Ravenscroft, Bill Lee, Max Smith, Bib Stevens, Paul Wexler, Mary Wickes, Barbara Luddy, Lisa Daniels, Helene Stanley, Don Barclay, Dale McKennon, Jeanne Bruns

Peter Pan

Rel. 1953, colour, 74 mins. Released by RKO Pictures. Based on the Story by J.M. Barrie. Production Supervisor: Ben Sharpsteen. Directors: Clyde Geronimi, Wilfred Jackson, Hamliton S. Luske. Story: Winston Hibler, Bill Peet, Joe Rinaldi, Ted Sears, Erdman Penner, Milt Banta, Ralph Wright. Animation Directors: Milt Kahl, Ward Kimball, Frank Thomas, Eric Larson, John

Lounsbery, Ollie Johnston, Wolfgang Reitherman, Marc Davis, Les Clark, Norman Ferguson. Music Supervision: Oliver Wallace. Songs: Sammy Fain, Sammy Cahn.

Pocahontas

Rel. 1995, colour, 78 mins. Released by Walt Disney Pictures. Directors: Mike Gabriel, Eric Goldberg. Producer: James Pentecost. Writers: Carl Bindor, Susannah Grant, Philip LaZebnik. Musical Director: Alan Menken. Editor: H. Lee Peterson. Art Director: Michael Giaimo. Songs: Alan Menken, Stephen Schwartz. Voices: Irene Bedard, Mel Gibson, David Ogden Stiers, John Kassir, Russell Means, Christian Bale, Linda Hunt, Danny Mann, Billy Connolly, Joe Baker, Frank Welker, Michelle St. John, James Apaumut Fall, Gordon Tootoosis.

The Rescuers

Rel. 1977, colour, 74 mins. Released by Buena Vista Distribution Co., Inc. Directors: Wolfgang Reitherman, John Lounsbery, Art Stevens. Assistant Directors: Jeff Patch, Richard Rich. Executive Producers: Ron Miller. Producer: Wolfgang Reitherman. Production Manager: Don Duckwall. Story: Larry Clemmons, Ken Anderson, Vance Gerry, Frank Thomas, Dave Michener, Ted Berman, Fred Lucky, Burny Mattinson, Dick Sebast, based on the original stories by Margery Sharpe. Animation Directors: Milt Kahl, Frank Thomas, Ollie Johnston, Don Bluth. Music: Artie Butler. Sound: Herb Taylor. Voices: Bob Newhart, Eva Gabor, Geraldine Page, Joe Flynn, Jeanette Nolan, Pat Buttram, Jim Jordan, John McIntire, Michelle Stacy, Berbard Fox, Larry Clemmons, James Macdonald, George Lindsey, Bill McMillan, Dub Taylor, John Fiedler.

Sleeping Beauty

Rel. 1959, colour, 75 mins. Walt Disney Studios. Director: Clyde Geronimi. Story Adaptation: Erdman Penner. Additional Story: Joe Rinaldi, Bill Peet, Ralph Wright, Winston Hibler, Ted Sears, Milt Banta, based on the story by Charles Perrault. Animation Directors: Milt Kahl, Frank Thomas, Ollie Johnston, Mark Davis, John Lounsbery. Editors: Roy M. Brewer, Jr., Donald Halliday Musical Adapter: George Bruns. Songs: George Bruns, Tom Adair, Winston Hibler, Erdman Penner, Sammy Fain, Jack Lawrence, Ted Sears. Sound: Robert Cook. Production Designers: Don da Gradi, Ken Anderson. Voices: Mary Costa, Bill Shirley, Eleanor Audley, Verna Felton, Barbara Jo Allen, Barbara Luddy.

Snow White and the Seven Dwarfs

Rel. 1937, colour, 82 mins. Walt Disney Studios. Director: Ben Sharpsteen. Supervising Director: David Hand; Musical Directors: Frank Churchill, Leigh Harline, Paul Smith; Songs: Larry Morey, Frank Churchill; Writers: Ted Sears, Otto Englander, Earl Hurd, Dorothy Ann Blank, Richard Creedon, Dick Richard, Merrill de Maris, Webb Smith, from the fairy tale by the Brothers Grimm. Voices: Adriana Caselotti, Harry Stockwell, Lucille La Verne, Scotty Mattraw, Roy Atwell, Pinto Colvig, Otis Harlan, Billy Gilbert, Moroni Olsen.

Tarzan

Rel. 1999, colour, 88 mins. Walt Disney Pictures. Directors: Kevin Lima, Chris Buck. Producer: Bonnie Arnold. Writers: Tab Murphy, Bob Tzudiker, Noni White. Based on the book *Tarzan of the Apes* by Edgar Rice Burroughs. Musical Score: Mark Mancina. Songs: Phil Collins. Voices: Tony Goldwyn, Minnie Driver, Glenn Close, Rosie O'Donnell, Brian Blessed, Nigel Hawthorne, Lance Henriksen, Wayne Knight.

Treasure Planet

Rel. 2003, colour, 91 minutes. Walt Disney Pictures. Produced and Directed by John Musker and Ron Clements. Screenplay: Ron Clements, John Musker, and Rob Edwards. Producer: Roy Conli. Animation Story: Ron Clements, John Musker, Ted Elliott, and Terry Rossio. Original Score: James Newton Howard. Original Songs: John Rzeznik. Voices: Joseph Gordon-Levitt, Brian Murray, Emma Thompson, David Hyde Pierce, Martin Short, Dane A. Davis, Michael Wincott, Laurie Metcalf, Roscoe Lee Browne, Patrick McGoohan.

Index